W9-BXD-450

Nine Algorithms That Changed the Future

Nine Algorithms That Changed the Future

The Ingenious Ideas That Drive Today's Computers

John MacCormick

with a foreword by Chris Bishop

PRINCETON UNIVERSITY PRESS
PRINCETON AND OXFORD

Published by Princeton University Press,
41 William Street, Princeton, New Jersey 08540

In the United Kingdom: Princeton University Press,
6 Oxford Street, Woodstock, Oxfordshire OX20 1TW

Library of Congress Cataloging-in-Publication Data

MacCormick, John, 1972–
Nine algorithms that changed the future : the ingenious ideas that drive today's computers / John MacCormick.
p. cm.
Includes bibliographical references and index.
ISBN 978-0-691-14714-7 (hardcover : alk. paper)
1. Computer science. 2. Computer algorithms.
3. Artificial intelligence. I. Title.

QA76M21453 2012
006.3–dc22 2011008867

A catalogue record for this book is available from the British Library

This book has been composed in Lucida using TEX

Typeset by T&T Productions Ltd, London

Printed on acid-free paper ∞

press.princeton.edu

Printed in the United States of America

10 9 8 7 6 5 4 3 2

The world has arrived at an age of cheap complex devices of great reliability; and something is bound to come of it.

—Vannevar Bush, "As We May Think," 1945

CONTENTS

FOREWORD

Computing is transforming our society in ways that are as profound as the changes wrought by physics and chemistry in the previous two centuries. Indeed, there is hardly an aspect of our lives that hasn't already been influenced, or even revolutionized, by digital technology. Given the importance of computing to modern society, it is therefore somewhat paradoxical that there is so little awareness of the fundamental concepts that make it all possible. The study of these concepts lies at the heart of computer science, and this new book by MacCormick is one of the relatively few to present them to a general audience.

One reason for the relative lack of appreciation of computer science as a discipline is that it is rarely taught in high school. While an introduction to subjects such as physics and chemistry is generally considered mandatory, it is often only at the college or university level that computer science can be studied in its own right. Furthermore, what is often taught in schools as "computing" or "ICT" (information and communication technology) is generally little more than skills training in the use of software packages. Unsurprisingly, pupils find this tedious, and their natural enthusiasm for the use of computer technology in entertainment and communication is tempered by the impression that the creation of such technology is lacking in intellectual depth. These issues are thought to be at the heart of the 50 percent decline in the number of students studying computer science at university over the last decade. In light of the crucial importance of digital technology to modern society, there has never been a more important time to re-engage our population with the fascination of computer science.

In 2008 I was fortunate in being selected to present the 180th series of Royal Institution Christmas Lectures, which were initiated by Michael Faraday in 1826. The 2008 lectures were the first time they had been given on the theme of computer science. When preparing these lectures I spent much time thinking about how to explain computer science to a general audience, and realized that there are very few resources, and almost no popular books, that address this need. This new book by MacCormick is therefore particularly welcome.

MacCormick has done a superb job of bringing complex ideas from computer science to a general audience. Many of these ideas have an extraordinary beauty and elegance which alone makes them worthy of attention. To give just one example: the explosive growth of web-based commerce is only possible because of the ability to send confidential information (such as credit card numbers, for example) secretly and securely across the Internet. The fact that secure communication can be established over "open" channels was for decades thought to be an intractable problem. When a solution was found, it turned out to be remarkably elegant, and is explained by MacCormick using precise analogies that require no prior knowledge of computer science. Such gems make this book an invaluable contribution to the popular science bookshelf, and I highly commend it.

Chris Bishop
Distinguished Scientist, *Microsoft Research Cambridge*
Vice President, *The Royal Institution of Great Britain*
Professor of Computer Science, *University of Edinburgh*

Nine Algorithms That Changed the Future

1

Introduction: What Are the Extraordinary Ideas Computers Use Every Day?

> This is a gift that I have ... a foolish extravagant spirit, full of forms, figures, shapes, objects, ideas, apprehensions, motions, revolutions.
>
> —WILLIAM SHAKESPEARE, *Love's Labour's Lost*

How were the great ideas of computer science born? Here's a selection:

- In the 1930s, before the first digital computer has even been built, a British genius founds the field of computer science, then goes on to prove that certain problems cannot be solved by any computer to be built in the future, no matter how fast, powerful, or cleverly designed.
- In 1948, a scientist working at a telephone company publishes a paper that founds the field of information theory. His work will allow computers to transmit a message with perfect accuracy even when most of the data is corrupted by interference.
- In 1956, a group of academics attend a conference at Dartmouth with the explicit and audacious goal of founding the field of artificial intelligence. After many spectacular successes and numerous great disappointments, we are still waiting for a truly intelligent computer program to emerge.
- In 1969, a researcher at IBM discovers an elegant new way to structure the information in a database. The technique is now used to store and retrieve the information underlying most online transactions.
- In 1974, researchers in the British government's lab for secret communications discover a way for computers to communicate securely even when another computer can observe everything that passes between them. The researchers are bound by government secrecy—but fortunately, three American professors

independently discover and extend this astonishing invention that underlies all secure communication on the internet.

- In 1996, two Ph.D. students at Stanford University decide to collaborate on building a web search engine. A few years later, they have created Google, the first digital giant of the internet era.

As we enjoy the astonishing growth of technology in the 21st century, it has become impossible to use a computing device—whether it be a cluster of the most powerful machines available or the latest, most fashionable handheld device—without relying on the fundamental ideas of computer science, all born in the 20th century. Think about it: have *you* done anything impressive today? Well, the answer depends on your point of view. Have you, perhaps, searched a corpus of billions of documents, picking out the two or three that are most relevant to your needs? Have you stored or transmitted many millions of pieces of information, without making a single mistake—despite the electromagnetic interference that affects all electronic devices? Did you successfully complete an online transaction, even though many thousands of other customers were simultaneously hammering the same server? Did you communicate some confidential information (for example, your credit card number) securely over wires that can be snooped by dozens of other computers? Did you use the magic of compression to reduce a multimegabyte photo down to a more manageable size for sending in an e-mail? Or did you, without even thinking about it, exploit the artificial intelligence in a hand-held device that self-corrects your typing on its tiny keyboard?

Each of these impressive feats relies on the profound discoveries listed earlier. Thus, most computer users employ these ingenious ideas many times every day, often without even realizing it! It is the objective of this book to explain these concepts—the great ideas of computer science that we use every day—to the widest possible audience. Each concept is explained without assuming any knowledge of computer science.

ALGORITHMS: THE BUILDING BLOCKS OF THE GENIUS AT YOUR FINGERTIPS

So far, I've been talking about great "ideas" of computer science, but computer scientists describe many of their important ideas as "algorithms." So what's the difference between an idea and an algorithm? What, indeed, *is* an algorithm? The simplest answer to this

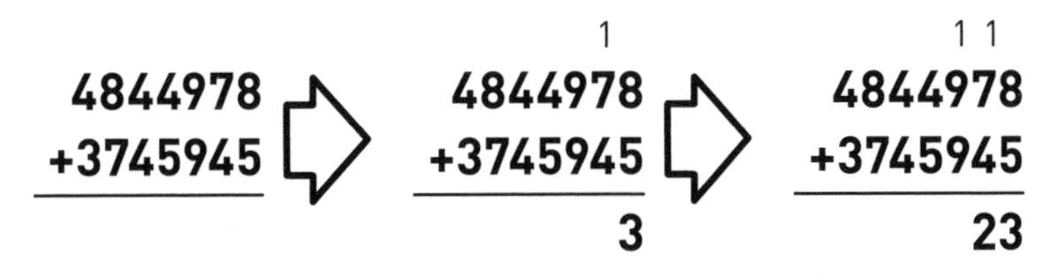

The first two steps in the algorithm for adding two numbers.

question is to say that an algorithm is a precise recipe that specifies the exact sequence of steps required to solve a problem. A great example of this is an algorithm we all learn as children in school: the algorithm for adding two large numbers together. An example is shown above. The algorithm involves a sequence of steps that starts off something like this: "First, add the final digits of the two numbers together, write down the final digit of the result, and carry any other digits into the next column on the left; second, add the digits in the next column together, add on any carried digits from the previous column..."—and so on.

Note the almost mechanical feel of the algorithm's steps. This is, in fact, one of the key features of an algorithm: each of the steps must be absolutely precise, requiring no human intuition or guesswork. That way, each of the purely mechanical steps can be programmed into a computer. Another important feature of an algorithm is that it always works, no matter what the inputs. The addition algorithm we learned in school does indeed have this property: no matter what two numbers you try to add together, the algorithm will eventually yield the correct answer. For example, although it would take a rather long time, you could certainly use this algorithm to add two 1000-digit numbers together.

You may be a little curious about this definition of an algorithm as a precise, mechanical recipe. Exactly how precise does the recipe need to be? What fundamental operations are permitted? For example, in the addition algorithm above, is it okay to simply say "add the two digits together," or do we have to somehow specify the entire set of addition tables for single-digit numbers? These details might seem innocuous or perhaps even pedantic, but it turns out that nothing could be further from the truth: the real answers to these questions lie right at the heart of computer science and also have connections to philosophy, physics, neuroscience, and genetics. The deep questions about what an algorithm really is all boil down to a proposition known as the *Church–Turing thesis*. We will revisit these issues in chapter 10, which discusses the theoretical limits of computation and some aspects of the Church–Turing thesis. Meanwhile, the informal notion of an algorithm as a very precise recipe will serve us perfectly well.

Now we know what an algorithm is, but what is the connection to computers? The key point is that computers need to be programmed with very precise instructions. Therefore, before we can get a computer to solve a particular problem for us, we need to develop an algorithm for that problem. In other scientific disciplines, such as mathematics and physics, important results are often captured by a single formula. (Famous examples include the Pythagorean theorem, $a^2 + b^2 = c^2$, or Einstein's $E = mc^2$.) In contrast, the great ideas of computer science generally describe *how* to solve a problem—using an algorithm, of course. So, the main purpose of this book is to explain what makes your computer into your own personal genius: the great algorithms your computer uses every day.

WHAT MAKES A GREAT ALGORITHM?

This brings us to the tricky question of which algorithms are truly "great." The list of potential candidates is rather large, but I've used a few essential criteria to whittle down that list for this book. The first and most important criterion is that the algorithms are used by ordinary computer users every day. The second important criterion is that the algorithms should address concrete, real-world problems—problems like compressing a particular file or transmitting it accurately over a noisy link. For readers who already know some computer science, the box on the next page explains some of the consequences of these first two criteria.

The third criterion is that the algorithms relate primarily to the *theory* of computer science. This eliminates techniques that focus on computer hardware, such as CPUs, monitors, and networks. It also reduces emphasis on design of infrastructure such as the internet. Why do I choose to focus on computer science theory? Part of my motivation is the imbalance in the public's perception of computer science: there is a widespread belief that computer science is mostly about programming (i.e., "software") and the design of gadgets (i.e., "hardware"). In fact, many of the most beautiful ideas in computer science are completely abstract and don't fall in either of these categories. By emphasizing these theoretical ideas, it is my hope that more people will begin to understand the nature of computer science as an intellectual discipline.

You may have noticed that I've been listing criteria to eliminate potential great algorithms, while avoiding the much more difficult issue of defining greatness in the first place. For this, I've relied on

The first criterion—everyday use by ordinary computer users—eliminates algorithms used primarily by computer professionals, such as compilers and program verification techniques. The second criterion—concrete application to a specific problem—eliminates many of the great algorithms that are central to the undergraduate computer science curriculum. This includes sorting algorithms like quicksort, graph algorithms such as Dijkstra's shortest-path algorithm, and data structures such as hash tables. These algorithms are indisputably great and they easily meet the first criterion, since most application programs run by ordinary users employ them repeatedly. But these algorithms are generic: they can be applied to a vast array of different problems. In this book, I have chosen to focus on algorithms for specific problems, since they have a clearer motivation for ordinary computer users.

Some additional details about the selection of algorithms for this book. Readers of this book are not expected to know any computer science. But if you do have a background in computer science, this box explains why many of your old favorites aren't covered in the book.

my own intuition. At the heart of every algorithm explained in the book is an ingenious trick that makes the whole thing work. The presence of an "aha" moment, when this trick is revealed, is what makes the explanation of these algorithms an exhilarating experience for me and hopefully also for you. Since I'll be using the word "trick" a great deal, I should point out that I'm not talking about the kind of tricks that are mean or deceitful—the kind of trick a child might play on a younger brother or sister. Instead, the tricks in this book resemble tricks of the trade or even magic tricks: clever techniques for accomplishing goals that would otherwise be difficult or impossible.

Thus, I've used my own intuition to pick out what I believe are the most ingenious, magical tricks out there in the world of computer science. The British mathematician G. H. Hardy famously put it this way in his book *A Mathematician's Apology*, in which he tried to explain to the public why mathematicians do what they do: "Beauty is the first test: there is no permanent place in the world for ugly mathematics." This same test of beauty applies to the theoretical ideas underlying computer science. So the final criterion for the algorithms presented in this book is what we might call Hardy's beauty test: I hope I have succeeded in conveying to the reader at least some portion of the beauty that I personally feel is present in each of the algorithms.

Let's move on to the specific algorithms I chose to present. The profound impact of search engines is perhaps the most obvious example of an algorithmic technology that affects all computer users, so it's not surprising that I included some of the core algorithms of web search. Chapter 2 describes how search engines use *indexing* to find documents that match a query, and chapter 3 explains *PageRank*—the original version of the algorithm used by Google to ensure that the most relevant matching documents are at the top of the results list.

Even if we don't stop to think about it very often, most of us are at least *aware* that search engines are using some deep computer science ideas to provide their incredibly powerful results. In contrast, some of the other great algorithms are frequently invoked without the computer user even realizing it. Public key cryptography, described in chapter 4, is one such algorithm. Every time you visit a secure website (with `https` instead of `http` at the start of its address), you use the aspect of public key cryptography known as *key exchange* to set up a secure session. Chapter 4 explains how this key exchange is achieved.

The topic of chapter 5, error correcting codes, is another class of algorithms that we use constantly without realizing it. In fact, error correcting codes are probably the single most frequently used great idea of all time. They allow a computer to recognize *and correct* errors in stored or transmitted data, without having to resort to a backup copy or a retransmission. These codes are everywhere: they are used in all hard disk drives, many network transmissions, on CDs and DVDs, and even in some computer memories—but they do their job so well that we are never even aware of them.

Chapter 6 is a little exceptional. It covers pattern recognition algorithms, which sneak into the list of great computer science ideas despite violating the very first criterion: that ordinary computer users must use them every day. Pattern recognition is the class of techniques whereby computers recognize highly variable information, such as handwriting, speech, and faces. In fact, in the first decade of the 21st century, most everyday computing did not use these techniques. But as I write these words in 2011, the importance of pattern recognition is increasing rapidly: mobile devices with small on-screen keyboards need automatic correction, tablet devices must recognize handwritten input, and all these devices (especially smartphones) are becoming increasingly voice-activated. Some websites even use pattern recognition to determine what kind of advertisements to display to their users. In addition, I have a personal bias toward pattern recognition, which is my own area of research. So chapter 6 describes three of the most interesting and successful pattern recognition techniques: nearest-neighbor classifiers, decision trees, and neural networks.

Compression algorithms, discussed in chapter 7, form another set of great ideas that help transform a computer into a genius at our fingertips. Computer users do sometimes apply compression directly, perhaps to save space on a disk or to reduce the size of a photo before e-mailing it. But compression is used even more often under the covers: without us being aware of it, our downloads or uploads may be compressed to save bandwidth, and data centers often compress customers' data to reduce costs. That 5 GB of space that your e-mail provider allows you probably occupies significantly less than 5 GB of the provider's storage!

Chapter 8 covers some of the fundamental algorithms underlying databases. The chapter emphasizes the clever techniques employed to achieve *consistency*—meaning that the relationships in a database never contradict each other. Without these ingenious techniques, most of our online life (including online shopping and interacting with social networks like Facebook) would collapse in a jumble of computer errors. This chapter explains what the problem of consistency really is and how computer scientists solve it without sacrificing the formidable efficiency we expect from online systems.

In chapter 9, we learn about one of the indisputable gems of theoretical computer science: digital signatures. The ability to "sign" an electronic document digitally seems impossible at first glance. Surely, you might think, any such signature must consist of digital information, which can be copied effortlessly by anyone wishing to forge the signature. The resolution of this paradox is one of the most remarkable achievements of computer science.

We take a completely different tack in chapter 10: instead of describing a great algorithm that already exists, we will learn about an algorithm that *would* be great if it existed. Astonishingly, we will discover that this particular great algorithm is impossible. This establishes some absolute limits on the power of computers to solve problems, and we will briefly discuss the implications of this result for philosophy and biology.

In the conclusion, we will draw together some common threads from the great algorithms and spend a little time speculating about what the future might hold. Are there more great algorithms out there or have we already found them all?

This is a good time to mention a caveat about the book's style. It's essential for any scientific writing to acknowledge sources clearly, but citations break up the flow of the text and give it an academic flavor. As readability and accessibility are top priorities for this book, there are no citations in the main body of the text. All sources are, however, clearly identified—often with amplifying comments—in the "Sources and Further Reading" section at the end of the book. This section also points to additional material that interested readers can use to find out more about the great algorithms of computer science.

While I'm dealing with caveats, I should also mention that a small amount of poetic license was taken with the book's title. Our *Nine Algorithms That Changed the Future* are—without a doubt—revolutionary, but are there exactly nine of them? This is debatable, and depends on exactly what gets counted as a separate algorithm. So let's see where the "nine" comes from. Excluding the introduction and conclusion, there are nine chapters in the book, each covering algorithms that have revolutionized a different type of computational task, such as cryptography, compression, or pattern recognition. Thus, the "Nine Algorithms" of the book's title really refer to nine classes of algorithms for tackling these nine computational tasks.

WHY SHOULD WE CARE ABOUT THE GREAT ALGORITHMS?

Hopefully, this quick summary of the fascinating ideas to come has left you eager to dive in and find out how they really work. But you may still be wondering: what is the ultimate goal here? So let me make some brief remarks about the true purpose of this book. It is definitely not a how-to manual. After reading the book, you won't be an expert on computer security or artificial intelligence or anything else. It's true that you may pick up some useful skills. For example: you'll be more aware of how to check the credentials of "secure" websites and "signed" software packages; you'll be able to choose judiciously between lossy and lossless compression for different tasks; and you may be able to use search engines more efficiently by understanding some aspects of their indexing and ranking techniques.

These, however, are relatively minor bonuses compared to the book's true objective. After reading the book, you *won't* be a vastly more skilled computer user. But you *will* have a much deeper appreciation of the beauty of the ideas you are constantly using, day in and day out, on all your computing devices.

Why is this a good thing? Let me argue by analogy. I am definitely not an expert on astronomy—in fact, I'm rather ignorant on the topic and wish I knew more. But every time I glance at the night sky, the small amount of astronomy that I do know enhances my enjoyment of this experience. Somehow, my understanding of what I am looking at leads to a feeling of contentment and wonder. It is my fervent hope that after reading this book, you will occasionally achieve this same sense of contentment and wonder while using a computer. You'll have a true appreciation of the most ubiquitous, inscrutable black box of our times: your personal computer, the genius at your fingertips.

2

Search Engine Indexing: Finding Needles in the World's Biggest Haystack

> Now, Huck, where we're a-standing you could touch that hole I got out of with a fishing-pole. See if you can find it.
>
> —MARK TWAIN, *Tom Sawyer*

Search engines have a profound effect on our lives. Most of us issue search queries many times a day, yet we rarely stop to wonder just how this remarkable tool can possibly work. The vast amount of information available and the speed and quality of the results have come to seem so normal that we actually get frustrated if a question can't be answered within a few seconds. We tend to forget that every successful web search extracts a needle from the world's largest haystack: the World Wide Web.

In fact, the superb service provided by search engines is not just the result of throwing a large amount of fancy technology at the problem. Yes, each of the major search engine companies runs an international network of enormous data centers, containing thousands of server computers and advanced networking equipment. But all of this hardware would be useless without the clever algorithms needed to organize and retrieve the information we request. So in this chapter and the one that follows, we'll investigate some of the algorithmic gems that are put to work for us every time we do a web search. As we'll soon see, two of the main tasks for a search engine are *matching* and *ranking*. This chapter covers a clever matching technique: the metaword trick. In the next chapter, we turn to the ranking task and examine Google's celebrated PageRank algorithm.

MATCHING AND RANKING

It will be helpful to begin with a high-level view of what happens when you issue a web search query. As already mentioned, there

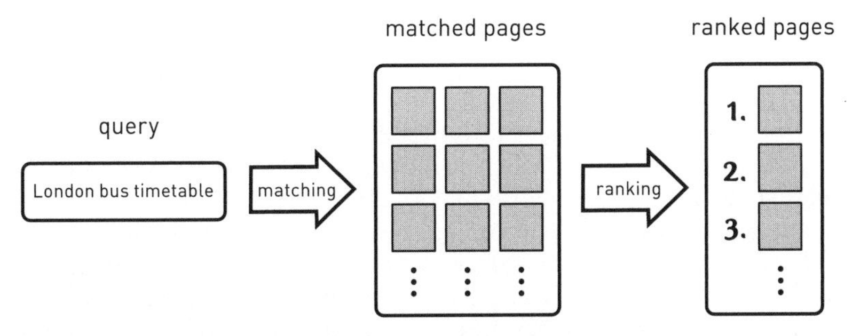

The two phases of web search: matching and ranking. There can be thousands or millions of matches after the first (matching) phase, and these must be sorted by relevance in the second (ranking) stage.

will be two main phases: matching and ranking. In practice, search engines combine matching and ranking into a single process for efficiency. But the two phases are conceptually separate, so we'll assume that matching is completed before ranking begins. The figure above shows an example, where the query is "London bus timetable." The matching phase answers the question "which web pages match my query?"—in this case, all pages that mention London bus timetables.

But many queries on real search engines have hundreds, thousands, or even millions of hits. And the users of search engines generally prefer to look through only a handful of results, perhaps five or ten at the most. Therefore, a search engine must be capable of picking the best few from a very large number of hits. A good search engine will not only pick out the best few hits, but display them in the most useful order—with the most suitable page listed first, then the next most suitable, and so on.

The task of picking out the best few hits in the right order is called "ranking." This is the crucial second phase that follows the initial matching phase. In the cutthroat world of the search industry, search engines live or die by the quality of their ranking systems. Back in 2002, the market share of the top three search engines in the United States was approximately equal, with Google, Yahoo, and MSN each having just under 30% of U.S. searches. (MSN was later rebranded first as Live Search and then as Bing.) In the next few years, Google made a dramatic improvement in its market share, crushing Yahoo and MSN down to under 20% each. It is widely believed that the phenomenal rise of Google to the top of the search industry was due to its ranking algorithms. So it's no exaggeration to say that search engines live or die according to the quality of their ranking algorithms. But as already mentioned, we'll be discussing ranking algorithms in the next chapter. For now, let's focus on the matching phase.

ALTAVISTA: THE FIRST WEB-SCALE MATCHING ALGORITHM

Where does our story of search engine matching algorithms begin? An obvious—but wrong—answer would be to start with Google, the greatest technology success story of the early 21st century. Indeed, the story of Google's beginnings as the Ph.D. project of two graduate students at Stanford University is both heartwarming and impressive. It was in 1998 that Larry Page and Sergey Brin assembled a ragtag bunch of computer hardware into a new type of search engine. Less than 10 years later, their company had become the greatest digital giant to rise in the internet age.

But the idea of web search had already been around for several years. Among the earliest commercial offerings were Infoseek and Lycos (both launched in 1994), and AltaVista, which launched its search engine in 1995. For a few years in the mid-1990s, AltaVista was the king of the search engines. I was a graduate student in computer science during this period, and I have clear memories of being wowed by the comprehensiveness of AltaVista's results. For the first time, a search engine had fully indexed all of the text on every page of the web—and, even better, results were returned in the blink of an eye. Our journey toward understanding this sensational technological breakthrough begins with a (literally) age-old concept: indexing.

PLAIN OLD INDEXING

The concept of an *index* is the most fundamental idea behind any search engine. But search engines did not invent indexes: in fact, the idea of indexing is almost as old as writing itself. For example, archaeologists have discovered a 5000-year-old Babylonian temple library that cataloged its cuneiform tablets by subject. So indexing has a pretty good claim to being the oldest useful idea in computer science.

These days, the word "index" usually refers to a section at the end of a reference book. All of the concepts you might want to look up are listed in a fixed order (usually alphabetical), and under each concept is a list of locations (usually page numbers) where that concept is referenced. So a book on animals might have an index entry that looks like "cheetah 124, 156," which means that the word "cheetah" appears on pages 124 and 156. (As a mildly amusing exercise, you could look up the word "index" in the index of this book. You should be brought back to this very page.)

The index for a web search engine works the same way as a book's index. The "pages" of the book are now web pages on the World Wide

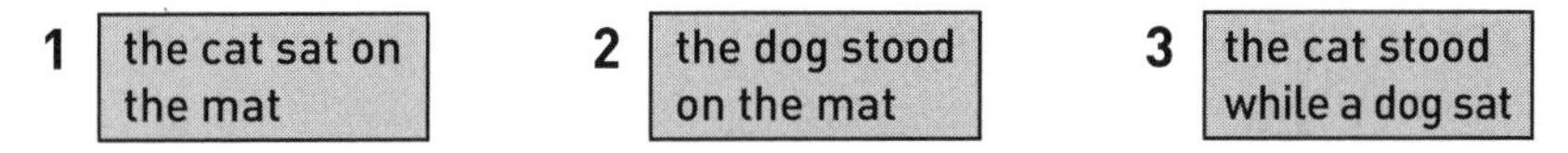

An imaginary World Wide Web that consists of only three pages, numbered 1, 2, and 3.

a	3
cat	1 3
dog	2 3
mat	1 2
on	1 2
sat	1 3
stood	2 3
the	1 2 3
while	3

A simple index with page numbers.

Web, and search engines assign a different page number to every single web page on the web. (Yes, there are a lot of pages—many billions at the last count—but computers are great at dealing with large numbers.) The figure above gives an example that will make this more concrete. Imagine that the World Wide Web consisted of only the 3 short web pages shown there, where the pages have been assigned page numbers 1, 2, and 3.

A computer could build up an index of these three web pages by first making a list of all the words that appear in any page and then sorting that list in alphabetical order. Let's call the result a *word list*—in this particular case it would be "a, cat, dog, mat, on, sat, stood, the, while." Then the computer would run through the pages word by word. For each word, it would make a note of the current page number next to the corresponding word in the word list. The final result is shown in the figure above. You can see immediately, for example, that the word "cat" occurs in pages 1 and 3, but not in page 2. And the word "while" appears only in page 3.

With this very simple approach, a search engine can already provide the answers to a lot of simple queries. For example, suppose you enter the query `cat`. The search engine can quickly jump to the entry for `cat` in the word list. (Because the word list is in alphabetical order, a computer can quickly find any entry, just like a human can quickly find a word in a dictionary.) And once it finds the entry for `cat`, the search engine can just give you the list of pages at that entry—in this case, 1 and 3. Modern search engines format the results nicely, with little snippets from each of the pages that were returned, but we will mostly ignore details like that and concentrate on how search engines know which page numbers are "hits" for the query you entered.

As another very simple example, let's check the procedure for the query `dog`. In this case, the search engine quickly finds the entry for `dog` and returns the hits 2 and 3. But how about a multiple-word query, like `cat dog`? This means you are looking for pages that contain both of the words "cat" and "dog." Again, this is pretty easy for the search engine to do with the existing index. It first looks up the two words individually to find which pages they occur on as individual words. This gives the answer 1, 3 for "cat" and 2, 3 for "dog." Then, the computer can quickly scan along both of the lists of hits, looking for any page numbers that occur on both lists. In this case, pages 1 and 2 are rejected, but page 3 occurs in both lists, so the final answer is a single hit on page 3. And a very similar strategy works for queries with more than two words. For example, the query `cat the sat` returns pages 1 and 3 as hits, since they are the common elements of the lists for "cat" (1, 3), "the" (1, 2, 3), and "sat" (1, 3).

So far, it sounds like building a search engine would be pretty easy. The simplest possible indexing technology seems to work just fine, even for multiword queries. Unfortunately, it turns out that this simple approach is completely inadequate for modern search engines. There are quite a few reasons for this, but for now we will concentrate on just one of the problems. This is the problem of how to do *phrase queries*. A phrase query is a query that searches for an exact phrase, rather than just the occurrence of some words anywhere on a page. On most search engines, phrase queries are entered using quotation marks. So, for example, the query `"cat sat"` has a very different meaning to the query `cat sat`. The query `cat sat` looks for pages that contain the two words "cat" and "sat" anywhere, in any order; whereas the query `"cat sat"` looks for pages that contain the word "cat" immediately followed by the word "sat." In our simple three-page example, `cat sat` results in hits on pages 1 and 3, but `"cat sat"` returns only one hit, on page 1.

How can a search engine efficiently perform a phrase query? Let's stick with the `"cat sat"` example. It seems like the first step should be to do the same thing as for the ordinary multiword query `cat sat`: retrieve from the word list the list of pages that each word occurs on, in this case 1, 3 for "cat," and the same thing—1, 3—for "sat." But here the search engine is stuck. It knows for sure that both words occur on both pages 1 and 3, but there is no way of telling whether the words occur next to each other in the right order. You might think that at this point the search engine could go back and look at the original web pages to see if the exact phrase is there or not. This would indeed be a possible solution, but it is very, very inefficient. It requires reading through the entire contents of every web page that *might* contain the phrase, and there could be a huge number of such pages. Remember, we are dealing with an extremely small example of only three pages here, but a real search engine has to give correct results on tens of billions of web pages.

THE WORD-LOCATION TRICK

The solution to this problem is the first really ingenious idea that makes modern search engines work well: the index should not store only page *numbers*, but also *locations* within the pages. These locations are nothing mysterious: they just indicate the position of a word within its page. So the third word has location 3, the 29th word has location 29, and so on. Our entire three-page data set is shown in the top figure on the next page, with the word locations added. Below that is the index that results from storing both page numbers and word locations. We'll call this way of building an index the "word-location trick." Let's look at a couple of examples to make sure we understand the word-location trick. The first line of the index is "a 3-5." This means the word "a" occurs exactly once in the data set, on page 3, and it is the fifth word on that page. The longest line of the index is "the 1-1 1-5 2-1 2-5 3-1." This line lets you know the exact locations of all occurrences of the word "the" in the data set. It occurs twice on page 1 (at locations 1 and 5), twice on page 2 (at locations 1 and 5), and once on page 3 (at location 1).

Now, remember why we introduced these in-page word locations: it was to solve the problem of how to do phrase queries efficiently. So let's see how to do a phrase query with this new index. We'll work with the same query as before, `"cat sat"`. The first steps are the same as with the old index: extract the locations of the individual words from the index, so for "cat" we get 1-2, 3-2, and for "sat" we get 1-3, 3-7. So far, so good: we know that the only possible hits for the phrase query `"cat sat"` can be on pages 1 and 3. But just like before, we are not yet sure whether that exact phrase occurs on those pages—it is possible that the two words do appear, but not next to each other in the correct order. Luckily, it is easy to check this from the location information. Let's concentrate on page 1 initially. From the index information, we know that "cat" appears at position 2 on page 1 (that's what the 1-2 means). And we know that "sat" appears at position 3 on page 1 (that's what the 1-3 means). But if "cat" is at position 2, and "sat" is at position 3, then we know "sat" appears immediately after "cat" (because 3 comes immediately after 2)—and

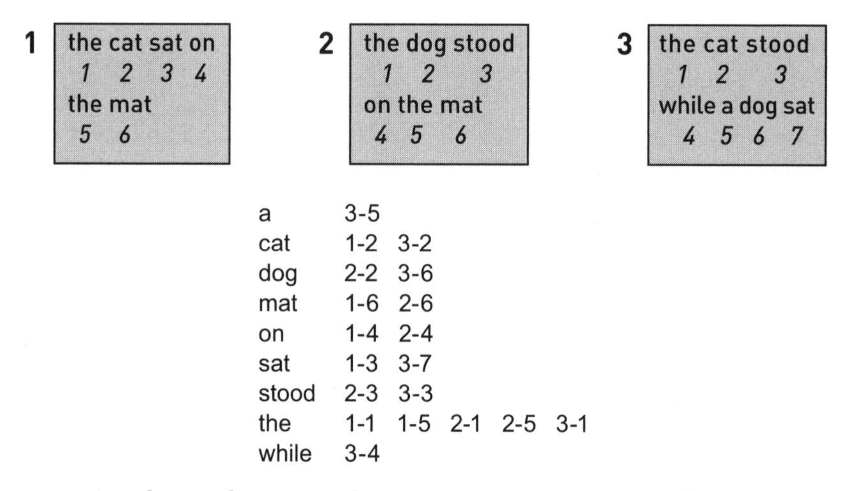

Top: Our three web pages with in-page word locations added. Bottom: A new index that includes both page numbers and in-page word locations.

so the entire phrase we are looking for, "cat sat," must appear on this page beginning at position 2!

I know I am laboring this point, but the reason for going through this example in excruciating detail is to understand *exactly* what information is used to arrive at this answer. Note that we have found a hit for the phrase `"cat sat"` by looking only at the index information (1-2, 3-2 for "cat," and 1-3, 3-7 for "sat"), not at the original web pages themselves. This is crucial, because we only had to look at the two entries in the index, rather than reading through all of the pages that might be hits—and there could be literally millions of such pages in a real search engine performing a real phrase query. To summarize: including the in-page word locations in the index has allowed us to find a phrase query hit by looking at only a couple of lines in the index, rather than reading through a large number of web pages. This simple word-location trick is one of the keys to making search engines work!

Actually, we haven't even finished working through the `"cat sat"` example. We finished processing the information for page 1, but not for page 3. But the reasoning for page 3 is similar: we see that "cat" appears at location 2, and "sat" occurs at location 7, so they cannot possibly occur next to each other—because 7 is not immediately after 2. So we know that page 3 is *not* a hit for the phrase query `"cat sat"`, even though it *is* a hit for the multiword query `cat sat`.

By the way, the word-location trick is important for more than just phrase queries. As one example, consider the problem of finding words that are near to each other. On some search engines, you can do this with the NEAR keyword in the query. In fact, the AltaVista search engine offered this facility from its early days and still does at the time of writing. As a specific example, suppose that on some particular search engine, the query `cat NEAR dog` finds pages in which the word "cat" occurs within five words of the word "dog." How can we perform this query efficiently on our data set? Using word locations, it's easy. The index entry for "cat" is 1-2, 3-2, and the index entry for "dog" is 2-2, 3-6. So we see immediately that page 3 is the only possible hit. And on page 3, "cat" appears at location 2, and "dog" appears at location 6. So the distance between the two words is 6 – 2, which is 4. Therefore, "cat" *does* appear within five words of "dog," and page 3 is a hit for the query `cat NEAR dog`. Again, note how efficiently we could perform this query: there was no need to read through the actual content of any web pages—instead, only two entries from the index were consulted.

It turns out that NEAR queries aren't very important to search engine users in practice. Almost no one uses NEAR queries, and most major search engines don't even support them. But despite this, the ability to perform NEAR queries is actually crucial to real-life search engines. This is because the search engines themselves are constantly performing NEAR queries behind the scenes. To understand why, we first have to take a look at one of the other major problems that confronts modern search engines: the problem of *ranking*.

RANKING AND NEARNESS

So far, we've been concentrating on the matching phase: the problem of efficiently finding all of the hits for a given query. But as emphasized earlier, the second phase, "ranking," is absolutely essential for a high-quality search engine: this is the phase that picks out the top few hits for display to the user.

Let's examine the concept of ranking a little more carefully. What does the "rank" of a page really depend on? The real question is not "Does this page *match* the query?" but rather "Is this page *relevant* to the query?" Computer scientists use the term "relevance" to describe how suitable or useful a given page is, in response to a particular query.

As a concrete example, suppose you are interested in what causes malaria, and you enter the query `malaria cause` into a search engine. To keep things simple, imagine there are only two hits for that query in the search engine—the two pages shown in the figure on the following page. Have a look at those pages now. It should be immediately clear to you, as a human, that page 1 is indeed about

also	1-19	
...		
cause	1-6	2-2
...		
malaria	1-8	2-19
...		
whom	2-15	

Top: Two example web pages that mention malaria.
Bottom: Part of the index built from the above two web pages.

the causes of malaria, whereas page 2 seems to be the description of some military campaign which just happens, by coincidence, to use the words "cause" and "malaria." So page 1 is undoubtedly more "relevant" to the query `malaria cause` than page 2. But computers are not humans, and there is no easy way for a computer to understand the topics of these two pages, so it might seem impossible for a search engine to rank these two hits correctly.

However, there is, in fact, a very simple way to get the ranking right in this case. It turns out that pages where the query words occur *near* each other are more likely to be relevant than pages where the query words are far apart. In the malaria example, we see that the words "malaria" and "cause" occur within two words of each other in page 1, but are separated by 17 words in page 2. (And remember, the search engine can find this out efficiently by looking at just the index entries, without having to go back and look at the web pages themselves.) So although the computer doesn't really "understand" the topic of this query, it can *guess* that page 1 is more relevant than page 2, because the query words occur much closer on page 1 than on page 2.

To summarize: although humans don't use NEAR queries much, search engines use the information about nearness constantly to improve their rankings—and the reason they can do this efficiently is because they use the word-location trick.

An example set of web pages that each have a title and a body.

We already know that the Babylonians were using indexing 5000 years before search engines existed. It turns out that search engines did not invent the word-location trick either: this is a well-known technique that was used in other types of information retrieval before the internet arrived on the scene. However, in the next section we will learn about a new trick that does appear to have been invented by search engine designers: the *metaword trick*. The cunning use of this trick and various related ideas helped to catapult the AltaVista search engine to the top of the search industry in the late 1990s.

THE METAWORD TRICK

So far, we've been using extremely simple examples of web pages. As you probably know, most web pages have quite a lot of structure, including titles, headings, links, and images, whereas we have been treating web pages as just ordinary lists of words. We're now going to find out how search engines take account of the structure in web pages. But to keep things as simple as possible, we will introduce only one aspect of structuring: we will allow our pages to have a *title* at the top of the page, followed by the *body* of the page. The figure above shows our familiar three-page example with some titles added.

Actually, to analyze web page structure in the same way that search engines do, we need to know a little more about how web pages are written. Web pages are composed in a special language that allows web browsers to display them in a nicely formatted way. (The most common language for this purpose is called HTML, but the details of HTML are not important for this discussion.) The formatting instructions for headings, titles, links, images, and the like are written using special words called *metawords*. As an example, the metaword used to start the title of a web page might be `<titleStart>`, and the metaword for ending the title might be `<titleEnd>`. Similarly, the body of the web page could be started with `<bodyStart>` and ended with `<bodyEnd>`. Don't let the symbols "<" and ">" confuse you. They appear on most computer keyboards and are often known by their mathematical meanings as "less than" and "greater than." But here, they have nothing whatsoever to do with math—they are just being used as convenient symbols to mark the metawords as different from regular words on a web page.

1	<titleStart> my cat <titleEnd> <bodyStart> the cat sat on the mat <bodyEnd>	2	<titleStart> my dog <titleEnd> <bodyStart> the dog stood on the mat <bodyEnd>	3	<titleStart> my pets <titleEnd> <bodyStart> the cat stood while a dog sat <bodyEnd>

The same set of web pages as in the last figure, but shown as they might be *written* with metawords, rather than as they would be displayed in a web browser.

Take a look at the figure above, which displays exactly the same content as the previous figure, but now showing how the web pages were actually written, rather than how they would be displayed in a web browser. Most web browsers allow you to examine the raw content of a web page by choosing a menu option called "view source"—I recommend experimenting with this the next time you get a chance. (Note that the metawords used here, such as `<titleStart>` and `<titleEnd>`, are fictitious, easily recognizable examples to aid our understanding. In real HTML, metawords are called *tags*. The tags for starting and ending titles in HTML are `<title>` and `</title>`—search for these tags after using the "view source" menu option.)

When building an index, it is a simple matter to include all of the metawords. No new tricks are needed: you just store the locations of the metawords in the same way as regular words. The figure on the next page shows the index built from the three web pages with metawords. Take a look at this figure and make sure you understand there is nothing mysterious going on here. For example, the entry for "mat" is 1-11, 2-11, which means that "mat" is the 11th word on page 1 and also the 11th word on page 2. The metawords work the same way, so the entry for "`<titleEnd>`," which is 1-4, 2-4, 3-4, means that "`<titleEnd>`" is the fourth word in page 1, page 2, and page 3.

We'll call this simple trick, of indexing metawords in the same way as normal words, the "metaword trick." It might seem ridiculously simple, but this metaword trick plays a crucial role in allowing search engines to perform accurate searches and high-quality rankings. Let's look at a simple example of this. Suppose for a moment that a search engine supports a special type of query using the `IN` keyword, so that a query like `boat IN TITLE` returns hits only for pages that have the word "boat" in the title of the web page, and `giraffe IN BODY` would find pages whose body contains "giraffe." Note that most real search engines do not provide `IN` queries in exactly this way, but some of them let you achieve the same effect by clicking on an "advanced search" option where you can specify that your query words must be in the title, or some other specific part of

a	3-10
cat	1-3 1-7 3-7
dog	2-3 2-7 3-11
mat	1-11 2-11
my	1-2 2-2 3-2
on	1-9 2-9
pets	3-3
sat	1-8 3-12
stood	2-8 3-8
the	1-6 1-10 2-6 2-10 3-6
while	3-9
<bodyEnd>	1-12 2-12 3-13
<bodyStart>	1-5 2-5 3-5
<titleEnd>	1-4 2-4 3-4
<titleStart>	1-1 2-1 3-1

The index for the web pages shown in the previous figure, including metawords.

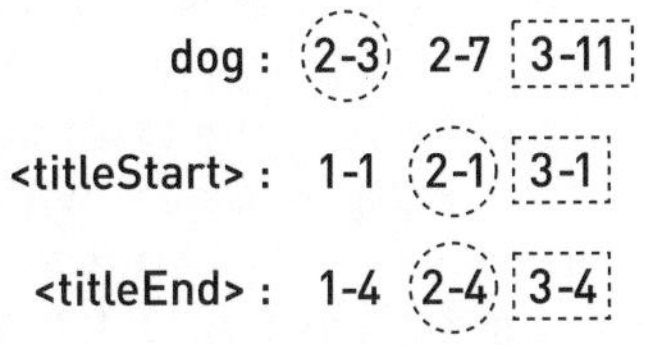

dog : 2-3 2-7 3-11

<titleStart> : 1-1 2-1 3-1

<titleEnd> : 1-4 2-4 3-4

How a search engine performs the search `dog IN TITLE`.

a document. We are pretending that the `IN` keyword exists purely to make our explanations easier. In fact, at the time of writing, Google lets you do a title search using the keyword `intitle:`, so the Google query `intitle:boat` finds pages with "boat" in the title. Try it for yourself!

Let's see how a search engine could efficiently perform the query `dog IN TITLE` on the three-page example shown in the last two figures. First, it extracts the index entry for "dog," which is 2-3, 2-7, 3-11. Then (and this might be a little unexpected, but bear with me for a second) it extracts the index entries for *both* `<titleStart>` and `<titleEnd>`. That results in 1-1, 2-1, 3-1 for `<titleStart>` and 1-4, 2-4, 3-4 for `<titleEnd>`. The information extracted so far is summarized in the figure above—you can ignore the circles and boxes for now.

The search engine then starts scanning the index entry for "dog," examining each of its hits and checking whether or not it occurs inside a title. The first hit for "dog" is the circled entry 2-3, corresponding to the third word of page number 2. By scanning along the entries for `<titleStart>`, the search engine can find out where the title for page 2 begins—that should be the first number that starts with "2-." In this case it arrives at the circled entry 2-1, which means that the title for page 2 begins at word number 1. In the same way, the search engine can find out where the title for page 2 ends. It just scans along the entries for `<titleEnd>`, looking for a number that starts with "2-," and therefore stops at the circled entry 2-4. So page 2's title ends at word 4.

Everything we know so far is summarized by the circled entries in the figure, which tell us the title for page 2 starts at word 1 and ends at word 4, and the word "dog" occurs at word 3. The final step is easy: because 3 is greater than 1 and less than 4, we are certain that this hit for the word "dog" does indeed occur in a title, and therefore page 2 should be a hit for the query `dog IN TITLE`.

The search engine can now move to the next hit for "dog." This happens to be 2-7 (the seventh word of page 2), but because we already know that page 2 is a hit, we can skip over this entry and move on to the next one, 3-11, which is marked by a box. This tells us that "dog" occurs at word 11 on page 3. So we start scanning past the current circled locations in the rows for `<titleStart>` and `<titleEnd>`, looking for entries that start with "3-." (It's important to note that we do not have to go back to the start of each row—we can pick up wherever we left off scanning from the previous hit.) In this simple example, the entry starting with "3-" happens to be the very next number in both cases—3-1 for `<titleStart>` and 3-4 for `<titleEnd>`. These are both marked by boxes for easy reference. Once again, we have the task of determining whether the current hit for "dog" at 3-11 is located inside a title or not. Well, the information in boxes tells us that on page 3, "dog" is at word 11, whereas the title begins at word 1 and ends at word 4. Because 11 is greater than 4, we know that this occurrence of "dog" occurs after the end of the title and is therefore *not* in the title—so page 3 is not a hit for the query `dog IN TITLE`.

So, the metaword trick allows a search engine to answer queries about the structure of a document in an extremely efficient way. The example above was only for searching inside page titles, but very similar techniques allow you to search for words in hyperlinks, image descriptions, and various other useful parts of web pages. And all of these queries can be answered as efficiently as the example above. Just like the queries we discussed earlier, the search engine does not need to go back and look at the original web pages: it can answer the query by consulting just a small number of index entries. And, just as importantly, it only needs to scan through each index entry *once.* Remember what happened when we had finished processing the first hit on page 2 and moved to the possible hit on page 3: instead of going back to the start of the entries for `<titleStart>` and `<titleEnd>`, the search engine could continue scanning from where it had left off. This is a crucial element in making the `IN` query efficient.

Title queries and other "structure queries" that depend on the *structure* of a web page are similar to the `NEAR` queries discussed earlier, in that humans rarely employ structure queries, but search engines use them internally all the time. The reason is the same as before: search engines live or die by their rankings, and rankings can be significantly improved by exploiting the structure of web pages. For example, pages that have "dog" in the title are much more likely to contain information about dogs than pages that mention "dog" only in the body of the page. So when a user enters the simple query `dog`, a search engine could internally perform a `dog IN TITLE` search (even though the user did not explicitly request that) to find pages that are most likely to be *about* dogs, rather than just happening to mention dogs.

INDEXING AND MATCHING TRICKS ARE NOT THE WHOLE STORY

Building a web search engine is no easy task. The final product is like an enormously complex machine with many different wheels, gears, and levers, which must all be set correctly for the system to be useful. Therefore, it is important to realize that the two tricks presented in this chapter do not by themselves solve the problem of building an effective search engine index. However, the word-location trick and the metaword trick certainly convey the *flavor* of how real search engines construct and use indexes.

The metaword trick did help AltaVista succeed—where others had failed—in finding efficient matches to the entire web. We know this because the metaword trick is described in a 1999 U.S. patent filing by AltaVista, entitled "Constrained Searching of an Index." However, AltaVista's superbly crafted matching algorithm was not enough to keep it afloat in the turbulent early days of the search industry. As we already know, efficient matching is only half the story for an effective search engine: the other grand challenge is to *rank* the matching pages. And as we will see in the next chapter, the emergence of a new type of ranking algorithm was enough to eclipse AltaVista, vaulting Google into the forefront of the world of web search.

3

PageRank: The Technology That Launched Google

> The Star Trek computer doesn't seem that interesting. They ask it random questions, it thinks for a while. I think we can do better than that.
>
> —LARRY PAGE (Google cofounder)

Architecturally speaking, the garage is typically a humble entity. But in Silicon Valley, garages have a special entrepreneurial significance: many of the great Silicon Valley technology companies were born, or at least incubated, in a garage. This is not a trend that began in the dot-com boom of the 1990s. Over 50 years earlier—in 1939, with the world economy still reeling from the Great Depression—Hewlett-Packard got underway in Dave Hewlett's garage in Palo Alto, California. Several decades after that, in 1976, Steve Jobs and Steve Wozniak operated out of Jobs' garage in Los Altos, California, after founding their now-legendary Apple computer company. (Although popular lore has it that Apple was founded in the garage, Jobs and Wozniak actually worked out of a bedroom at first. They soon ran out of space and moved into the garage.) But perhaps even more remarkable than the HP and Apple success stories is the launch of a search engine called Google, which operated out of a garage in Menlo Park, California, when first incorporated as a company in September 1998.

By that time, Google had in fact already been running its web search service for well over a year—initially from servers at Stanford University, where both of the cofounders were Ph.D. students. It wasn't until the bandwidth requirements of the increasingly popular service became too much for Stanford that the two students, Larry Page and Sergey Brin, moved the operation into the now-famous Menlo Park garage. They must have been doing something right, because only three months after its legal incorporation as a company, Google was named by *PC Magazine* as one of the top 100 websites for 1998.

And here is where our story really begins: in the words of *PC Magazine*, Google's elite status was awarded for its "uncanny knack for returning extremely relevant results." You may recall from the last chapter that the first commercial search engines had been launched four years earlier, in 1994. How could the garage-bound Google overcome this phenomenal four-year deficit, leapfrogging the already-popular Lycos and AltaVista in terms of search quality? There is no simple answer to this question. But one of the most important factors, especially in those early days, was the innovative algorithm used by Google for ranking its search results: an algorithm known as *PageRank*.

The name "PageRank" is a pun: it's an algorithm that ranks web pages, but it's also the ranking algorithm of Larry Page, its chief inventor. Page and Brin published the algorithm in 1998, in an academic conference paper, "The Anatomy of a Large-scale Hypertextual Web Search Engine." As its title suggests, this paper does much more than describe PageRank. It is, in fact, a complete description of the Google system as it existed in 1998. But buried in the technical details of the system is a description of what may well be the first algorithmic gem to emerge in the 21st century: the PageRank algorithm. In this chapter, we'll explore how and why this algorithm is able to find needles in haystacks, consistently delivering the most relevant results as the top hits to a search query.

THE HYPERLINK TRICK

You probably already know what a hyperlink is: it is a phrase on a web page that takes you to another web page when you click on it. Most web browsers display hyperlinks underlined in blue so that they stand out easily.

Hyperlinks are a surprisingly old idea. In 1945 — around the same time that electronic computers themselves were first being developed — the American engineer Vannevar Bush published a visionary essay entitled "As We May Think." In this wide-ranging essay, Bush described a slew of potential new technologies, including a machine he called the *memex*. A memex would store documents and automatically index them, but it would also do much more. It would allow "associative indexing, ... whereby any item may be caused at will to select immediately and automatically another"—in other words, a rudimentary form of hyperlink!

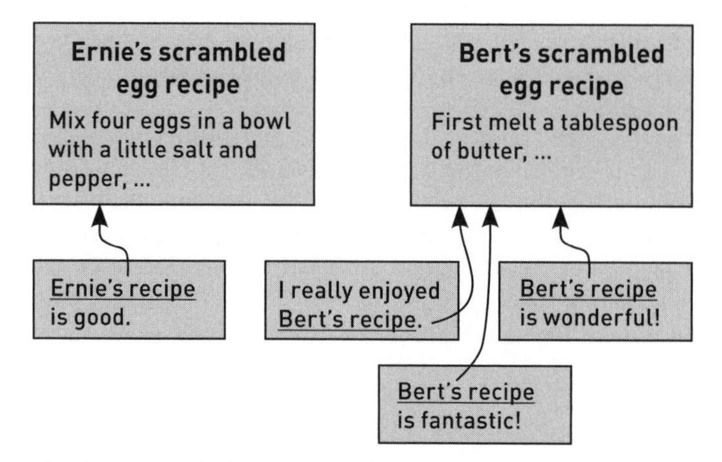

The basis of the hyperlink trick. Six web pages are shown, each represented by a box. Two of the pages are scrambled egg recipes, and the other four are pages that have hyperlinks to these recipes. The hyperlink trick ranks Bert's page above Ernie's, because Bert has three incoming links and Ernie only has one.

Hyperlinks have come along way since 1945. They are one of the most important tools used by search engines to perform ranking, and they are fundamental to Google's PageRank technology, which we'll now begin to explore in earnest.

The first step in understanding PageRank is a simple idea we'll call the *hyperlink trick*. This trick is most easily explained by an example. Suppose you are interested in learning how to make scrambled eggs and you do a web search on that topic. Now any real web search on scrambled eggs turns up millions of hits, but to keep things really simple, let's imagine that only two pages come up—one called "Ernie's scrambled egg recipe" and the other called "Bert's scrambled egg recipe." These are shown in the figure above, together with some other web pages that have hyperlinks to either Bert's recipe or Ernie's. To keep things simple (again), let's imagine that the four pages shown are the *only* pages on the entire web that link to either of our two scrambled egg recipes. The hyperlinks are shown as underlined text, with arrows to show where the link goes to.

The question is, which of the two hits should be ranked higher, Bert or Ernie? As humans, it's not much trouble for us to read the pages that link to the two recipes and make a judgment call. It seems that both of the recipes are reasonable, but people are much more enthusiastic about Bert's recipe than Ernie's. So in the absence of any other information, it probably makes more sense to rank Bert above Ernie.

Unfortunately, computers are not good at understanding what a web page actually means, so it is not feasible for a search engine to examine the four pages linking to the hits and make an assessment of how strongly each recipe is recommended. On the other hand, computers are excellent at counting things. So one simple approach is to simply *count* the number of pages that link to each of the recipes—in this case, one for Ernie, and three for Bert—and rank the recipes according to how many incoming links they have. Of course, this approach is not nearly as accurate as having a human read all the pages and determine a ranking manually, but it is nevertheless a useful technique. It turns out that, if you have no other information, the number of incoming links that a web page has can be a helpful indicator of how useful, or "authoritative," the page is likely to be. In this case, the score is Bert 3, Ernie 1, so Bert's page gets ranked above Ernie's when the search engine's results are presented to the user.

You can probably already see some problems with this "hyperlink trick" for ranking. One obvious issue is that sometimes links are used to indicate *bad* pages rather than good ones. For example, imagine a web page that linked to Ernie's recipe by saying, "I tried Ernie's recipe, and it was awful." Links like this one, that criticize a page rather than recommend it, do indeed cause the hyperlink trick to rank pages more highly than they deserve. But it turns out that, in practice, hyperlinks are more often recommendations than criticisms, so the hyperlink trick remains useful despite this obvious flaw.

THE AUTHORITY TRICK

You may already be wondering why all the incoming links to a page should be treated equally. Surely a recommendation from an expert is worth more than one from a novice? To understand this in detail, we will stick with the scrambled eggs example from before, but with a different set of incoming links. The figure on the following page shows the new setup: Bert and Ernie each now have the same number of incoming links (just one), but Ernie's incoming link is from my own home page, whereas Bert's is from the famous chef Alice Waters.

If you had no other information, whose recipe would you prefer? Obviously, it's better to choose the one recommended by a famous chef, rather than the one recommended by the author of a book about computer science. This basic principle is what we'll call the "authority trick": links from pages with high "authority" should result in a higher ranking than links from pages with low authority.

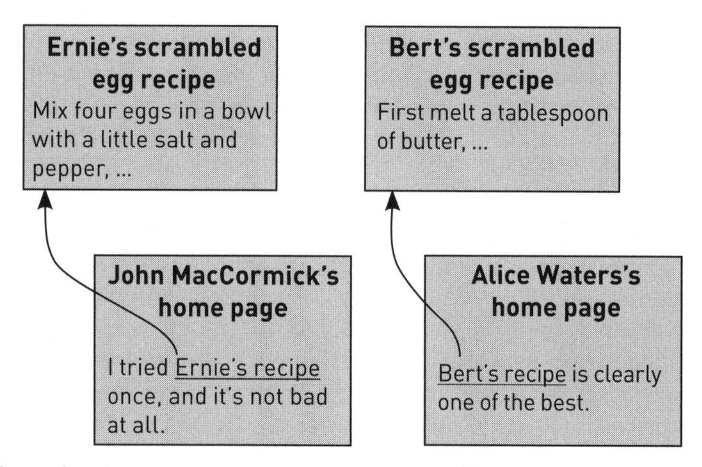

The basis for the authority trick. Four web pages are shown: two scrambled egg recipes and two pages that link to the recipes. One of the links is from the author of this book (who is *not* a famous chef) and one is from the home page of the famous chef Alice Waters. The authority trick ranks Bert's page above Ernie's, because Bert's incoming link has greater "authority" than Ernie's.

This principle is all well and good, but in its present form it is useless to search engines. How can a computer automatically determine that Alice Waters is a greater authority on scrambled eggs than me? Here is an idea that might help: let's combine the hyperlink trick with the authority trick. All pages start off with an authority score of 1, but if a page has some incoming links, its authority is calculated by adding up the authority of all the pages that point to it. In other words, if pages X and Y link to page Z, then the authority of Z is just the authority of X plus the authority of Y.

The figure on the next page gives a detailed example, calculating authority scores for the two scrambled egg recipes. The final scores are shown in circles. There are two pages that link to my home page; these pages have no incoming links themselves, so they get scores of 1. My home page gets the total score of all its incoming links, which adds up to 2. Alice Waters's home page has 100 incoming links that each have a score of 1, so she gets a score of 100. Ernie's recipe has only one incoming link, but it is from a page with a score of 2, so by adding up all the incoming scores (in this case there is only one number to add), Ernie gets a score of 2. Bert's recipe also has only one incoming link, valued at 100, so Bert's final score is 100. And because 100 is greater than 2, Bert's page gets ranked above Ernie's.

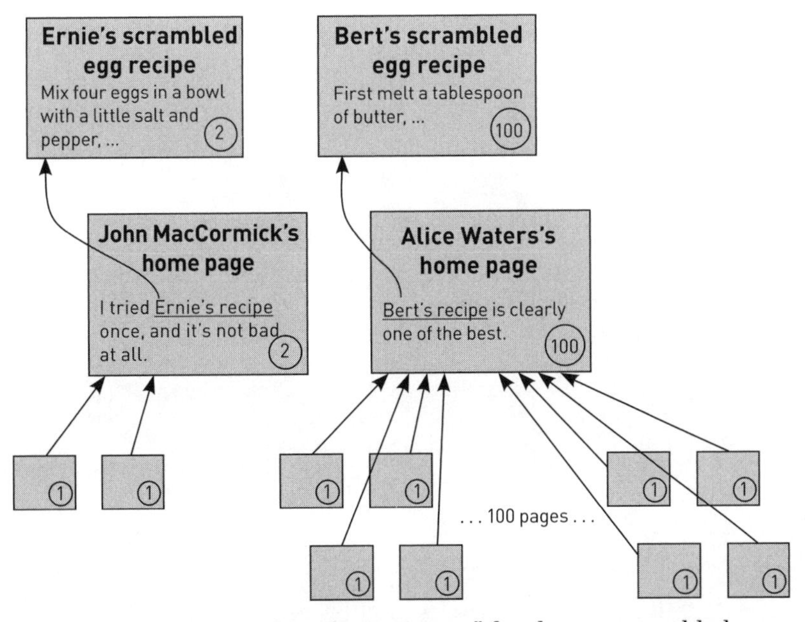

A simple calculation of "authority scores" for the two scrambled egg recipes. The authority scores are shown in circles.

THE RANDOM SURFER TRICK

It seems like we have hit on a strategy for automatically calculating authority scores that really works, without any need for a computer to actually understand the content of a page. Unfortunately, there can be a major problem with the approach. It is quite possible for hyperlinks to form what computer scientists call a "cycle." A cycle exists if you can get back to your starting point just by clicking on hyperlinks.

The figure on the following page gives an example. There are 5 web pages labeled A, B, C, D, and E. If we start at A, we can click through from A to B, and then from B to E—and from E we can click through to A, which is where we started. This means that A, B, and E form a cycle.

It turns out that our current definition of "authority score" (combining the hyperlink trick and the authority trick) gets into big trouble whenever there is a cycle. Let's see what happens on this particular example. Pages C and D have no incoming links, so they get a score of 1. C and D both link to A, so A gets the sum of C and D, which is $1 + 1 = 2$. Then B gets the score 2 from A, and E gets 2 from B. (The situation so far is summarized by the left-hand panel of the

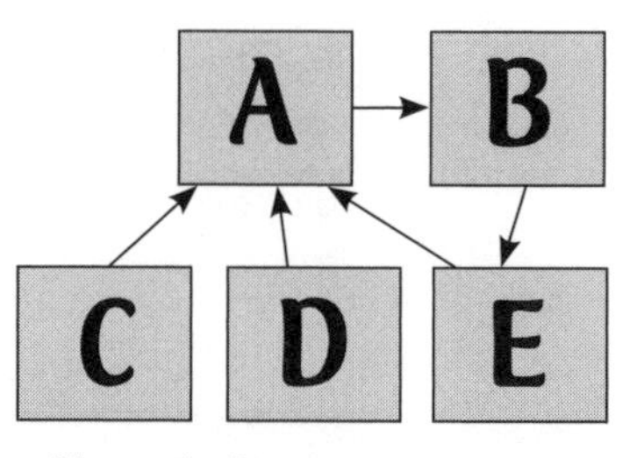

An example of a cycle of hyperlinks. Pages A, B, and E form a cycle because you can start at A, click through to B, then E, and then return to your starting point at A.

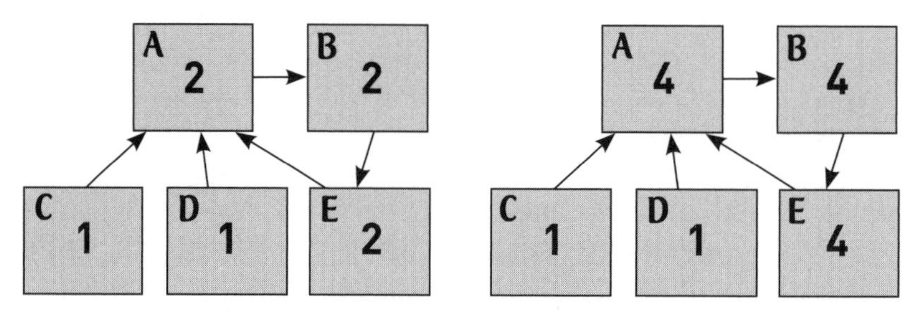

The problem caused by cycles. A, B, and E are always out of date, and their scores keep growing forever.

figure above.) But now A is out of date: it still gets 1 each from C and D, but it also gets 2 from E, for a total of 4. But now B is out of date: it gets 4 from A. But then E needs updating, so it gets 4 from B. (Now we are at the right-hand panel of the figure above.) And so on: now A is 6, so B is 6, so E is 6, so A is 8, ... You get the idea, right? We have to go on forever with the scores always increasing as we go round the cycle.

Calculating authority scores this way creates a chicken-and-egg problem. If we knew the true authority score for A, we could compute the authority scores for B and E. And if we knew the true scores for B and E, we could compute the score for A. But because each depends on the other, it seems as if this would be impossible.

Fortunately, we can solve this chicken-and-egg problem using a technique we'll call the *random surfer trick*. Beware: the initial description of the random surfer trick bears no resemblance to the hyperlink and authority tricks discussed so far. Once we've covered the basic mechanics of the random surfer trick, we'll do some analysis to uncover its remarkable properties: it combines the desirable features of the hyperlink and authority tricks, but works even when cycles of hyperlinks are present.

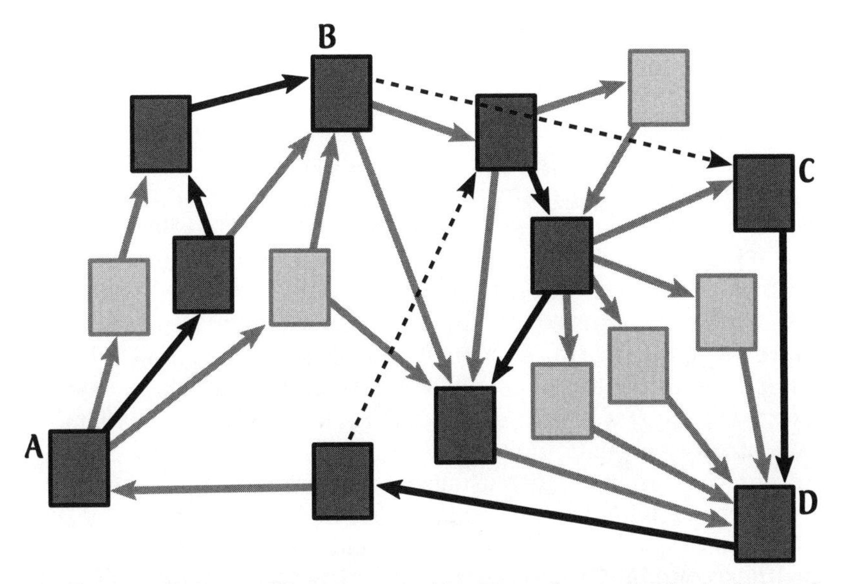

The random surfer model. Pages visited by the surfer are darkly shaded, and the dashed arrows represent random restarts. The trail starts at page *A* and follows randomly selected hyperlinks interrupted by two random restarts.

The trick begins by imagining a person who is randomly surfing the internet. To be specific, our surfer starts off at a single web page selected at random from the entire World Wide Web. The surfer then examines all the hyperlinks on the page, picks one of them at random, and clicks on it. The new page is then examined and one of its hyperlinks is chosen at random. This process continues, with each new page being selected randomly by clicking a hyperlink on the previous page. The figure above shows an example, in which we imagine that the entire World Wide Web consists of just 16 web pages. Boxes represent the web pages, and arrows represent hyperlinks between the pages. Four of the pages are labeled for easy reference later. Web pages visited by the surfer are darkly shaded, hyperlinks clicked by the surfer are colored black, and the dashed arrows represent random restarts, which are described next.

There is one twist in the process: every time a page is visited, there is some fixed *restart probability* (say, 15%) that the surfer does *not* click on one of the available hyperlinks. Instead, he or she restarts the procedure by picking another page randomly from the whole web. It might help to think of the surfer having a 15% chance of getting bored by any given page, causing him or her to follow a new chain of links instead. To see some examples, take a closer look at the figure above. This particular surfer started at page *A* and followed three random hyperlinks before getting bored by page *B* and restarting on page *C*. Two more random hyperlinks were followed before the next restart. (By the way, all the random surfer examples in this chapter use a restart probability of 15%, which is the same value used by Google cofounders Page and Brin in the original paper describing their search engine prototype.)

It's easy to simulate this process by computer. I wrote a program to do just that and ran it until the surfer had visited 1000 pages. (Of course, this doesn't mean 1000 distinct pages. Multiple visits to the same page are counted, and in this small example, all of the pages were visited many times.) The results of the 1000 simulated visits are shown in the top panel of the figure on the next page. You can see that page *D* was the most frequently visited, with 144 visits.

Just as with public opinion polls, we can improve the accuracy of our simulation by increasing the number of random samples. I reran the simulation, this time waiting until the surfer had visited one million pages. (In case you're wondering, this takes less than half a second on my computer!) With such a large number of visits, it's preferable to present the results as percentages. This is what you can see in the bottom panel of the figure on the facing page. Again, page *D* was the most frequently visited, with 15% of the visits.

What is the connection between our random surfer model and the authority trick that we would like to use for ranking web pages? The percentages calculated from random surfer simulations turn out to be exactly what we need to measure a page's authority. So let's define the *surfer authority score* of a web page to be the percentage of time that a random surfer would spend visiting that page. Remarkably, the surfer authority score incorporates both of our earlier tricks for ranking the importance of web pages. We'll examine these each in turn.

First, we had the hyperlink trick: the main idea here was that a page with many incoming links should receive a high ranking. This is also true in the random surfer model, because a page with many incoming links has many chances to be visited. Page *D* in the lower panel on the next page is a good example of this: it has five incoming links—more than any other page in the simulation—and ends up having the highest surfer authority score (15%).

Second, we had the authority trick. The main idea was that an incoming link from a highly authoritative page should improve a page's ranking more than an incoming link from a less authoritative page. Again, the random surfer model takes account of this. Why? Because an incoming link from a popular page will have more opportunities to be followed than a link from an unpopular page. To

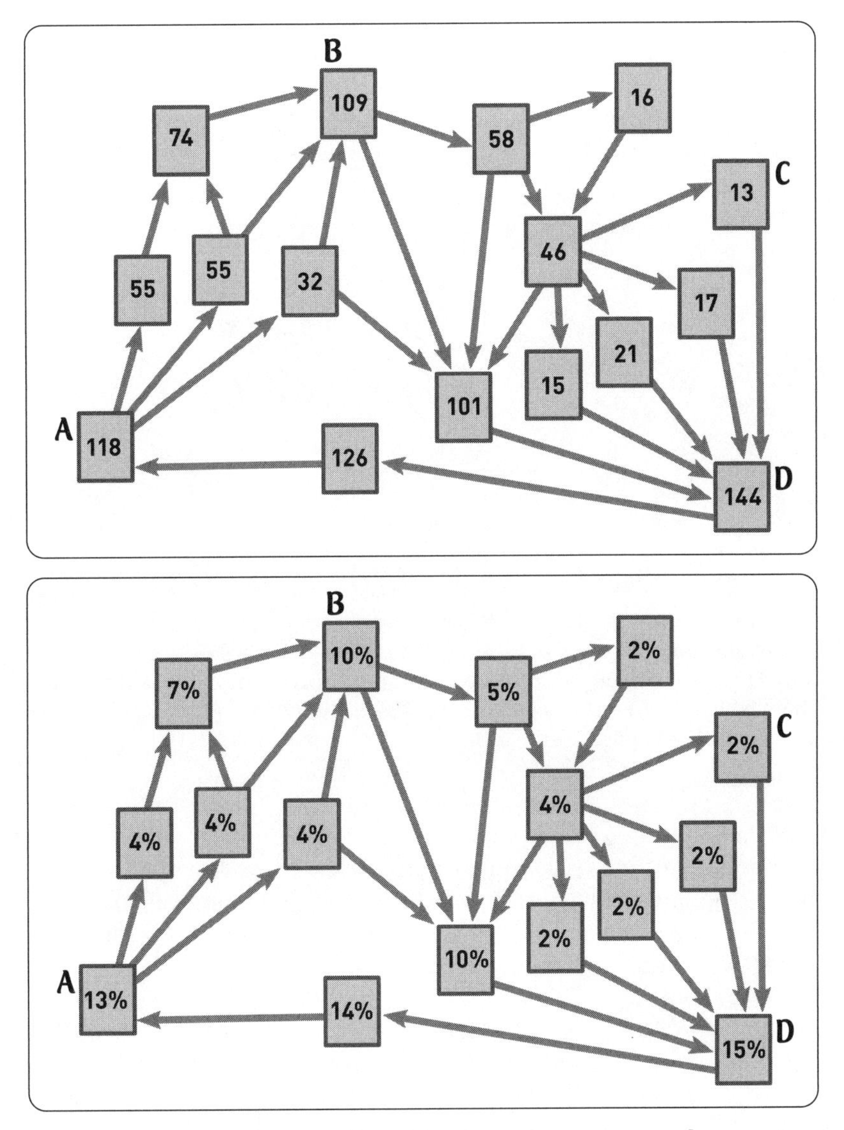

Random surfer simulations. Top: Number of visits to each page in a 1000-visit simulation. Bottom: Percentage of visits to each page in a simulation of one million visits.

see an instance of this in our simulation example, compare pages *A* and *C* in the lower panel above: each has exactly one incoming link, but page *A* has a much higher surfer authority score (13% vs. 2%) because of the quality of its incoming link.

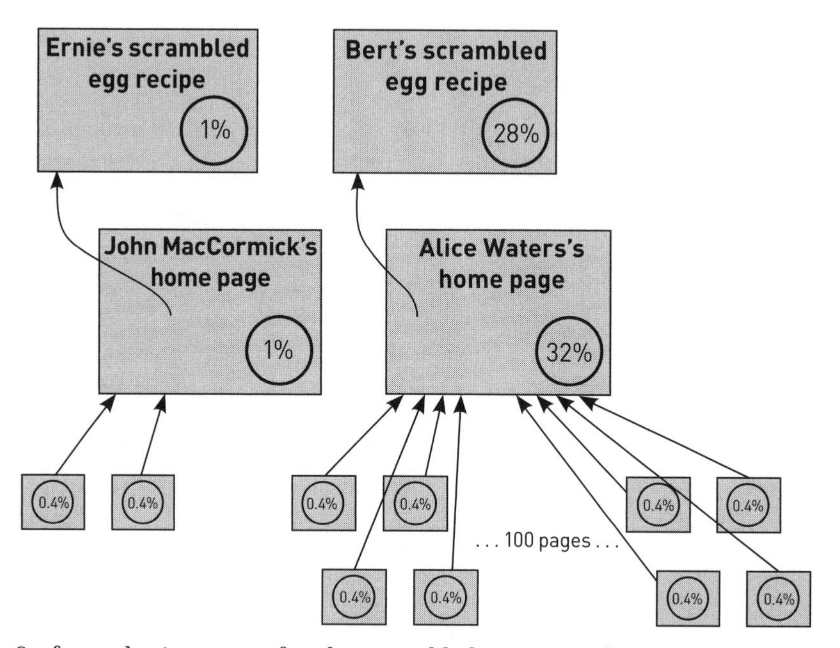

Surfer authority scores for the scrambled egg example on page 29. Bert and Ernie each have exactly one incoming link conferring authority on their pages, but Bert's page will be ranked higher in a web search query for "scrambled eggs."

Notice that the random surfer model simultaneously incorporates both the hyperlink trick and authority trick. In other words, the quality and quantity of incoming links at each page are all taken into account. Page *B* demonstrates this: it receives its relatively high score (10%) due to three incoming links from pages with moderate scores, ranging from 4% to 7%.

The beauty of the random surfer trick is that, unlike the authority trick, it works perfectly well whether or not there are cycles in the hyperlinks. Going back to our earlier scrambled egg example (page 29), we can easily run a random surfer simulation. After several million visits, my own simulation produced the surfer authority scores shown in the figure above. Notice that, as with our earlier calculation using the authority trick, Bert's page receives a much higher score than Ernie's (28% vs. 1%)—despite the fact that each has exactly one incoming link. So Bert would be ranked higher in a web search query for "scrambled eggs."

Now let's turn to the more difficult example from earlier: the figure on page 30, which caused an insurmountable problem for our

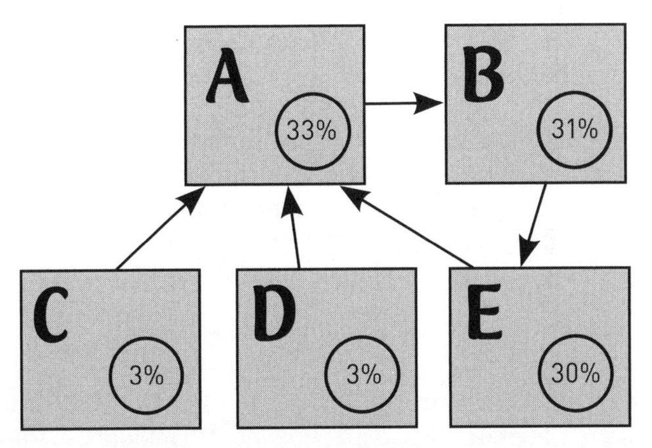

Surfer authority scores for the earlier example with a cycle of hyperlinks (page 30). The random surfer trick has no trouble computing appropriate scores, despite the presence of a cycle ($A \rightarrow B \rightarrow E \rightarrow A$).

original authority trick because of the cycle of hyperlinks. Again, it's easy to run a computer simulation of random surfers, producing the surfer authority scores in the figure above. The surfer authority scores determined by this simulation tell us the final ranking that would be used by a search engine when returning results: page *A* is highest, followed by *B*, then *E*, with *C* and *D* sharing last place.

PAGERANK IN PRACTICE

The random surfer trick was described by Google's cofounders in their now-famous 1998 conference paper, "The Anatomy of a Large-scale Hypertextual Web Search Engine." In combination with many other techniques, variants of this trick are still used by the major search engines. There are, however, numerous complicating factors, which mean that the actual techniques employed by modern search engines differ somewhat from the random surfer trick described here.

One of these complicating factors strikes at the heart of PageRank: the assumption that hyperlinks confer legitimate authority is sometimes questionable. We already learned that although hyperlinks can represent criticisms rather than recommendations, this tends not to be a significant problem in practice. A much more severe problem is that people can abuse the hyperlink trick to artificially inflate the ranking of their own web pages. Suppose you run a website called BooksBooksBooks.com that sells (surprise, surprise) books. Using automated technology, it's relatively easy to create a large number—say, 10,000—of different web pages that all have links to BooksBooksBooks.com. Thus, if search engines computed PageRank authorities exactly as described here, BooksBooksBooks.com might undeservedly get a score thousands of times higher than other bookstores, resulting in a high ranking and thus more sales.

Search engines call this kind of abuse *web spam*. (The terminology comes from an analogy with e-mail spam: unwanted messages in your e-mail inbox are similar to unwanted web pages that clutter the results of a web search.) Detecting and eliminating various types of web spam are important ongoing tasks for all search engines. For example, in 2004, some researchers at Microsoft found over 300,000 websites that had *exactly* 1001 pages linking to them—a very suspicious state of affairs. By inspecting these websites manually, the researchers found that the vast majority of these incoming hyperlinks were web spam.

Hence, search engines are engaged in an arms race against web spammers and are constantly trying to improve their algorithms in order to return realistic rankings. This drive to improve PageRank has spawned a great deal of academic and industrial research into other algorithms that use the hyperlink structure of the web for ranking pages. Algorithms of this kind are often referred to as *link-based ranking algorithms*.

Another complicating factor relates to the efficiency of PageRank computations. Our surfer authority scores were computed by running random simulations, but running a simulation of that kind on the entire web would take far too long to be of practical use. So search engines do not compute their PageRank values by simulating random surfers: they use mathematical techniques that give the same answers as our own random surfer simulations, but with far less computational expense. We studied the surfer-simulation technique because of its intuitive appeal, and because it describes *what* the search engines calculate, not *how* they calculate it.

It's also worth noting that commercial search engines determine their rankings using a lot more than just a link-based ranking algorithm like PageRank. Even in their original, published description of Google back in 1998, Google's cofounders mentioned several other features that contributed to the ranking of search results. As you might expect, the technology has moved on from there: at the time of writing, Google's own website states that "more than 200 signals" are used in assessing the importance of a page.

Despite the many complexities of modern search engines, the beautiful idea at the heart of PageRank—that authoritative pages can confer authority on other pages via hyperlinks—remains valid.

It was this idea that helped Google to dethrone AltaVista, transforming Google from small startup to king of search in a few heady years. Without the core idea of PageRank, most web search queries would drown in a sea of thousands of matching, but irrelevant, web pages. PageRank is indeed an algorithmic gem that allows a needle to rise effortlessly to the top of its haystack.

4

Public Key Cryptography: Sending Secrets on a Postcard

> Who knows those most secret things of me that are hidden from the world?
>
> —Bob Dylan, *Covenant Woman*

Humans love to gossip, and they love secrets. And since the goal of cryptography is to communicate secrets, we are all natural cryptographers. But humans can communicate secretly more easily than computers. If you want to tell a secret to your friend, you can just whisper in your friend's ear. It's not so easy for computers to do that. There's no way for one computer to "whisper" a credit card number to another computer. If the computers are connected by the internet, they have no control over where that credit card number goes, and which other computers get to find it out. In this chapter we'll find out how computers get around this problem, using one of the most ingenious and influential computer science ideas of all time: public key cryptography.

At this point, you may be wondering why the title of this chapter refers to "sending secrets on a postcard." The figure on the facing page reveals the answer: communicating via postcards can be used as an analogy to demonstrate the power of public key cryptography. In real life, if you wanted to send a confidential document to someone, you would, of course, enclose the document in a securely sealed envelope before sending it. This doesn't guarantee confidentiality, but it is a sensible step in the right direction. If, on the other hand, you chose to write your confidential message on the back of a postcard before sending it, confidentiality is obviously violated: anyone who comes in contact with the postcard (postal workers, for example) can just look at the postcard and read the message.

This is precisely the problem that computers face when trying to communicate confidentially with each other on the internet. Because

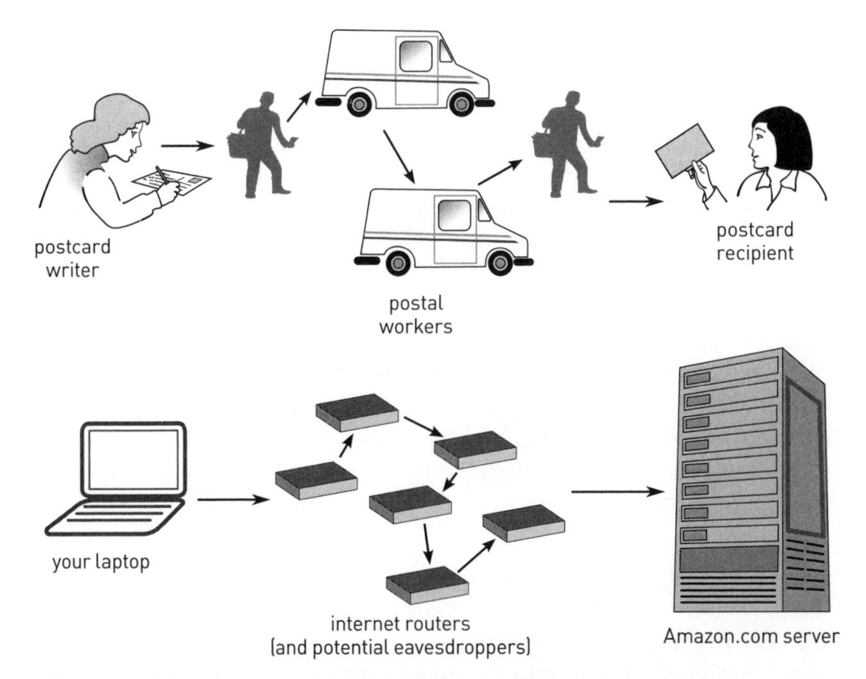

The postcard analogy: It's obvious that sending a postcard through the mail system will not keep the contents of the postcard secret. For the same reason, a credit card number sent from your laptop to Amazon.com can easily be snooped by an eavesdropper if it is not properly encrypted.

any message on the internet typically travels through numerous computers called routers, the contents of the message can be seen by anyone with access to the routers—and this includes potentially malicious eavesdroppers. Thus, every single piece of data that leaves your computer and enters the internet might as well be written on a postcard!

You may have already thought of a quick fix for this postcard problem. Why don't we just use a secret code to encrypt each message before writing it on a postcard? Actually, this works just fine if you already know the person to whom you're sending the postcard. This is because you could have agreed, at some time in the past, on what secret code to use. The real problem is when you send a postcard to someone you don't know. If you use a secret code on this postcard, the postal workers will not be able to read your message, but neither will the intended recipient! The real power of public key cryptography is that it allows you to employ a secret code that only the recipient can decrypt—despite the fact that you had no chance to secretly agree on what code to use.

Note that computers face the same problem of communicating with recipients they don't "know." For example, the first time you purchase something from Amazon.com using your credit card, your computer must transmit your credit card number to a server computer at Amazon. But your computer has never communicated before with the Amazon server, so there has been no opportunity in the past for these two computers to agree on a secret code. And any agreement they try to make can be observed by all routers on the internet route between them.

Let's switch back to the postcard analogy. Admittedly, the situation sounds like a paradox: the recipient will see exactly the same information as the postal workers, but somehow the recipient will learn how to decode the message, whereas the postal workers will not. Public key cryptography provides a resolution to this paradox. This chapter explains how.

ENCRYPTING WITH A SHARED SECRET

Let's start with a very simple thought experiment. We'll abandon the postcard analogy for something even simpler: verbal communication in a room. Specifically, you're in a room with your friend Arnold and your enemy Eve. You want to secretly communicate a message to Arnold, without Eve being able to understand the message. Maybe the message is a credit card number, but let's keep things simple and suppose that it's an incredibly short credit card number—just a single digit between 1 and 9. Also, the only way you're allowed to communicate with Arnold is by speaking out loud so that Eve can overhear. No sneaky tricks, like whispering or passing him a handwritten note, are permitted.

To be specific, let's assume the credit card number you're trying to communicate is the number 7. Here's one way you could go about it. First, try to think of some number that Arnold knows but Eve doesn't. Let's say, for example, that you and Arnold are very old friends and lived on the same street as children. In fact, suppose you both often played in the front yard of your family's house at 322 Pleasant Street. Also, suppose that Eve didn't know you as a child and, in particular, she doesn't know the address of this house where you and Arnold used to play. Then you can say to Arnold: "Hey Arnold, remember the number of my family's house on Pleasant Street where we used to play as children? Well, if you take that house number, and add on the 1-digit credit card number I'm thinking of right now, you get 329."

The addition trick: The message 7 is encrypted by adding it to the shared secret, 322. Arnold can decrypt it by subtracting the shared secret, but Eve cannot.

Now, as long as Arnold remembers the house number correctly, he can work out the credit card number by subtracting off the house number from the total you told him: 329. He calculates 329 minus 322 and gets 7, which is the credit card number you were trying to communicate to him. Meanwhile, Eve has no idea what the credit card number is, despite the fact that she heard every word you said to Arnold. The figure above demonstrates the whole process.

Why does this method work? Well, you and Arnold have a thing that computer scientists call a *shared secret*: the number 322. Because you both know this number, but Eve doesn't, you can use the shared secret to secretly communicate any other number you want, just by adding it on, announcing the total, and letting the other party subtract the shared secret. Hearing the total is of no use to Eve, because she doesn't know what number to subtract from it.

Believe it or not, if you understood this simple "addition trick" of adding a shared secret to a private message like a credit card number, then you already understand how the vast majority of encryption on the internet actually works! Computers are constantly using this trick, but for it to be truly secure there are a few more details that need to be taken care of.

First, the shared secrets that computers use need to be much longer than the house number 322. If the secret is too short, anyone eavesdropping on the conversation can just try out all the possibilities. For example, suppose we used a 3-digit house number to encrypt a *real* 16-digit credit card number using the addition trick.

Note that there are 999 possible 3-digit house numbers, so an adversary like Eve who overheard our conversation could work out a list of 999 possible numbers, of which one must be the credit card number. It would take a computer almost no time at all to try out 999 credit card numbers, so we need to use a lot more than 3 digits in a shared secret if it is going to be useful.

In fact, when you hear about a type of encryption being a certain number of bits, as in the phrase "128-bit encryption," this is actually a description of how long the shared secret is. The shared secret is often called a "key," since it can be used to unlock, or "decrypt," a message. If you work out 30% of the number of bits in the key, that tells you the approximate number of digits in the key. So because 30% of 128 is about 38, we know that 128-bit encryption uses a key that is a 38-digit number.[1] A 38-digit number is bigger than a billion billion billion billion, and because it would take any known computer billions of years to try out that many possibilities, a shared secret of 38 digits is considered to be very secure.

There's one more wrinkle that prevents the simple version of the addition trick from working in real life: the addition produces results that can be analyzed statistically, meaning that someone could work out your key based on analyzing a large number of your encrypted messages. Instead, modern encryption techniques, called "block ciphers," use a variant of the addition trick.

First, long messages are broken up into small "blocks" of a fixed size, typically around 10–15 characters. Second, rather than simply adding a block of the message and the key together, each block is transformed several times according to a fixed set of rules that are similar to addition but cause the message and the key to be mixed up more aggressively. For example, the rules could say something like "add the first half of the key to the last half of the block, reverse the result and add the second half of the key to the last half of the block"—although in reality the rules are quite a bit more complicated. Modern block ciphers typically use 10 or more "rounds" of these operations, meaning the list of operations is applied repeatedly. After a sufficient number of rounds, the original message is well and truly mixed up and will resist statistical attacks, but anyone who knows the key can run all the operations in reverse to obtain the original, decrypted message.

---

[1]For those who know about computer number systems, I'm referring here to decimal digits, not binary digits (bits). For those who know about logarithms, the conversion factor of 30% for transforming from bits to decimal digits comes from the fact that $\log_{10} 2 \approx 0.3$.

At the time of writing, the most popular block cipher is the Advanced Encryption Standard, or AES. AES can be used with a variety of different settings, but a typical application might use blocks of 16 characters, with 128-bit keys, and 10 rounds of mixing operations.

ESTABLISHING A SHARED SECRET IN PUBLIC

So far, so good. We've already found out how the vast majority of encryption on the internet actually works: chop the message up into blocks and use a variant of the addition trick to encrypt each block. But it turns out that this is the easy part. The hard part is *establishing* a shared secret in the first place. In the example given above, where you were in a room with Arnold and Eve, we actually cheated a bit—we used the fact that you and Arnold had been playmates as children and therefore already knew a shared secret (your family's house number) that Eve couldn't possibly know. What if you, Arnold, and Eve were all strangers, and we tried to play the same game? Is there any way that you and Arnold can set up a shared secret without Eve also knowing it? (Remember, no cheating—you can't whisper anything to Arnold or give him a note that Eve can't see. All communication must be public.)

At first this might seem impossible, but it turns out that there is an ingenious way of solving the problem. Computer scientists call the solution *Diffie-Hellman key exchange*, but we're going to call it the *paint-mixing trick*.

The Paint-Mixing Trick

To understand the trick, we're going to forget about communicating credit card numbers for a while, and instead imagine that the secret you would like to share is a particular color of paint. (Yes, this is a little weird, but as we'll soon see, it's also a very useful way of thinking about the problem.) So now suppose that you are in a room with Arnold and Eve and each of you has a huge collection of various pots of paint. You are each given the same choice of colors—there are many different colors available, and each of you has many pots of each color. So running out of paint is not going to be a problem. Each pot is clearly labeled with its color, so it's easy to give specific instructions to someone else about how to mix various colors together: you just say something like "mix one pot of 'sky blue' with six pots of 'eggshell' and five pots of 'aquamarine'." But there are hundreds or thousands of colors of every conceivable shade, so it's impossible to work out which exact colors went into a mixture just by looking at it. And it's impossible to work out which colors went into a mixture by trial and error, because there are just too many colors to try.

Now, the rules of the game are going to change just a little bit. Each of you is going to have a corner of the room curtained off for privacy, as a place where you store your paint collection and where you can go to secretly mix paints without the others seeing. But the rules about communication are just the same as before: any communication between you, Arnold, and Eve must be out in the open. You can't invite Arnold into your private mixing area! Another rule regulates how you can share mixtures of paint. You can give a batch of paint to one of the other people in the room, but only by placing that batch on the ground in the middle of the room and waiting for someone else to pick it up. This means that you can never be sure who is going to pick up your batch of paint. The best way is to make enough for everybody, and leave several separate batches in the middle of the room. That way anyone who wants one of your batches can get it. This rule is really just an extension of the fact that all communication must be public: if you give a certain mixture to Arnold without giving it to Eve too, you have had some kind of "private" communication with Arnold, which is against the rules.

Remember that this paint-mixing game is meant to explain how to establish a shared secret. At this point you may well be wondering what on earth mixing paints has got to do with cryptography, but don't worry. You are about to learn an amazing trick that is actually used by computers to establish shared secrets in a public place like the internet!

First, we need to know the objective of the game. The objective is for you and Arnold to each produce the *same* mixture of paint, without telling Eve how to produce it. If you achieve this, we'll say that you and Arnold have established a "shared secret mixture." You are allowed to have as much public conversation as you like, and you are also allowed to carry pots of paint back and forth between the middle of the room and your private mixing area.

Now we begin our journey into the ingenious ideas behind public key cryptography. Our paint-mixing trick will be broken down into four steps.

Step 1. You and Arnold each choose a "private color."

Your private color is not the same thing as the shared secret mixture that you will eventually produce, but it will be one of the ingredients in the shared secret mixture. You can choose any color you want as your private color, but you have to remember it. Obviously, your private color will almost certainly be different from Arnold's, since there are so many colors to choose from. As an example, let's say your private color is lavender and Arnold's is crimson.

Step 2. One of you publicly announces the ingredients of a new, different color that we'll call the "public color."

Again, you can choose anything you like. Let's say you announce that the public color is daisy-yellow. Note that there is only one public color (not two separate ones for you and Arnold), and, of course, Eve knows what the public color is because you announce it publicly.

Step 3. You and Arnold each create a mixture by combining one pot of the public color with one pot of your private color. This produces your "public-private mixture."

Obviously, Arnold's public-private mixture will be different from yours, because his private color is different from yours. If we stick with the above example, then your public-private mixture will contain one pot each of lavender and daisy-yellow, whereas Arnold's public-private mixture consists of crimson and daisy-yellow.

At this point, you and Arnold would like to give each other samples of your public-private mixtures, but remember it's against the rules to directly give a mixture of paint to one of the other people in the room. The only way to give a mixture to someone else is to make several batches of it and leave them in the middle of the room so that anyone who wants one can take it. This is exactly what you and Arnold do: each of you makes several batches of your public-private mixture and leaves them in the middle of the room. Eve can steal a batch or two if she wants, but as we will learn in a minute, they will do her no good at all. The figure on the following page shows the situation after this third step of the paint-mixing trick.

OK, now we're getting somewhere. If you think hard at this point, you might see the final trick that would allow you and Arnold to each create an identical shared secret mixture without letting Eve in on the secret. Here's the answer:

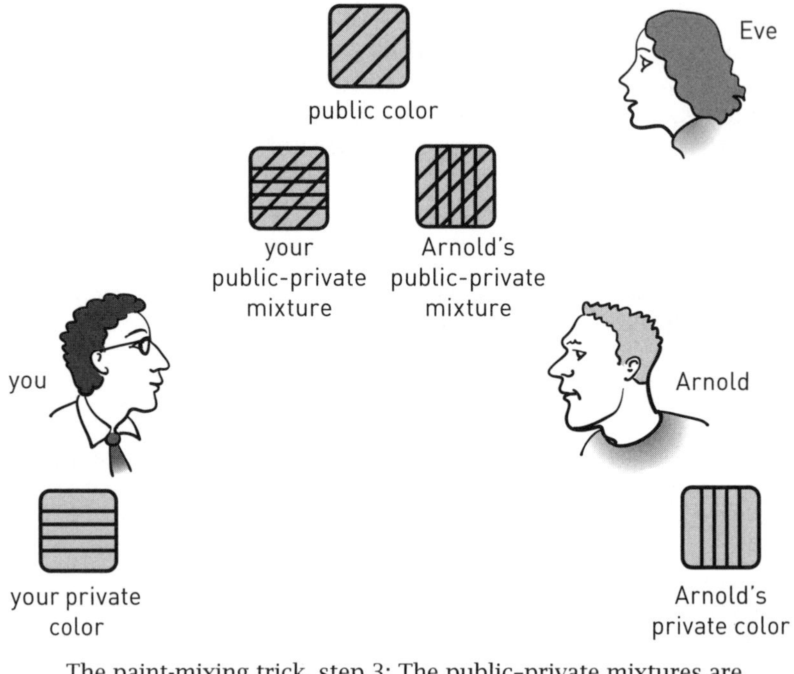

The paint-mixing trick, step 3: The public-private mixtures are available to anyone who wants them.

> **Step 4.** You pick up a batch of Arnold's public-private mixture and take it back to your corner. Now add one pot of your private color. Meanwhile, Arnold picks up a batch of *your* public-private mixture and takes it back to his corner, where he adds it to a pot of *his* private color.

Amazingly, you have both just created identical mixtures! Let's check: you added your private color (lavender) to Arnold's public-private mixture (crimson and daisy-yellow), resulting in a final mixture of 1 lavender, 1 crimson, 1 daisy-yellow. What about Arnold's final mixture? Well, he added his private color (crimson) to your public-private mixture (lavender and daisy-yellow), resulting in a final mixture of 1 crimson, 1 lavender, 1 daisy-yellow. This is exactly the same as your final mixture. It really is a shared secret mixture. The figure on the next page shows the situation after this final step of the paint-mixing trick.

Now, what about Eve? Why can't she create a batch of this shared secret mixture? The reason is that she doesn't know your private

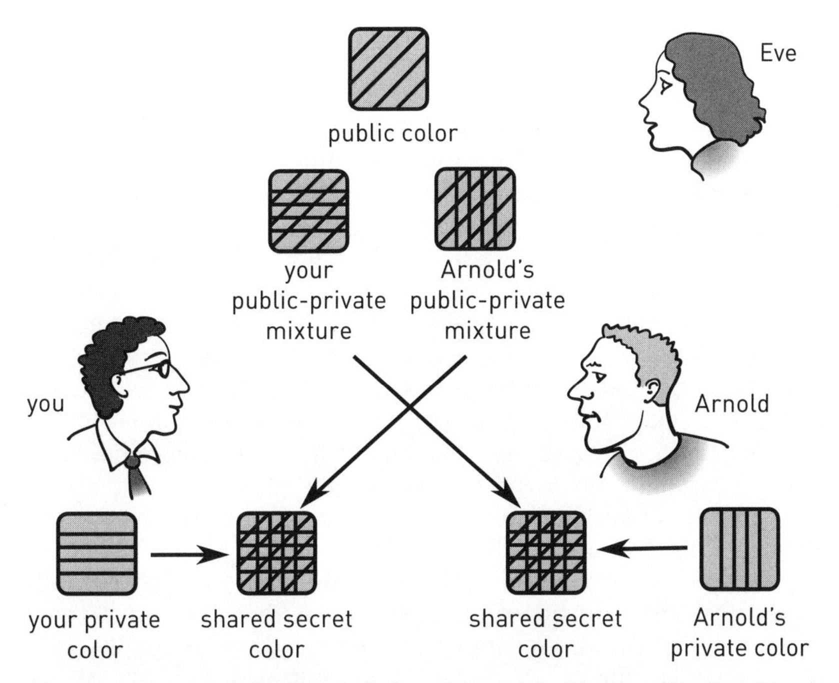

The paint-mixing trick, step 4: Only you and Arnold can make the shared secret color, by combining the mixtures shown by arrows.

color or Arnold's private color, and she needs at least one of them to create the shared secret mixture. You and Arnold have thwarted her, because you never left your private colors exposed, on their own, in the middle of the room. Instead, you each combined your private color with the public color before exposing it, and Eve has no way of "unmixing" the public-private mixtures to obtain a pure sample of one of the private colors.

Thus, Eve has access *only* to the two public-private mixtures. If she mixes one batch of your public-private mixture with one batch of Arnold's public-private mixture, the result will contain 1 crimson, 1 lavender, and 2 daisy-yellow. In other words, compared to the shared secret mixture, Eve's mixture has an extra daisy-yellow. Her mixture is too yellow, and because there's no way to "unmix" paint, she can't remove that extra yellow. You might think Eve could get around this by adding more crimson and lavender, but remember she doesn't know your private colors, so she wouldn't know that these are the colors that need to be added. She can only add the *combination* of crimson plus daisy-yellow or lavender plus daisy-yellow, and these will always result in her mixture being too yellow.

Paint-Mixing with Numbers

If you understand the paint-mixing trick, you understand the essence of how computers establish shared secrets on the internet. But, of course, they don't really use paint. Computers use numbers, and to mix the numbers they use mathematics. The actual math they use isn't too complicated, but it's complicated enough to be confusing at first. So, for our next step toward understanding how shared secrets are established on the internet, we will use some "pretend" math. The real point is that to translate the paint-mixing trick into numbers, we need a *one-way action*: something that can be *done*, but can't be *undone*. In the paint-mixing trick the one-way action was "mixing paint." It's easy to mix some paints together to form a new color, but it's impossible to "unmix" them and get the original colors back. That's why paint-mixing is a one-way action.

We found out earlier that we would be using some pretend math. Here is what we are going to pretend: *multiplying two numbers together is a one-way action*. As I'm sure you realize, this is definitely a pretense. The opposite of multiplication is division, and it's easy to undo a multiplication just by performing a division. For example, if we start with the number 5 and then multiply it by 7, we get 35. It's easy to undo this multiplication by starting with 35 and dividing by 7. That gets us back to the 5 we started with.

But despite that, we are going to stick with the pretense and play another game between you, Arnold, and Eve. And this time, we'll assume you all know how to multiply numbers together, but none of you knows how to divide one number by another number. The objective is almost the same as before: you and Arnold are trying to establish a shared secret, but this time the shared secret will be a number rather than a color of paint. The usual communication rules apply: all communication must be public, so Eve can hear any conversations between you and Arnold.

OK, now all we have to do is translate the paint-mixing trick into numbers:

Step 1. Instead of choosing a "private color," you and Arnold each choose a "private number."

Let's say you choose 4 and Arnold chooses 6. Now think back to the remaining steps of the paint-mixing trick: announcing the public color, making a public–private mixture, publicly swapping your public-private mixture with Arnold's, and finally adding your private color to Arnold's public-private mixture to get the shared secret color. It shouldn't be too hard to see how to translate this into numbers, using multiplication as the one-way action instead of paint-mixing. Take a couple of minutes to see if you can work out this example for yourself, before reading on.

The solution isn't too hard to follow; you've already both chosen your private numbers (4 and 6), so the next step is

> **Step 2.** One of you announces a "public number" (instead of the public color in the paint-mixing trick).

Let's say you choose 7 as the public number.

The next step in the paint-mixing trick was to create a public-private mixture. But we already decided that instead of mixing paints we would be multiplying numbers. So all you have to do is

> **Step 3.** Multiply your private number (4) and the public number (7) to get your "public-private number," 28.

You can announce this publicly so that Arnold and Eve both know your public-private number is 28 (there's no need to carry pots of paint around anymore). Arnold does the same thing with his private number: he multiplies it by the public number, and announces his public-private number, which is 6×7, or 42. The figure on the following page shows the situation at this point in the process.

Remember the last step of the paint-mixing trick? You took Arnold's public-private mixture, and added a pot of your private color to produce the shared secret color. Exactly the same thing happens here, using multiplication instead of paint-mixing:

> **Step 4.** You take Arnold's public-private number, which is 42, and multiply it by your private number, 4, which results in the *shared secret number*, 168.

Meanwhile, Arnold takes *your* public-private number, 28, and multiplies it by *his* private number, 6, and—amazingly—gets the same

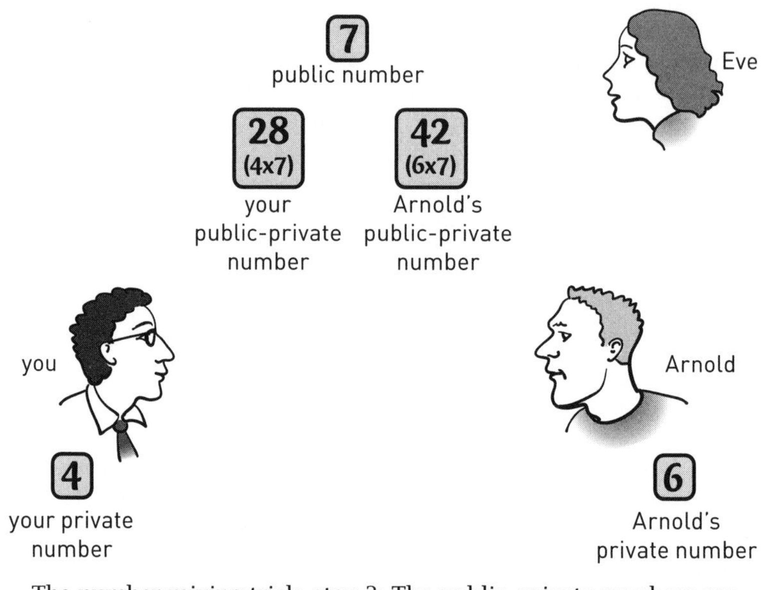

The number-mixing trick, step 3: The public–private numbers are available to anyone who wants them.

shared secret number, since $28 \times 6 = 168$. The final result is shown in the figure on the facing page.

Actually, when you think about it the right way, this isn't amazing at all. When Arnold and you managed to both produce the same shared secret color, it was because you mixed together the same three original colors, but in a different order: each of you kept one of the colors private, combining it with a publicly available mixture of the other two. The same thing has happened here with numbers. You both arrived at the same shared secret by multiplying together the same three numbers: 4, 6, and 7. (Yes, as you can check for yourself, $4 \times 6 \times 7 = 168$.) But *you* arrived at the shared secret by keeping 4 private and "mixing" (i.e., multiplying) it with the publicly available mixture of 6 and 7 (i.e., 42) that had been announced by Arnold. On the other hand, *Arnold* arrived at the shared secret by keeping 6 private and mixing it with the publicly available mixture of 4 and 7 (i.e., 28) that you had announced.

Just as we did in the paint-mixing trick, let's now verify that Eve has no chance of working out the shared secret. Eve gets to hear the value of each public–private number as it is announced. So she hears you say "28," and Arnold say "42." And she also knows the public number, which is 7. So *if* Eve knew how to do division, she could work out all your secrets immediately, just by observing that $28 \div 7 = 4$, and $42 \div 7 = 6$. And she could go on to compute the

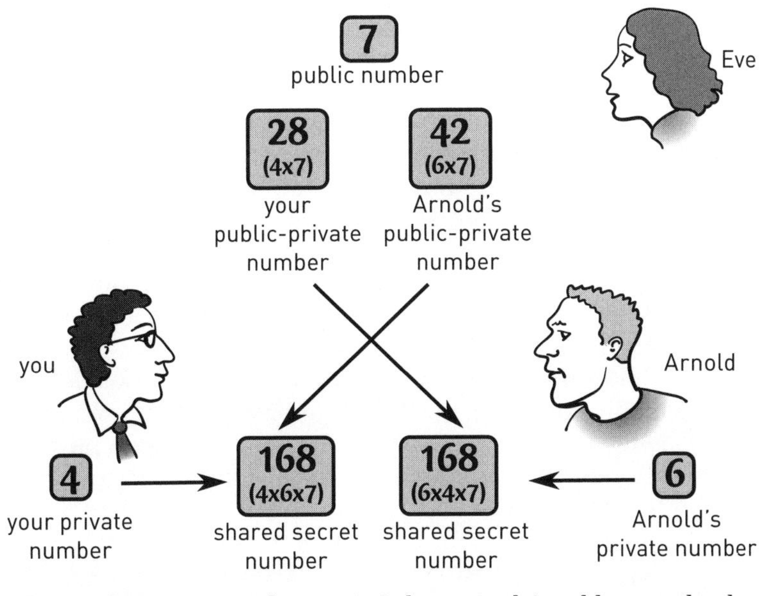

The number-mixing trick, step 4: Only you and Arnold can make the shared secret number, by multiplying together the numbers shown by arrows.

shared secret by calculating $4 \times 6 \times 7 = 168$. However, luckily, we are using pretend math in this game: we assumed that multiplication was a one-way action and therefore Eve *doesn't* know how to divide. So she is stuck with the numbers 28, 42, and 7. She can multiply some of them together, but that doesn't tell her anything about the shared secret. For example, if she takes $28 \times 42 = 1176$, she is way off. Just as in the paint-mixing game her result was too yellow, here her result has too many 7's. The shared secret has only one factor of 7 in it, since $168 = 4 \times 6 \times 7$. But Eve's attempt at cracking the secret has two factors of 7 in it, since $1176 = 4 \times 6 \times 7 \times 7$. And there's no way she can get rid of that extra 7, since she doesn't know how to do division.

Paint-Mixing in Real Life

We have now covered all of the fundamental concepts needed for computers to establish shared secrets on the internet. The only flaw in the paint-mixing-with-numbers scheme is that it uses "pretend math," in which we pretended that none of the parties could do division. To complete the recipe, we need a real-life math operation that is easy to do (like mixing paint) but practically impossible to undo (like unmixing paint). When computers do this in real life, the mixing operation is a thing called *discrete exponentiation* and the unmixing operation is called the *discrete logarithm*. And because there is no known method for a computer to calculate discrete logarithms efficiently, discrete exponentiation turns out to be just the kind of one-way action we are looking for. To explain discrete exponentiation properly, we're going to need two simple mathematical ideas. And we'll also need to write a few formulas. If you don't like formulas, just skip the rest of this section—you already understand almost everything about this topic. On the other hand, if you really want to know how computers do this magic, read on.

The first important math idea we need is called *clock arithmetic*. This is actually something we are all familiar with: there are only 12 numbers on a clock, so every time the hour hand goes past 12, it starts counting again from 1. An activity that starts at 10 o'clock and lasts 4 hours finishes at 2 o'clock, so we might say that $10 + 4 = 2$ in this 12-hour clock system. In mathematics, clock arithmetic works the same way, except for two details: (i) the size of the clock can be any number (rather than the familiar 12 numbers on a regular clock), and (ii) the numbers start counting from 0 rather than 1.

The figure on the next page gives an example using the clock size 7. Note that the numbers on the clock are 0, 1, 2, 3, 4, 5, and 6. To do clock arithmetic with clock size 7, just add and multiply numbers together as normal—but whenever an answer is produced, you only count the *remainder* after dividing by 7. So to compute $12 + 6$, we first do the addition as normal, obtaining 18. Then we notice that 7 goes into 18 twice (making 14), with 4 left over. So the final answer is

$$12 + 6 = 4 \quad \text{(clock size 7)}$$

In the examples below, we'll be using 11 as the clock size. (As discussed later, the clock size in a real implementation would be much, much larger. We are using a small clock size to keep the explanation as simple as possible.) Taking the remainder after dividing by 11 isn't too hard, since the multiples of 11 all have repeated digits like 66 and 88. Here are a few examples of calculations with a clock size of 11:

$$7 + 9 + 8 = 24 = 2 \quad \text{(clock size 11)}$$
$$8 \times 7 = 56 = 1 \quad \text{(clock size 11)}$$

The second math idea we need is *power notation*. This is nothing fancy: it's just a quick way of writing down lots of multiplications of the same number. Instead of writing $6 \times 6 \times 6 \times 6$, which is just 6

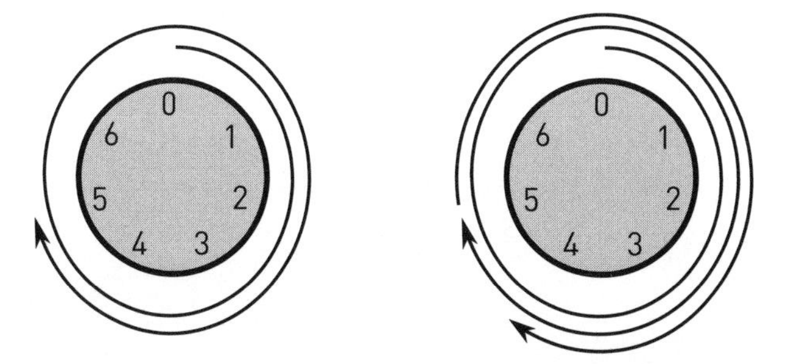

Left: When using a clock size of 7, the number 12 is simplified to the number 5—just start at zero and count 12 units in a clockwise direction, as shown by the arrow. Right: Again using a clock size of 7, we find that $12 + 6 = 4$—starting at 5, where we ended in the left figure, add on another 6 units in clockwise direction.

multiplied by itself 4 times in a row, you can write 6^4. And you can combine power notation with clock arithmetic. For example,

$$3^4 = 3 \times 3 \times 3 \times 3 = 81 = 4 \quad \text{(clock size 11)}$$
$$7^2 = 7 \times 7 = 49 = 5 \quad \text{(clock size 11)}$$

The table on the following page shows the first ten powers of 2, 3, and 6 when using clock size 11. These will be useful in the example we're about to work through. So before plunging on, make sure you're comfortable with how this table was generated. Let's take a look at the last column. The first entry in this column is 6, which is the same thing as 6^1. The next entry represents 6^2, or 36, but since we're using clock size 11 and 36 is 3 more than 33, the entry in the table is a 3. To calculate the third entry in this column, you might think that we need to work out $6^3 = 6 \times 6 \times 6$, but there is an easier way. We have already computed 6^2 for the clock size we're interested in—it turned out to be 3. To get 6^3, we just need to multiply the previous result by 6. This gives $3 \times 6 = 18 = 7$ (clock size 11). And the next entry is $7 \times 6 = 42 = 9$ (clock size 11), and so on down the column.

OK, we are finally ready to establish a shared secret, as used by computers in real life. As usual, you and Arnold will be trying to share a secret, while Eve eavesdrops and tries to work out what the secret is.

Step 1. You and Arnold each separately choose a *private number*.

n	2^n	3^n	6^n
1	2	3	6
2	4	9	3
3	8	5	7
4	5	4	9
5	10	1	10
6	9	3	5
7	7	9	8
8	3	5	4
9	6	4	2
10	1	1	1

This table shows the first ten powers of 2, 3, and 6 when using clock size 11. As explained in the text, each entry can be computed from the one above it by some very simple arithmetic.

To keep the math as easy as possible, we'll use very small numbers in this example. So suppose you choose 8 as your private number, and Arnold chooses 9. These two numbers—8 and 9—are not themselves shared secrets, but just like the private colors you chose in the paint-mixing trick, these numbers will be used as *ingredients* to "mix up" a shared secret.

Step 2. You and Arnold publicly agree on two *public numbers*: a clock size (we'll use 11 in this example) and another number, called the *base* (we'll use the base 2).

These public numbers—11 and 2—are analogous to the public color that you and Arnold agreed on at the start of the paint-mixing trick. Note that the paint-mixing analogy does break down a little here: whereas we needed only one public color, two public numbers are needed.

Step 3. You and Arnold each separately create a *public-private number* (PPN) by mixing up your private number with the public numbers, using power notation and clock arithmetic.

Specifically, the mixing is done according to the formula

$$\text{PPN} = \text{base}^{\text{private number}} \quad (\text{clock size})$$

This formula might look a little weird written out in words, but it's simple in practice. In our example, we can work out the answers by consulting the table on the previous page:

$$\text{your PPN} = 2^8 = 3 \quad (\text{clock size } 11)$$
$$\text{Arnold's PPN} = 2^9 = 6 \quad (\text{clock size } 11)$$

You can see the situation after this step in the figure on the following page. These public-private numbers are precisely analogous to the "public-private mixtures" that you made in the third step of the paint-mixing trick. There, you mixed one pot of the public color with one part of your private color to make your public-private mixture. Here, you have mixed your private number with the public numbers using power notation and clock arithmetic.

Step 4. You and Arnold each separately take the other's public-private number and mix it in with your own private number.

This is done according to the formula

$$\text{shared secret} = \text{other person's PPN}^{\text{private number}} \quad (\text{clock size})$$

Again this looks a little weird written out in words, but by consulting the table on the previous page, it works out simply in numbers:

$$\text{your shared secret} = 6^8 = 4 \quad (\text{clock size } 11)$$
$$\text{Arnold's shared secret} = 3^9 = 4 \quad (\text{clock size } 11)$$

The final situation is shown in the figure on page 57.

Naturally, your shared secret and Arnold's shared secret end up being the same number (in this case, 4). It depends on some sophisticated mathematics in this case, but the basic idea is the same as before: although you mixed your ingredients in a different order,

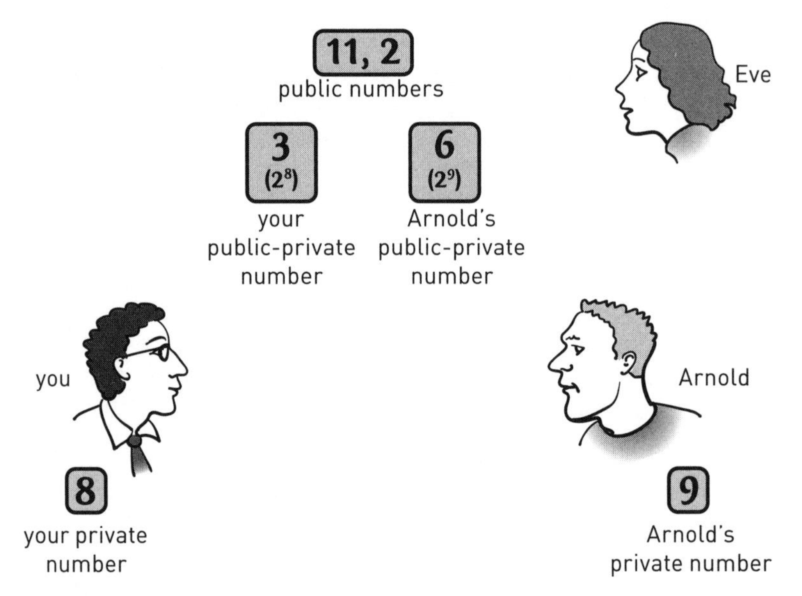

Real-life number-mixing, step 3: The public-private numbers (3 and 6), computed using powers and clock arithmetic, are available to anyone who wants them. The "2^8" shown below the 3 reminds us how the 3 was computed, but the fact that $3 = 2^8$ in clock size 11 is not made public. Similarly, the "2^9" shown below the 6 remains private.

both you and Arnold used the same ingredients and therefore produced the same shared secret.

And as with the earlier versions of this trick, Eve is left out in the cold. She knows the two public numbers (2 and 11), and she also knows the two public-private numbers (3 and 6). But she can't use any of this knowledge to compute the shared secret number, because she can't access either of the secret ingredients (the private numbers) held by you and Arnold.

PUBLIC KEY CRYPTOGRAPHY IN PRACTICE

The final version of the paint-mixing trick, mixing numbers using powers and clock arithmetic, is one of the ways that computers actually establish shared secrets on the internet. The particular method described here is called the Diffie–Hellman key exchange protocol, named for Whitfield Diffie and Martin Hellman, who first published the algorithm in 1976. Whenever you go to a secure website (one that starts with "`https:`" rather than "`http:`"), your own computer and the web server it's communicating with create a shared secret, using the Diffie–Hellman protocol or one of several alternatives that work

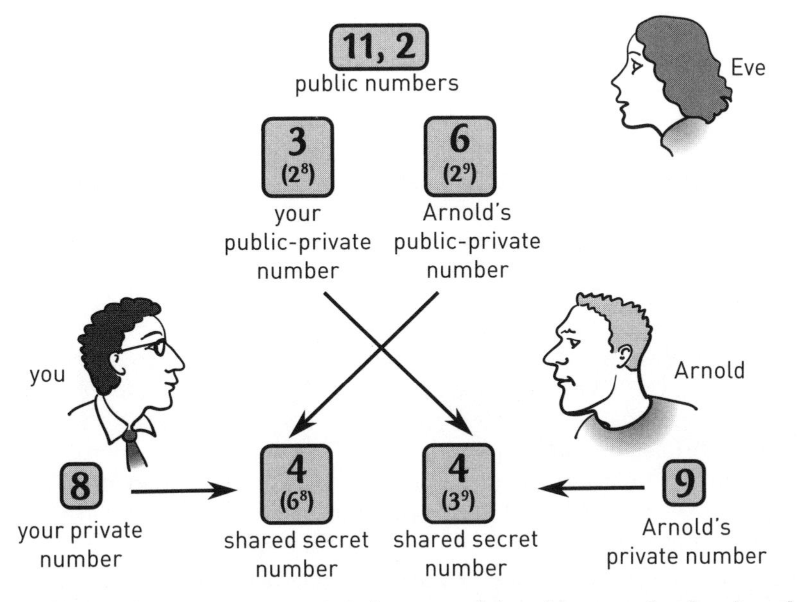

Real-life number-mixing, step 4: Only you and Arnold can make the shared secret number, by combining together the elements shown with arrows, using powers and clock arithmetic.

in a similar way. And once this shared secret is established, the two computers can encrypt all their communication using a variant of the addition trick described earlier.

It's important to realize that when the Diffie–Hellman protocol is used in practice, the actual numbers involved are far larger than the examples we worked through here. We used a very small clock size (11), so that the calculations would be easy. But if you choose a small public clock size, then the number of possible private numbers is also small (since you can only use private numbers that are smaller than the clock size). And that means someone could use a computer to try out all the possible private numbers until they find one that produces your public-private number. In the example above, there were only 11 possible private numbers, so this system would be ludicrously easy to crack. In contrast, real implementations of the Diffie–Hellman protocol typically use a clock size that is a few hundred digits long, which creates an unimaginably large number of possible private numbers (much more than a trillion trillion). And even then, the public numbers must be chosen with some care, to make sure they have the correct mathematical properties—check out the box on the next page if you're interested in this.

The most important property for Diffie-Hellman public numbers is that the clock size must be a prime number—so it has no divisors other than 1 and itself. Another intriguing requirement is that the base must be a *primitive root* of the clock size. This means that the powers of the base eventually cycle through every possible value on the clock. If you look at the table on page 54, you'll notice that 2 and 6 are both primitive roots of 11, but 3 is not—the powers of 3 cycle through the values 3, 9, 5, 4, 1 and miss 2, 6, 7, 8, and 10.

When choosing a clock size and base for the Diffie-Hellman protocol, certain mathematical properties must be satisfied.

The Diffie-Hellman approach described here is just one of many cunning techniques for communicating via (electronic) postcards. Computer scientists call Diffie-Hellman a *key exchange algorithm*. Other public key algorithms work differently and allow you to directly encrypt a message for your intended recipient, using public information announced by that recipient. In contrast, a key exchange algorithm allows you to establish a shared secret using the public information from the recipient, but the encryption itself is done via the addition trick. For most communication on the internet, this latter option—the one we have learned about in this chapter—is preferable, as it requires much less computational power.

But there are some applications in which fully fledged public key cryptography is required. Perhaps the most interesting of these applications is digital signatures, which will be explained in chapter 9. As you will discover when you read that chapter, the flavor of the ideas in the fully fledged type of public key cryptography is similar to what we have already seen: secret information is "mixed" with public information in a mathematically irreversible way, just as paint colors can be mixed irreversibly. The most famous public key cryptosystem is the one known as RSA, after the three inventors who first published it: Ronald **R**ivest, Adi **S**hamir, and Leonard **A**dleman. Chapter 9 uses RSA as the main example of how digital signatures work.

There is a fascinating and complex story behind the invention of these early public key algorithms. Diffie and Hellman were indeed the first people to publish Diffie-Hellman, in 1976. Rivest, Shamir, and Adleman were indeed the first to publish RSA, in 1978. But that is not the whole story! It was later discovered that the British government had already known of similar systems for several years. Unfortunately for the inventors of these precursors to Diffie-Hellman and RSA, they were mathematicians working in the British government's communications laboratory, GCHQ. The results of their work were recorded in secret internal documents and were not declassified until 1997.

RSA, Diffie-Hellman, and other public key cryptosystems are not just ingenious ideas. They have evolved into commercial technologies and internet standards with great importance for businesses and individuals alike. The vast majority of the online transactions we perform every day could not be completed securely without public key cryptography. The RSA inventors patented their system in the 1970s, and their patent did not expire until late 2000. A celebratory party was held at the Great American Music Hall in San Francisco on the night the patent expired—a celebration, perhaps, of the fact that public key cryptography is here to stay.

5

Error-Correcting Codes: Mistakes That Fix Themselves

> It is one thing to show a man that he is in an error, and another to put him in possession of truth.
>
> —JOHN LOCKE, *Essay Concerning Human Understanding* (1690)

These days, we're used to accessing computers whenever we need them. Richard Hamming, a researcher working at the Bell Telephone Company labs in the 1940s, was not so lucky: the company computer he needed was used by other departments and available to him only on weekends. You can imagine his frustration, therefore, at the crashes that kept recurring due to the computer's errors in reading its own data. Here is what Hamming himself had to say on the matter:

> Two weekends in a row I came in and found that all my stuff had been dumped and nothing was done. I was really aroused and annoyed because I wanted those answers and two weekends had been lost. And so I said, "Dammit, if the machine can detect an error, why can't it locate the position of the error and correct it?"

There can be few more clear-cut cases of necessity being the mother of invention. Hamming had soon created the first ever *error-correcting code*: a seemingly magical algorithm that detects and corrects errors in computer data. Without these codes, our computers and communication systems would be drastically slower, less powerful, and less reliable than they are today.

THE NEED FOR ERROR DETECTION AND CORRECTION

Computers have three fundamental jobs. The most important job is to perform computations. That is, given some input data, the computer must transform the data in some way to produce a useful answer. But the ability to compute answers would be essentially useless without the other two very important jobs that computers perform: storing data and transmitting data. (Computers mostly store data in their memory and on disk drives. And they typically transmit data over the internet.) To emphasize this point, imagine a computer that could neither store nor transmit information. It would, of course, be almost useless. Yes, you could do some complex computations (for example, preparing an intricate financial spreadsheet detailing the budget for a company), but then you would be unable to send the results to a colleague or even to save the results so you could come back and work on them later. Therefore, transmission and storage of data are truly essential for modern computers.

But there is a huge challenge associated with transmitting and storing data: the data must be *exactly right*—because in many cases, even one tiny mistake can render the data useless. As humans, we are also familiar with the need to store and transmit information without any errors. For example, if you write down someone's phone number, it is essential that every digit is recorded correctly and in the right order. If there is even one mistake in one of the digits, the phone number is probably useless to you or anyone else. And in some cases, errors in data can actually be *worse* than useless. For example, an error in the file that stores a computer program can make that program crash or do things it was not intended to. (It might even delete some important files or crash before you get a chance to save your work.) And an error in some computerized financial records could result in actual monetary loss (if, say, you thought you were buying a stock priced at $5.34 per share but the actual cost was $8.34).

But, as humans, the amount of error-free information we need to store is relatively small, and it's not too hard to avoid mistakes just by checking carefully whenever you know some information is important—things like bank account numbers, passwords, e-mail addresses, and the like. On the other hand, the amount of information that computers need to store and transmit without making any errors is absolutely immense. To get some idea of the scale, consider this. Suppose you have some kind of computing device with a storage capacity of 100 gigabytes. (At the time of writing, this is the typical capacity of a low-cost laptop.) This 100 gigabytes is equivalent to about 15 million pages of text. So even if this computer's storage system makes just one error per million pages, there would still be (on average) 15 mistakes on the device when filled to capacity. And the same lesson applies to transmission of data too: if you download a 20-megabyte software program, and your computer misinterprets just one in every million characters it receives, there will probably still be over 20 errors in your downloaded program—every one of which could cause a potentially costly crash when you least expect it.

The moral of the story is that, for a computer, being accurate 99.9999% of the time is not even close to good enough. Computers must be able to store and transmit literally billions of pieces of information without making a single mistake. But computers have to deal with communication problems just like other devices. Telephones are a good example here: it's obvious that they don't transmit information perfectly, because phone conversations often suffer from distortions, static, or other types of noise. But telephones are not alone in their suffering: electrical wires are subject to all sorts of fluctuations; wireless communications suffer interference all the time; and physical media such as hard disks, CDs, and DVDs can be scratched, damaged, or simply misread because of dust or other physical interference. How on earth can we hope to achieve an error rate of less than one in many billions, in the face of such obvious communication errors? This chapter will reveal the ideas behind the ingenious computer science that makes this magic happen. It turns out that if you use the right tricks, even extremely unreliable communication channels can be used to transmit data with incredibly low error rates—so low that in practice, errors can be completely eliminated.

THE REPETITION TRICK

The most fundamental trick for communicating reliably over an unreliable channel is one that we are all familiar with: to make sure that some information has been communicated correctly, you just need to repeat it a few times. If someone dictates a phone number or bank account number to you over a bad telephone connection, you will probably ask them to repeat it at least once to make sure there were no mistakes.

Computers can do exactly the same thing. Let's suppose a computer at your bank is trying to transmit your account balance to you over the internet. Your account balance is actually $5213.75, but unfortunately the network is not very reliable and every single digit has a 20% chance being changed to something else. So the first time your balance is transmitted, it might arrive as $5293.75. Obviously, you have no way of knowing whether or not this is correct. All of the digits *might* be right, but one or more of them might be wrong and you have no way of telling. But by using the repetition trick, you can make a very good guess as to the true balance. Imagine that you ask for your balance to be transmitted five times, and receive the following responses:

transmission 1:	$	5	2	9	3	.	7	5
transmission 2:	$	5	2	1	3	.	7	5
transmission 3:	$	5	2	1	3	.	1	1
transmission 4:	$	5	4	4	3	.	7	5
transmission 5:	$	7	2	1	8	.	7	5

Notice that some of the transmissions have more than one digit wrong, and there's even one transmission (number 2) with no errors at all. The crucial point is that you have no way of knowing where the errors are, so there is no way you can pick out transmission 2 as being the correct one. Instead, what you can do is examine each digit separately, looking at all transmissions of that one digit, and pick the value that occurs most often. Here are the results again, with the most common digits listed at the end:

transmission 1:	$	5	2	9	3	.	7	5
transmission 2:	$	5	2	1	3	.	7	5
transmission 3:	$	5	2	1	3	.	1	1
transmission 4:	$	5	4	4	3	.	7	5
transmission 5:	$	7	2	1	8	.	7	5
most common digit:	$	5	2	1	3	.	7	5

Let's look at some examples to make the idea absolutely clear. Examining the first digit in the transmission, we see that in transmissions 1–4, the first digit was a 5, whereas in transmission 5, the first digit was a 7. In other words, four of the transmissions said "5" and only one said "7." So although you can't be absolutely sure, the *most likely* value for the first digit of your bank balance is 5. Moving on to the second digit, we see that 2 occurred four times, and 4 only once, so 2 is the most likely second digit. The third digit is a bit more interesting, because there are three possibilities: 1 occurs three times, 9 occurs once, and 4 occurs once. But the same principle applies, and 1 is the most likely true value. By doing this for all the digits, you can arrive at a final guess for your complete bank balance: $5213.75, which in this case is indeed correct.

Well, that was easy. Have we solved the problem already? In some ways, the answer is yes. But you might be a little dissatisfied because of two things. First, the error rate for this communication channel was only 20%, and in some cases computers might need to communicate over channels that are much worse than that. Second, and perhaps more seriously, the final answer happened to be correct in the above example, but there is no guarantee that the answer will always be right: it is just a guess, based on what we think is most likely to be the true bank balance. Luckily, both of these objections can be addressed very easily: we just increase the number of retransmissions until the reliability is as high as we want.

For example, suppose the error rate was 50% instead of the 20% in the last example. Well, you could ask the bank to transmit your balance 1000 times instead of just 5. Let's concentrate on just the first digit, since the others work out the same way. Since the error rate is 50%, about half of them will be transmitted correctly, as a 5, and the other half will be changed to some other random values. So there will be about 500 occurrences of 5, and only about 50 each of the other digits (0–4 and 6–9). Mathematicians can calculate the chances of one of the other digits coming up more often than the 5: it turns out that even if we transmitted a new bank balance every second using this method, we would have to wait many trillions of years before we expect to make a wrong guess for the bank balance. The moral of the story is that by repeating an unreliable message often enough, you can make it as reliable as you want. (In these examples, we assumed the errors occur *at random*. If, on the other hand, a malicious entity is deliberately interfering with the transmission and choosing which errors to create, the repetition trick is much more vulnerable. Some of the codes introduced later work well even against this type of malicious attack.)

So, by using the repetition trick, the problem of unreliable communication can be solved, and the chance of a mistake essentially eliminated. Unfortunately, the repetition trick is not good enough for modern computer systems. When transmitting a small piece of data like a bank balance, it is not too costly to retransmit 1000 times, but it would obviously be completely impractical to transmit 1000 copies of a large (say, 200-megabyte) software download. Clearly, computers need to use something more sophisticated than the repetition trick.

THE REDUNDANCY TRICK

Even though computers don't use the repetition trick as it was described above, we covered it first so that we could see the most basic principle of reliable communication in action. This basic principle is that you can't just send the original message; you need to send something extra to increase the reliability. In the case of the repetition trick, the extra thing you send is just more copies of the original message. But it turns out there are many other types of extra stuff you can send to improve the reliability. Computer scientists call the extra stuff "redundancy." Sometimes, the redundancy is added on to the original message. We'll see this "adding on" technique when we look at the next trick (the checksum trick). But first, we will look at another way of adding redundancy, which actually transforms the original message into a longer "redundant" one—the original message is deleted and replaced by a different, longer one. When you receive the longer message, you can then transform it back into the original, even if it has been corrupted by a poor communication channel. We'll call this simply the *redundancy trick*.

An example will make this clear. Recall that we were trying to transmit your bank balance of $5213.75 over an unreliable communication channel that randomly altered 20% of the digits. Instead of trying to transmit just "$5213.75," let's transform this into a longer (and therefore "redundant") message that contains the same information. In this case, we'll simply spell out the balance in English words, like this:

```
five two one three point seven five
```

Let's again suppose that about 20% of the characters in this message get flipped randomly to something else due to a poor communication channel. The message might end up looking something like this:

```
fiqe kwo one thrxp point sivpn fivq
```

Although it's a little annoying to read, I think you will agree that anyone who knows English can guess that this corrupted message represents the true bank balance of $5213.75.

The key point is that because we used a *redundant* message, it is possible to reliably detect and correct any single change to the message. If I tell you that the characters "fiqe" represent a number in English and that only one character has been altered, you can be absolutely certain that the original message was "five," because there is no other English number that can be obtained from "fiqe" by altering only one character. In stark contrast, if I tell you that the digits "367" represent a number but one of the digits has been altered, you have no way of knowing what the original number was, because there is no redundancy in this message.

Although we haven't yet explored exactly how redundancy works, we have already seen that it has something to do with making the message *longer*, and that each part of the message should conform to some kind of well-known *pattern*. In this way, any single change can be first identified (because it does not fit in with a known pattern) and then corrected (by changing the error to fit with the pattern).

Computer scientists call these known patterns "code words." In our example, the code words are just numbers written in English, like "one," "two," "three," and so on.

Now it's time to explain exactly how the redundancy trick works. Messages are made up of what computer scientists call "symbols." In our simple example, the symbols are the numeric digits 0–9 (we'll ignore the dollar sign and decimal point to make things even easier). Each symbol is assigned a code word. In our example, the symbol 1 is assigned the code word "one," 2 is assigned "two," and so on.

To transmit a message, you first take each symbol and translate it into its corresponding code word. Then you send the transformed message over the unreliable communication channel. When the message is received, you look at each part of a message and check whether it is a valid code word. If it is valid (e.g., "five"), you just transform it back into the corresponding symbol (e.g., 5). If it is not a valid code word (e.g., "fiqe"), you find out which code word it matches most closely (in this case, "five"), and transform *that* into the corresponding symbol (in this case, 5). Examples of using this code are shown in the figure above.

Encoding

1	→	one
2	→	two
3	→	three
4	→	four
5	→	five

Decoding

five	→	5	(exact match)
fiqe	→	5	(closest match)
twe	→	2	(closest match)

A code using English words for digits.

That's really all there is to it. Computers actually use this redundancy trick all the time to store and transmit information. Mathematicians have worked out fancier codewords than the English-language ones we were using as an example, but otherwise the workings of reliable computer communication are the same. The figure on the facing page gives a real example. This is the code computer scientists call the (7, 4) Hamming code, and it is one of the codes discovered by Richard Hamming at Bell Labs in 1947, in response to the weekend computer crashes described earlier. (Because of Bell's requirement that he patent the codes, Hamming did not publish them until three years later, in 1950.) The most obvious difference to our previous code is that everything is done in terms of zeros and ones. Because every piece of data stored or transmitted by a computer is converted into strings of zeros and ones, any code used in real life is restricted to just these two digits.

Encoding

0000 → 0000000
0001 → 0001011
0010 → 0010111
0011 → 0011100
0100 → 0100110

Decoding

0010111 → 0010 (exact match)
0010110 → 0010 (closest match)
1011100 → 0011 (closest match)

A real code used by computers. Computer scientists call this code the (7, 4) Hamming code. Note that the "Encoding" box lists only five of the 16 possible 4-digit inputs. The remaining inputs also have corresponding code words, but they are omitted here.

But apart from that, everything works exactly the same as before. When encoding, each group of four digits has redundancy added to it, generating a code word of seven digits. When decoding, you first look for an exact match for the seven digits you received, and if that fails, you take the closest match. You might be worried that, now we are working with only ones and zeros, there might be more than one equally close match and you could end up choosing the wrong decoding. However, this particular code has been designed cunningly so that any single error in a 7-digit codeword can be corrected unambiguously. There is some beautiful mathematics behind the design of codes with this property, but we won't be pursuing the details here.

It's worth emphasizing why the redundancy trick is preferred to the repetition trick in practice. The main reason is the relative *cost* of the two tricks. Computer scientists measure the cost of error-correction systems in terms of "overhead." Overhead is just the amount of extra information that needs to be sent to make sure a message is received correctly. The overhead of the repetition trick is enormous, since you have to send several entire copies of the message. The overhead of the redundancy trick depends on the exact set of code words that you use. In the example above that used English words, the redundant message was 35 characters long, whereas the original message consisted of only 6 numeric digits, so the overhead of this particular application of the redundancy trick is also quite large. But mathematicians have worked out sets of code words that have much lower redundancy, yet still get incredibly high performance in terms of the chance of an error going undetected. The low overhead of these code words is the reason that computers use the redundancy trick instead of the repetition trick.

The discussion so far has used examples of *transmitting* information using codes, but everything we have discussed applies equally well to the task of *storing* information. CDs, DVDs, and computer hard drives all rely heavily on error-correcting codes to achieve the superb reliability we observe in practice.

THE CHECKSUM TRICK

So far, we've looked at ways to simultaneously *detect* and *correct* errors in data. The repetition trick and the redundancy trick are both ways of doing this. But there's another possible approach to this whole problem: we can forget about *correcting* errors and concentrate only on *detecting* them. (The 17th-century philosopher John Locke was clearly aware of the distinction between error detection and error correction—as you can see from the opening quotation of this chapter.) For many applications, merely detecting an error is sufficient, because if you detect an error, you just request another copy of the data. And you can keep on requesting new copies, until you get one that has no errors in it. This is a very frequently used strategy. For example, almost all internet connections use this technique. We'll call it the "checksum trick," for reasons that will become clear very soon.

To understand the checksum trick, it will be more convenient to pretend that all of our messages consist of numbers only. This is a very realistic assumption, since computers store all information in the form of numbers and only translate the numbers into text or images when presenting that information to humans. But, in any case, it is important to understand that any particular choice of symbols for the messages does not affect the techniques described in this chapter. Sometimes it is more convenient to use numeric symbols (the digits 0–9), and sometimes it is more convenient to use alphabetic symbols (the characters a–z). But in either case, we can agree on some translation between these sets of symbols. For example, one obvious translation from alphabetic to numeric symbols would be a → 01, b → 02, . . . , z → 26. So it really doesn't matter whether we investigate a technique for transmitting numeric messages or alphabetic messages; the technique can later be applied to any type of message by first doing a simple, fixed translation of the symbols.

At this point, we have to learn what a checksum actually is. There are many different types of checksums, but for now we will stick with the least complicated type, which we'll call a "simple checksum."

Computing the simple checksum of a numeric message is really, really easy: you just take the digits of the message, add them all up, throw away everything in the result except for the last digit, and the remaining digit is your simple checksum. Here's an example: suppose the message is

4 6 7 5 6

Then the sum all the digits is $4 + 6 + 7 + 5 + 6 = 28$, but we keep only the last digit, so the simple checksum of this message is 8.

But how are checksums used? That's easy: you just append the checksum of your original message to the end of the message before you send it. Then, when the message is received by someone else, they can calculate the checksum again, compare it with the one you sent, and see if it is correct. In other words, they "check" the "sum" of the message—hence the terminology "checksum." Let's stick with the above example. The simple checksum of the message "46756" is 8, so we transmit the message and its checksum as

4 6 7 5 6 8

Now, the person receiving the message has to know that you are using the checksum trick. Assuming they do know, they can immediately recognize that the last digit, the 8, is not part of the original message, so they put it to one side and compute the checksum of everything else. If there were no errors in the transmission of the message, they will compute $4 + 6 + 7 + 5 + 6 = 28$, keep the last digit (which is 8), check that it is equal to the checksum they put aside earlier (which it is), and therefore conclude that the message was transmitted correctly. On the other hand, what happens if there *was* an error in transmitting the message? Suppose the 7 was randomly changed to a 3. Then you would receive the message

4 6 3 5 6 8

You would set aside the 8 for later comparison and compute the checksum as $4+6+3+5+6 = 24$, keeping only the last digit (4). This is *not* equal to the 8 that was set aside earlier, so you would be sure that the message was corrupted during transmission. At this point, you request that the message is retransmitted, wait until you receive a new copy, then again compute and compare the checksum. And you can keep doing this until you get a message whose checksum is correct.

All of this seems almost too good to be true. Recall that the "overhead" of an error-correcting system is the amount of extra information you have to send in addition to the message itself. Well, here we seem to have the ultimate low-overhead system, since no matter how long the message is, we only have to add one extra digit (the checksum) to detect an error!

Alas, it turns out that this system of simple checksums *is* too good to be true. Here is the problem: the simple checksum described above can detect at most *one* error in the message. If there are two or more errors, the simple checksum might detect them, but then again it might not. Let's look at some examples of this:

						checksum
original message	4	6	7	5	6	8
message with one error	1	6	7	5	6	5
message with two errors	1	5	7	5	6	4
message with two (different) errors	2	8	7	5	6	8

The original message (46756) is the same as before, and so is its checksum (8). In the next line is a message with one error (the first digit is a 1 instead of a 4), and the checksum turns out to be 5. In fact, you can probably convince yourself that changing any *single* digit results in a checksum that differs from 8, so you are guaranteed to detect any single mistake in the message. It's not hard to prove that this is always true: if there is only one error, a simple checksum is absolutely guaranteed to detect it.

In the next line of the table, we see a message with two errors: each of the first two digits has been altered. In this case, the checksum happens to be 4. And since 4 is different from the original checksum, which was 8, the person receiving this message would in fact detect that an error had been made. However, the crunch comes in the last line of the table. Here is another message with two errors, again in the first two digits. But the values are different, and it so happens that the checksum for this two-error message is 8—the same as the original! So a person receiving this message would fail to detect that there are errors in the message.

Luckily, it turns out that we can get around this problem by adding a few more tweaks to our checksum trick. The first step is to define a new type of checksum. Let's call it a "staircase" checksum because it helps to think of climbing a staircase while computing it. Imagine you are at the bottom of a staircase with the stairs numbered 1, 2, 3, and so on. To calculate a staircase checksum, you add up the digits just like before, but each digit gets multiplied by the number of the stair you are on, and you have to move up one step for each digit. At the end, you throw away everything except the last digit, just as with the simple checksum. So if the message is

4 6 7 5 6

like before, then the staircase checksum is calculated by first calculating the staircase sum

$$\begin{aligned}(1 \times 4) + (2 \times 6) + (3 \times 7) + (4 \times 5) + (5 \times 6)& \\ &= 4 + 12 + 21 + 20 + 30 \\ &= 87\end{aligned}$$

Then throw away everything except the last digit, which is 7. So the staircase checksum of "46756" is 7.

What is the point of all this? Well, it turns out that if you include *both* the simple and staircase checksums, then you are guaranteed to detect any two errors in any message. So our new checksum trick is to transmit the original message, then two extra digits: the simple checksum first, then the staircase checksum. For example, the message "46756" would now be transmitted as

4 6 7 5 6 8 7

When you receive the message, you again have to know by prior agreement exactly what trick has been applied. But assuming you do know, it is easy to check for errors just as with the simple checksum trick. In this case you first set aside the last two digits (the 8, which is the simple checksum, and the 7, which is the staircase checksum). You then compute the simple checksum of the rest of the message (46756, which comes to 8), and you compute the staircase checksum too (which comes to 7). If *both* the computed checksum values match the ones that were sent (and in this case they do), you are guaranteed that the message is either correct, or has at least three errors.

The next table shows this in practice. It is identical to the previous table except that the staircase checksum has been added to each row, and a new row has been added as an extra example. When there is one error, we find that both the simple and staircase checksums differ from the original message (5 instead of 8, and 4 instead of 7). When there are two errors, it is possible for both checksums to differ, as in the third row of the table where we see 4 instead of 8, and 2 instead of 7. But as we already found out, sometimes the simple checksum will not change when there are two errors. The fourth row shows an example, where the simple checksum is still 8. But because the staircase checksum differs from the original (9 instead of 7), we still know that this message has errors. And in the last row, we see that it can work out the other way around too: here is an example of two errors that results in a different simple checksum (9 instead of 8), but the same staircase checksum (7). But, again, the point is that we can still detect the error because at least one of the two checksums differs from the original. And although it would take some slightly technical math to prove it, this is no accident: it turns out that you will always be able to detect the errors if there are no more than two of them.

						simple and staircase checksums
original message	4	6	7	5	6	8 7
message with one error	1	6	7	5	6	5 4
message with two errors	1	5	7	5	6	4 2
message with two (different) errors	2	8	7	5	6	8 9
message with two (again different) errors	6	5	7	5	6	9 7

Now that we have a grasp of the fundamental approach, we need to be aware that the checksum trick just described is guaranteed to work only for relatively short messages (fewer than 10 digits). But very similar ideas can be applied to longer messages. It is possible to define checksums by certain sequences of simple operations like adding up the digits, multiplying the digits by "staircases" of various shapes, and swapping some of the digits around according to a fixed pattern. Although that might sound complicated, computers can compute these checksums blindingly fast and it turns out to be an extremely useful, practical way of detecting errors in a message.

The checksum trick described above produces only two checksum digits (the simple digit and the staircase digit), but real checksums usually produce many more digits than that—sometimes as many as 150 digits. (Throughout the remainder of this chapter, I am talking about the ten *decimal* digits, 0–9, not the two *binary* digits, 0 and 1, which are more commonly used in computer communication.) The important point is that the number of digits in the checksum (whether 2, as in the example above, or about 150, as for some checksums used in practice) is *fixed*. But although the length of the checksums produced by any given checksum algorithm is fixed, you can compute checksums of messages that are as long as you want. So for very long messages, even a relatively large checksum like 150 digits ends up being minuscule in proportion to the message itself. For example, suppose you use a 100-digit checksum to verify the correctness of a 20-megabyte software package downloaded from the web. The checksum is less than one-thousandth of 1% of the size of the software package. I'm sure you would agree this is an acceptable level of overhead! And a mathematician will tell you that the chance of failing to detect an error when using a checksum of this length is so incredibly tiny that it is for all practical purposes impossible.

As usual, there are a few important technical details here. It's not true that any 100-digit checksum system has this incredibly high resistance to failure. It requires a certain type of checksum that computer scientists call a *cryptographic hash function*—especially if the changes to the message might be made by a malicious opponent, instead of the random vagaries of a poor communication channel. This is a very real issue, because it is possible that an evil hacker might try to alter that 20-megabyte software package in such a way that it has the same 100-digit checksum, but is actually a different piece of software that will take control of your computer! The use of cryptographic hash functions eliminates this possibility.

THE PINPOINT TRICK

Now that we know about checksums, we can go back to the original problem of both detecting *and* correcting communication errors. We already know how to do this, either inefficiently using the repetition trick or efficiently using the redundancy trick. But let's return to this now, because we never really found out how to create the code words that form the key ingredient in this trick. We did have the example of using English words to describe numerals, but this particular set of code words is less efficient than the ones computers actually use. And we also saw the real example of a Hamming code, but without any explanation of how the code words were produced in the first place.

So now we will learn about another possible set of code words that can be used to perform the redundancy trick. Because this is a very special case of the redundancy trick that allows you to quickly pinpoint an error, we'll call this the "pinpoint trick."

Just as we did with the checksum trick, we will work entirely with numerical messages consisting of the digits 0–9, but you should keep in mind that this is just for convenience. It is very simple to take an alphabetical message and translate it into numbers, so the technique described here can be applied to any message whatsoever.

To keep things simple, we'll assume that the message is exactly 16 digits long, but, again, this doesn't limit the technique in practice. If you have a long message, just break it into 16-digit chunks and work with each chunk separately. If the message is shorter than 16 digits, fill it up with zeroes, until it is 16 digits long.

The first step in the pinpoint trick is to rearrange the 16 digits of the message into a square that reads left to right, top to bottom. So if the actual message is

4 8 3 7 5 4 3 6 2 2 5 6 3 9 9 7

it gets rearranged into

4	8	3	7
5	4	3	6
2	2	5	6
3	9	9	7

Next, we compute a simple checksum of each row and add it to the right-hand side of the row:

4	8	3	7	2
5	4	3	6	8
2	2	5	6	5
3	9	9	7	8

These simple checksums are computed just like before. For example, to get the second row checksum you compute $5 + 4 + 3 + 6 = 18$ and then take the last digit, which is 8.

The next step in the pinpoint trick is to compute simple checksums for each column and add these in a new row at the bottom:

4	8	3	7	2
5	4	3	6	8
2	2	5	6	5
3	9	9	7	8
4	3	0	6	

Again, there's nothing mysterious about the simple checksums. For example, the third column is computed from $3+3+5+9 = 20$, which becomes 0 when we take the last digit.

The next step in the pinpoint trick is to reorder everything so it can be stored or transmitted one digit at a time. You do this in the obvious way, reading digits from left to right, top to bottom. So we end up with the following 24-digit message:

4 8 3 7 2 5 4 3 6 8 2 2 5 6 5 3 9 9 7 8 4 3 0 6

Now imagine you have received a message that has been transmitted using the pinpoint trick. What steps do you follow to work out the original message and correct any communication errors? Let's work through an example. The original 16-digit message will be the same as the one above, but to make things interesting, suppose there was a communication error and one of the digits was altered. Don't worry about which is the altered digit yet—we will be using the pinpoint trick to determine that very shortly.

So let's suppose the 24-digit message you *received* is

4 8 3 7 2 5 4 3 6 8 2 7 5 6 5 3 9 9 7 8 4 3 0 6

Your first step will be to lay the digits out in a 5-by-5 square, recognizing that the last column and last row correspond to checksum digits that were sent with the original message:

4	8	3	7	2
5	4	3	6	8
2	7	5	6	5
3	9	9	7	8
4	3	0	6	

Next, compute simple checksums of the first four digits in each row and column, recording the results in a newly created row and column next to the checksum values that you received:

4	8	3	7	2	2
5	4	3	6	8	8
2	7	5	6	5	0
3	9	9	7	8	8
4	3	0	6		
4	8	0	6		

It is crucial to bear in mind that there are two sets of checksum values here: the ones you were *sent*, and the ones you *calculated*. Mostly, the two sets of values will be the same. In fact, if they are all identical, you can conclude that the message is very likely correct. But if there was a communication error, some of the calculated checksum values will differ from the sent ones. Notice that in the current example, there are two such differences: the 5 and 0 in the third row differ, and so do the 3 and 8 in the second column. The offending checksums are highlighted in boxes:

4	8	3	7	2	2
5	4	3	6	8	8
2	7	5	6	5	0
3	9	9	7	8	8
4	3	0	6		
4	8	0	6		

Here is the key insight: the location of these differences tells you exactly where the communication error occurred! It *must* be in the third row (because every other row had the correct checksum), and it *must* be in the second column (because every other column had the correct checksum). And as you can see from the following diagram, this narrows it down to exactly one possibility—the 7 highlighted in a solid box:

4	8	3	7	2	2
5	4	3	6	8	8
2	7	5	6	5	0
3	9	9	7	8	8
4	3	0	6		
4	8	0	6		

But that's not all—we have located the error, but not yet corrected it. Fortunately, this is easy: we just have to replace the erroneous 7 with a number that will make both of the checksums correct. We can see that the second column was meant to have a checksum of 3, but it came out to 8 instead—in other words, the checksum needs to be reduced by 5. So let's reduce the erroneous 7 by 5, which leaves 2:

4	8	3	7	2	2
5	4	3	6	8	8
2	2	5	6	5	5
3	9	9	7	8	8
4	3	0	6		
4	3	0	6		

You can even double-check this change, by examining the third row—it now has a checksum of 5, which agrees with the received checksum. The error has been both located and corrected! The final obvious step is to extract the corrected original 16-digit message from the 5-by-5 square, by reading top to bottom, left to right (and ignoring the final row and column, of course). This gives

4 8 3 7 5 4 3 6 2 2 5 6 3 9 9 7

which really is the same message that we started with.

In computer science, the pinpoint trick goes by the name of "two-dimensional parity." The word *parity* means the same thing as a simple checksum, when working with the binary numbers computers normally use. And the parity is described as *two-dimensional* because the message gets laid out in a grid with two dimensions (rows and columns). Two-dimensional parity has been used in some real computer systems, but it is not as effective as certain other redundancy tricks. I chose to explain it here because it is very easy to visualize and conveys the flavor of how one can both find and correct errors without requiring the sophisticated math behind the codes popular in today's computer systems.

ERROR CORRECTION AND DETECTION IN THE REAL WORLD

Error-correcting codes sprang into existence in the 1940s, rather soon after the birth of the electronic computer itself. In retrospect, it's not hard to see why: early computers were rather unreliable, and their components frequently produced errors. But the true roots of error-correcting codes lie even earlier, in communication systems such as telegraphs and telephones. So it is not altogether surprising that the two major events triggering the creation of error-correcting codes both occurred in the research laboratories of the Bell Telephone Company. The two heroes of our story, Claude Shannon and Richard Hamming, were both researchers at Bell Labs. Hamming we have met already: it was his annoyance at the weekend crashes of a company computer that led directly to his invention of the first error-correcting codes, now known as Hamming codes.

However, error-correcting codes are just one part of a larger discipline called *information theory*, and most computer scientists trace the birth of the field of information theory to a 1948 paper by Claude Shannon. This extraordinary paper, entitled "The Mathematical Theory of Communication," is described in one biography of Shannon as "the Magna Carta of the information age." Irving Reed (co-inventor of the Reed–Solomon codes mentioned below) said of the same paper: "Few other works of this century have had greater impact on science and engineering. By this landmark paper ... he has altered most profoundly all aspects of communication theory and practice." Why the high praise? Shannon demonstrated through mathematics that it was possible, in principle, to achieve surprisingly high rates of error-free communication over a noisy, error-prone link. It was not until many decades later that scientists came close to achieving Shannon's theoretical maximum communication rate in practice.

Incidentally, Shannon was apparently a man of extremely diverse interests. As one of the four main organizers of the 1956 Dartmouth AI conference (discussed at the end of chapter 6), he was intimately involved in the founding of another field: artificial intelligence. But it doesn't stop there. He also rode unicycles and built an improbable-sounding unicycle with an elliptical (i.e., noncircular) wheel, meaning that the rider moved up and down as the unicycle moved forward!

Shannon's work placed Hamming codes in a larger theoretical context and set the stage for many further advances. Hamming codes were thus used in some of the earliest computers and are still widely used in certain types of memory systems. Another important family of codes is known as the *Reed–Solomon* codes. These codes can be adapted to correct for a large number of errors per codeword. (Contrast this with the (7, 4) Hamming code in the figure on page 67, which can correct only one error in each 7-digit code word.) Reed–Solomon codes are based on a branch of mathematics called finite field algebra, but you can think of them, very roughly, as combining the features of the staircase checksum and the two-dimensional pinpoint trick. They are used in CDs, DVDs, and computer hard drives.

Checksums are also widely used in practice, typically for detecting rather than correcting errors. Perhaps the most pervasive example is Ethernet, the networking protocol used by almost every computer on the planet these days. Ethernet employs a checksum called CRC-32 to detect errors. The most common internet protocol, called TCP (for Transmission Control Protocol), also uses checksums for each chunk, or *packet*, of data that it sends. Packets whose checksums are incorrect are simply discarded, because TCP is designed to automatically retransmit them later if necessary. Software packages published on the internet are often verified using checksums; popular ones include a checksum called MD5, and another called SHA-1. Both are intended to be cryptographic hash functions, providing protection against malicious alteration of the software as well as random communication errors. MD5 checksums have about 40 digits,

SHA-1 produces about 50 digits, and there are some even more error-resistant checksums in the same family, such as SHA-256 (about 75 digits) and SHA-512 (about 150 digits).

The science of error-correcting and error-detecting codes continues to expand. Since the 1990s, an approach known as *low-density parity-check codes* has received considerable attention. These codes are now used in applications ranging from satellite TV to communication with deep space probes. So the next time you enjoy some high-definition satellite TV on the weekend, spare a thought for this delicious irony: it was the frustration of Richard Hamming's weekend battle with an early computer that led to our own weekend entertainment today.

6

Pattern Recognition: Learning from Experience

> The Analytical Engine has no pretensions whatever to *originate* anything. It can do whatever we *know how to order it* to perform.
>
> —Ada Lovelace, from her 1843 notes on the Analytical Engine

In each previous chapter, we've looked at an area in which the ability of computers far outstrips the ability of humans. For example, a computer can typically encrypt or decrypt a large file within a second or two, whereas it would take a human many years to perform the same computations by hand. For an even more extreme example, imagine how long it would take a human to manually compute the PageRank of billions of web pages according to the algorithm described in chapter 3. This task is so vast that, in practice, it is impossible for a human. Yet the computers at web search companies are constantly performing these computations.

In this chapter, on the other hand, we examine an area in which humans have a natural advantage: the field of *pattern recognition*. Pattern recognition is a subset of artificial intelligence and includes tasks such as face recognition, object recognition, speech recognition, and handwriting recognition. More specific examples would include the task of determining whether a given photograph is a picture of your sister, or determining the city and state written on a hand-addressed envelope. Thus, pattern recognition can be defined more generally as the task of getting computers to act "intelligently" based on input data that contains a lot of variability.

The word "intelligently" is in quotation marks here for good reason: the question of whether computers can ever exhibit true intelligence is highly controversial. The opening quotation of this chapter represents one of the earliest salvos in this debate: Ada Lovelace commenting, in 1843, on the design of an early mechanical computer called the Analytical Engine. Lovelace is sometimes described as the world's first computer programmer because of her profound insights about the Analytical Engine. But in this pronouncement, she emphasizes that computers lack originality: they must slavishly follow the instructions of their human programmers. These days, computer scientists disagree on whether computers can, in principle, exhibit intelligence. And the debate becomes even more complex if philosophers, neuroscientists, and theologians are thrown into the mix.

Fortunately, we don't have to resolve the paradoxes of machine intelligence here. For our purposes, we might as well replace the word "intelligent" with "useful." So the basic task of pattern recognition is to take some data with extremely high variability—such as photographs of different faces in different lighting conditions, or samples of many different words handwritten by many different people—and do something useful with it. Humans can unquestionably process such data intelligently: we can recognize faces with uncanny accuracy, and read the handwriting of virtually anyone without having to see samples of their writing in advance. It turns out that computers are vastly inferior to humans at such tasks. But some ingenious algorithms have emerged that enable computers to achieve good performance on certain pattern recognition tasks. In this chapter, we will learn about three of these algorithms: nearest-neighbor classifiers, decision trees, and artificial neural networks. But first, we need a more scientific description of the problem we are trying to solve.

WHAT'S THE PROBLEM?

The tasks of pattern recognition might seem, at first, to be almost absurdly diverse. Can computers use a single toolbox of pattern recognition techniques to recognize handwriting, faces, speech, and more? One possible answer to this question is staring us (literally) in the face: our own human brains achieve superb speed and accuracy in a wide array of recognition tasks. Could we write a computer program to achieve the same thing?

Before we can discuss the techniques that such a program might use, we need to somehow unify the bewildering array of tasks and define a single problem that we are trying to solve. The standard approach here is to view pattern recognition as a *classification* problem. We assume that the data to be processed is divided up into sensible chunks called *samples*, and that each sample belongs to one of a fixed set of possible *classes*. For example, in a face recognition problem, each sample would be a picture of a face, and the classes would be the identities of the people the system can recognize. In some problems, there are only two classes. A common example of this is in medical diagnosis for a particular disease, where the two classes might be "healthy" and "sick," while each data sample could consist of all the test results for a single patient (e.g., blood pressure, weight, x-ray images, and possibly many other things). So the computer's task is to process new data samples that it has never seen before and *classify* each sample into one of the possible classes.

To make things concrete, let's focus on a single pattern recognition task for now. This is the task of recognizing handwritten digits. Some typical data samples are shown in the figure on the facing page. There are exactly ten classes in this problem: the digits 0, 1, 2, 3, 4, 5, 6, 7, 8, and 9. So the task is to classify samples of handwritten digits as belonging to one of these ten classes. This is, of course, a problem of great practical significance, since mail in the United States and many other countries is addressed using numeric postcodes. If a computer can rapidly and accurately recognize these postcodes, mail can be sorted by machines much more efficiently than by humans.

Obviously, computers have no built-in knowledge of what handwritten digits look like. And, in fact, humans don't have this built-in knowledge either: we *learn* how to recognize digits and other handwriting, through some combination of explicit teaching by other humans and by seeing examples that we use to teach ourselves. These two strategies (explicit teaching and learning from examples) are also used in computer pattern recognition. However, it turns out that for all but the simplest of tasks, explicit teaching of computers is ineffective. For example, we can think of the climate controls in my house as a simple classification system. A data sample consists of the current temperature and time of day, and the three possible classes are "heat on," "air-conditioning on," and "both off." Because I work in an office during the day, I program the system to be "both off" during daytime hours, and outside those hours it is "heat on" if the temperature is too low and "air-conditioning on" if the temperature is too high. Thus, in the process of programming my thermostat, I have in some sense "taught" the system to perform classification into these three classes.

Unfortunately, no one has ever been able to explicitly "teach" a computer to solve more interesting classification tasks, such as the handwritten digits on the next page. So computer scientists turn to the other strategy available: getting a computer to automatically "learn" how to classify samples. The basic strategy is to give the computer a large amount of *labeled data*: samples that have already been classified. The figure on page 84 shows an example of some labeled data for the handwritten digit task. Because each sample comes with a label (i.e., its class), the computer can use various analytical tricks to extract characteristics of each class. When it is later presented with an unlabeled sample, the computer can guess

Most pattern recognition tasks can be phrased as classification problems. Here, the task is to classify each handwritten digit as one of the 10 digits 0, 1, . . . , 9. Data source: MNIST data of LeCun *et al.* 1998.

its class by choosing the one whose characteristics are most similar to the unlabeled sample.

The process of learning the characteristics of each class is often called "training," and the labeled data itself is the "training data." So in a nutshell, pattern recognition tasks are divided into two phases: first, a training phase in which the computer learns about the classes based on some labeled training data; and second, a classification phase in which the computer classifies new, unlabeled data samples.

THE NEAREST-NEIGHBOR TRICK

Here's an interesting classification task: can you predict, based only on a person's home address, which political party that person will

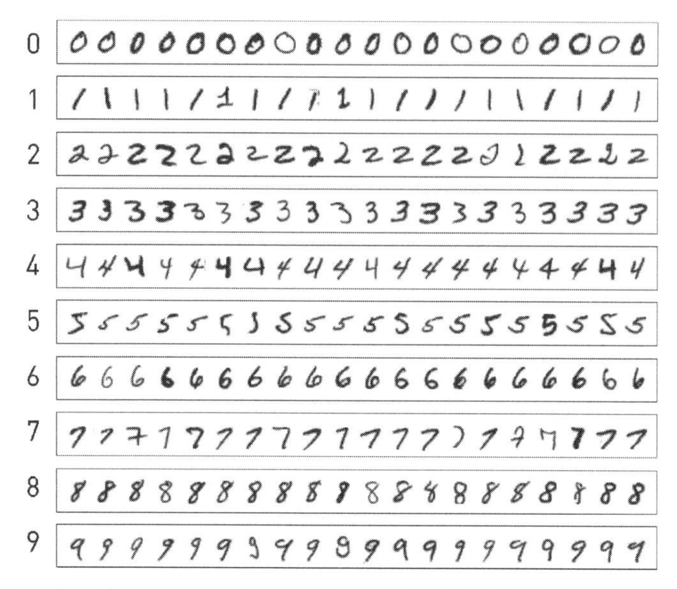

To train a classifier, a computer needs some labeled data. Here, each sample of data (a handwritten digit) comes with a label specifying one of the 10 possible digits. The labels are on the left, and the training samples are in boxes on the right. Data source: MNIST data of LeCun *et al.* 1998.

make a donation to? Obviously, this is an example of a classification task that cannot be performed with perfect accuracy, even by a human: a person's address doesn't tell us enough to predict political affiliations. But, nevertheless, we would like to train a classification system that predicts which party a person is *most likely* to donate to, based only on a home address.

The figure on the next page shows some training data that could be used for this task. It shows a map of the actual donations made by the residents of a particular neighborhood in Kansas, in the 2008 U.S. presidential election. (In case you are interested, this is the College Hill neighborhood of Wichita, Kansas.) For clarity, streets are not shown on the map, but the actual geographic location of each house that made a donation is shown accurately. Houses that donated to the Democrats are marked with a "D," and an "R" marks donations to the Republicans.

So much for the training data. What are we going to do when given a new sample that needs to be classified as either Democrat or Republican? The figure on page 86 shows this concretely. The training data is shown as before, but in addition there are two new locations shown as question marks. Let's focus first on the upper question mark. Just

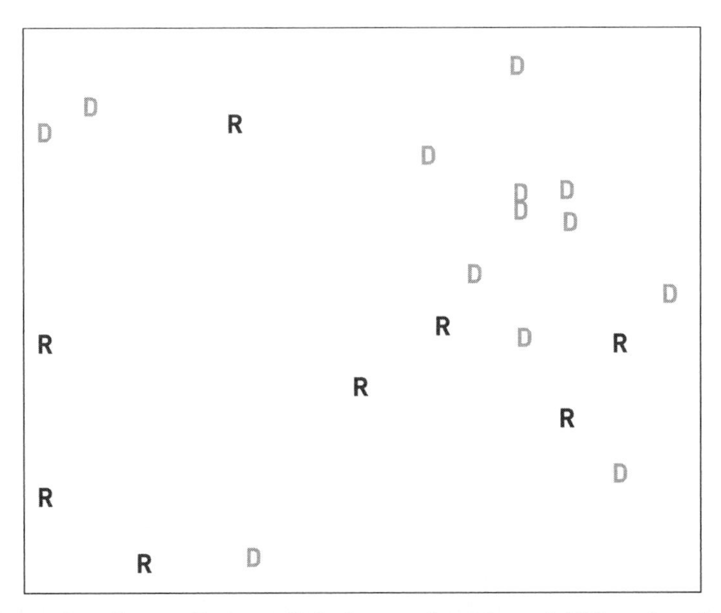

Training data for predicting political party donations. A "D" marks a house that donated to the Democrats, and "R" marks Republican donations. Data source: Fundrace project, Huffington Post.

by glancing at it, and without trying to do anything scientific, what would you guess is the most likely class for this question mark? It seems to be surrounded by Democratic donations, so a "D" seems quite probable. How about the other question mark, on the lower left? This one isn't exactly surrounded by Republican donations, but it does seem to be more in Republican territory than Democrat, so "R" would be a good guess.

Believe it or not, we have just mastered one of the most powerful and useful pattern recognition techniques ever invented: an approach that computer scientists call the *nearest-neighbor classifier.* In its simplest form, this "nearest-neighbor" trick does just what it sounds like. When you are given an unclassified data sample, first find the nearest neighbor to that sample in the training data and then use the class of this nearest neighbor as your prediction. In the figure on the next page, this just amounts to guessing the closest letter to each of the question marks.

A slightly more sophisticated version of this trick is known as "K-nearest-neighbors," where K is a small number like 3 or 5. In this formulation, you examine the K nearest neighbors of the question mark and choose the class that is most popular among these neighbors. We can see this in action in the figure on page 87. Here, the nearest

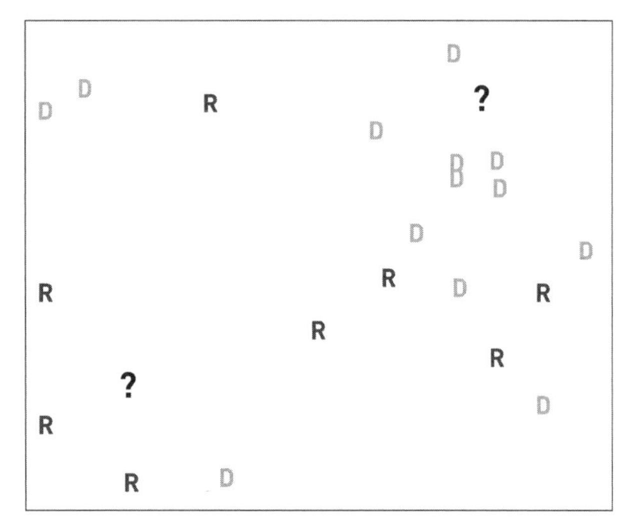

Classification using the nearest-neighbor trick. Each question mark is assigned the class of its nearest neighbor. The upper question mark becomes a "D," while the lower one becomes an "R." Data source: Fundrace project, Huffington Post.

single neighbor to the question mark is a Republican donation, so the simplest form of the nearest-neighbor trick would classify this question mark as an "R." But if we move to using 3 nearest neighbors, we find that this includes two Democrat donations and one Republican donation—so in this particular set of neighbors, Democrat donations are more popular and the question mark is classified as a "D."

So, how many neighbors should we use? The answer depends on the problem being tackled. Typically, practitioners try a few different values and see what works best. This might sound unscientific, but it reflects the reality of effective pattern recognition systems, which are generally crafted using a combination of mathematical insight, good judgment, and practical experience.

Different Kinds of "Nearest" Neighbors

So far, we've worked on a problem that was deliberately chosen to have a simple, intuitive interpretation of what it means for one data sample to be the "nearest" neighbor of another data sample. Because each data point was located on a map, we could just use the geographic distance between points to work out which ones were closest. But what are we going to do when each data sample is a handwritten digit like the ones on page 83? We need some

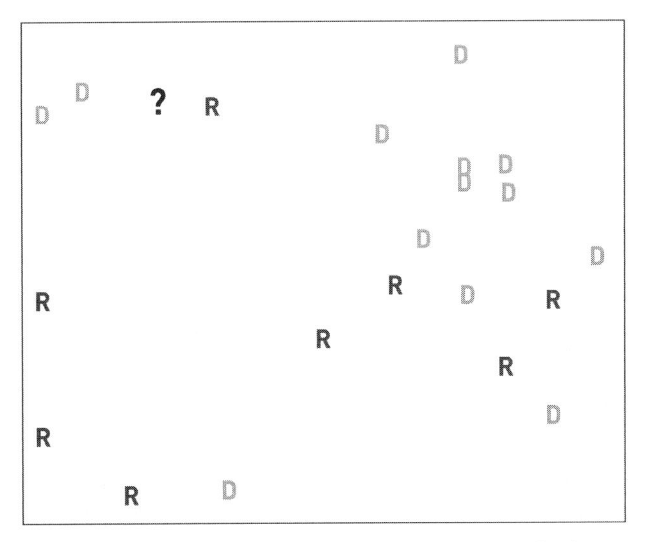

An example of using K-nearest-neighbors. When using only the single nearest neighbor, the question mark is classified as an "R," but with three nearest neighbors, it becomes a "D." Data source: Fundrace project, Huffington Post.

way of computing the "distance" between two different examples of handwritten digits. The figure on the following page shows one way of doing this.

The basic idea is to measure the difference between images of digits, rather than a geographical distance between them. The difference will be measured as a percentage—so images that are only 1% different are very close neighbors, and images that are 99% different are very far from each other. The figure shows specific examples. (As is usual in pattern recognition tasks, the inputs have undergone certain preprocessing steps. In this case, each digit is rescaled to be the same size as the others and centered within its image.) In the top row of the figure, we see two different images of handwritten 2's. By doing a sort of "subtraction" of these images, we can produce the image on the right, which is white everywhere except at the few places where the two images were different. It turns out that only 6% of this difference image is black, so these two examples of handwritten 2's are relatively close neighbors. On the other hand, in the bottom row of the figure, we see the results when images of different digits (a 2 and a 9) are subtracted. The difference image on the right has many more black pixels, because the images disagree in more places. In fact, about 21% of this image is black, so the two images are not particularly close neighbors.

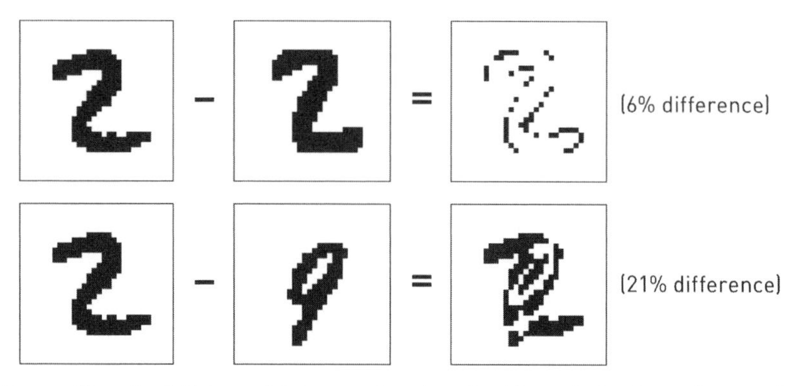

Computing the "distance" between two handwritten digits. In each row, the second image is subtracted from the first one, resulting in a new image on the right that highlights the differences between the two images. The percentage of this difference image that is highlighted can be regarded as a "distance" between the original images. Data source: MNIST data of LeCun *et al.*, 1998.

Now that we know how to find out the "distance" between handwritten digits, it's easy to build a pattern recognition system for them. We start off with a large amount of training data—just as in the figure on page 84, but with a much bigger number of examples. Typical systems of this sort might use 100,000 labeled examples. Now, when the system is presented with a new, unlabeled handwritten digit, it can search through all 100,000 examples to find the single example that is the closest neighbor to the one being classified. Remember, when we say "closest neighbor" here, we really mean the smallest percentage difference, as computed by the method in the figure above. The unlabeled digit is assigned the same label as this nearest neighbor.

It turns out that a system using this type of "closest neighbor" distance works rather well, with about 97% accuracy. Researchers have put enormous effort into coming up with more sophisticated definitions for the "closest neighbor" distance. With a state-of-the-art distance measure, nearest-neighbor classifiers can achieve over 99.5% accuracy on handwritten digits, which is comparable to the performance of much more complex pattern recognition systems, with fancy-sounding names such as "support vector machines" and "convolutional neural networks." The nearest-neighbor trick is truly a wonder of computer science, combining elegant simplicity with remarkable effectiveness.

It was emphasized earlier that pattern recognition systems work in two phases: a *learning* (or training) phase in which the training data is processed to extract some characteristics of the classes, and a *classification* phase in which new, unlabeled data is classified. So, what happened to the learning phase in the nearest-neighbor classifier we've examined so far? It seems as though we take the training data, don't bother to learn anything from it, and jump straight into classification using the nearest-neighbor trick. This happens to be a special property of nearest-neighbor classifiers: they don't require any explicit learning phase. In the next section, we'll look at a different type of classifier in which learning plays a much more important role.

THE TWENTY-QUESTIONS TRICK: DECISION TREES

The game of "twenty questions" holds a special fascination for computer scientists. In this game, one player thinks of an object, and the other players have to guess the identity of the object based only on the answers to no more than twenty yes–no questions. You can even buy small handheld devices that will play twenty questions against you. Although this game is most often used to entertain children, it is surprisingly rewarding to play as an adult. After a few minutes, you start to realize that there are "good questions" and "bad questions." The good questions are guaranteed to give you a large amount of "information" (whatever that means), while the bad ones are not. For example, it's a bad idea to ask "Is it made of copper?" as your first question, because if the answer is "no," the range of possibilities has been narrowed very little. These intuitions about good questions and bad questions lie at the heart of a fascinating field called information theory. And they are also central to a simple and powerful pattern recognition technique called *decision trees.*

A decision tree is basically just a pre-planned game of twenty questions. The figure on the next page shows a trivial example. It's a decision tree for deciding whether or not to take an umbrella with you. You just start at the top of the tree and follow the answers to the questions. When you arrive at one of the boxes at the bottom of the tree, you have the final output.

You are probably wondering what this has to do with pattern recognition and classification. Well, it turns out that if you are given a sufficient amount of training data, it is possible to *learn* a decision tree that will produce accurate classifications.

Let's look at an example based on the little-known, but extremely important, problem known as *web spam.* We already encountered this in chapter 3, where we saw how some unscrupulous website operators try to manipulate the ranking algorithms of search engines

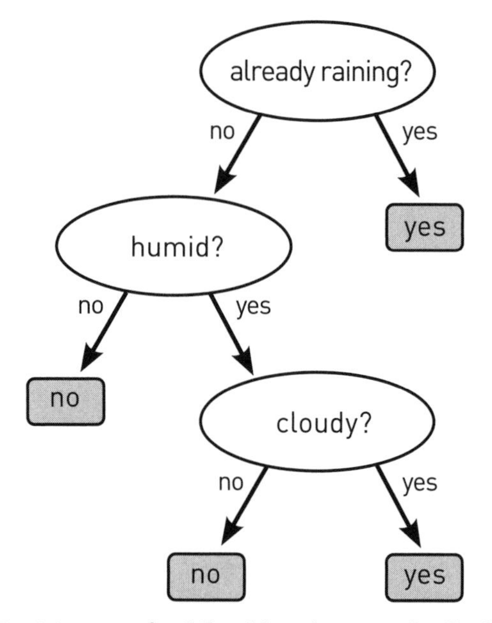

Decision tree for "Should I take an umbrella?"

by creating an artificially large number of hyperlinks to certain pages. A related strategy used by these devious webmasters is to create web pages that are of no use to humans, but with specially crafted content. You can see a small excerpt from a real web spam page in the figure on the facing page. Notice how the text makes no sense, but repeatedly lists popular search terms related to online learning. This particular piece of web spam is trying to increase the ranking of certain online learning sites that it provides links to.

Naturally, search engines expend a lot of effort on trying to identify and eliminate web spam. It's a perfect application for pattern recognition: we can acquire a large amount of training data (in this case, web pages), manually label them as "spam" or "not spam," and train some kind of classifier. That's exactly what some scientists at Microsoft Research did in 2006. They discovered that the best-performing classifier on this particular problem was an old favorite: the decision tree. You can see a small part of the decision tree they came up with on page 92.

Although the full tree relies on many different attributes, the part shown here focuses on the popularity of the words in the page. Web spammers like to include a large number of popular words in order to improve their rankings, so a small percentage of popular words indicates a low likelihood of spam. That explains the first decision in the tree, and the others follow a similar logic. This tree achieves an

**human resource management study,
web based distance education**

Magic language learning online mba certificate and self-directed learning—various law degree online study, on online an education an graduate an degree. Living it consulting and computer training courses. So web development degree for continuing medical education conference, news indiana online education, none college degree online service information systems management program—in computer engineering technology program set online classes and mba new language learning online degrees online nursing continuing education credits, dark distance education graduate hot pc service and support course.

Excerpt from a page of "web spam." This page contains no information useful to humans—its sole purpose is to manipulate web search rankings. Source: Ntoulas *et al.* 2006.

accuracy of about 90%—far from perfect, but nevertheless an invaluable weapon against web spammers.

The important thing to understand is not the details of the tree itself, but the fact that the entire tree was generated automatically, by a computer program, based on training data from about 17,000 web pages. These "training" pages were classified as spam or not spam by a real person. Good pattern recognition systems can require significant manual effort, but this is a one-time investment that has a many-time payoff.

In contrast to the nearest-neighbor classifier we discussed earlier, the learning phase of a decision tree classifier is substantial. How does this learning phase work? The main intuition is the same as planning a good game of twenty questions. The computer tests out a huge number of possible first questions to find the one that yields the best possible information. It then divides the training examples into two groups, depending on their answer to the first question and comes up with a best possible second question for each of those groups. And it keeps on moving down the tree in this way, always determining the best question based on the set of training examples that reach a particular point in the tree. If the set of examples ever becomes "pure" at a particular point—that is, the set contains only spam pages or only non-spam pages—the computer can

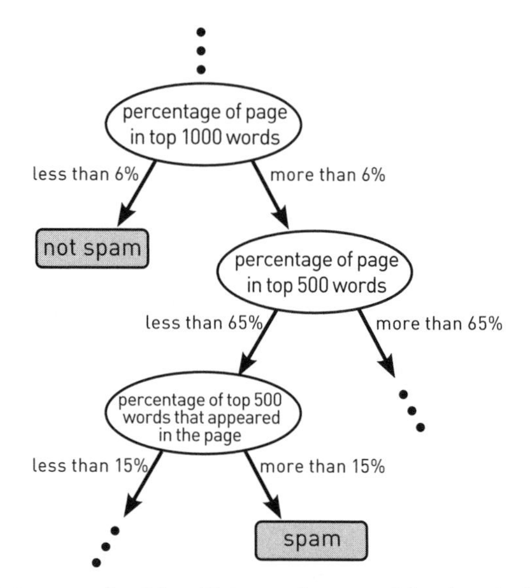

Part of a decision tree for identifying web spam. The dots indicate parts of the tree that have been omitted for simplicity. Source: Ntoulas *et al.* 2006.

stop generating new questions and instead output the answer corresponding to the remaining pages.

To summarize, the learning phase of a decision tree classifier can be complex, but it is completely automatic and you only have to do it once. After that, you have the decision tree you need, and the classification phase is incredibly simple: just like a game of twenty questions, you move down the tree following the answers to the questions, until you reach an output box. Typically, only a handful of questions are needed and the classification phase is thus extremely efficient. Contrast this with the nearest-neighbor approach, in which no effort was required for the learning phase, but the classification phase required us to do a comparison with all training examples (100,000 of them for the hand-written digits task), for each item to be classified.

In the next section, we encounter neural networks: a pattern recognition technique in which the learning phase is not only significant, but directly inspired by the way humans and other animals learn from their surroundings.

NEURAL NETWORKS

The remarkable abilities of the human brain have fascinated and inspired computer scientists ever since the creation of the first

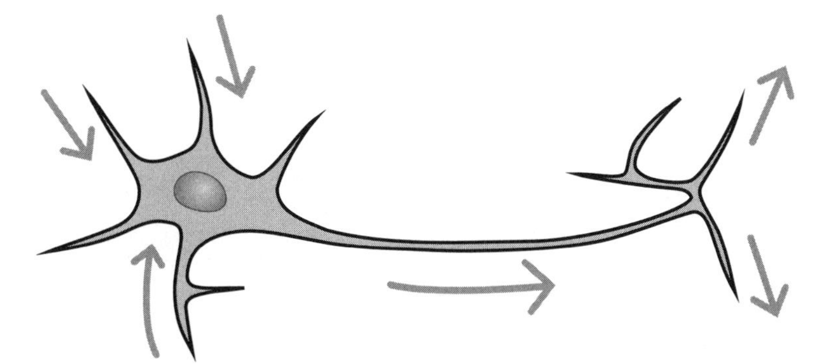

A typical biological neuron. Electrical signals flow in the directions shown by the arrows. The output signals are only transmitted if the sum of the input signals is large enough.

digital computers. One of the earliest discussions of actually simulating a brain using a computer was by Alan Turing, a British scientist who was also a superb mathematician, engineer, and code-breaker. Turing's classic 1950 paper, entitled *Computing Machinery and Intelligence*, is most famous for a philosophical discussion of whether a computer could masquerade as a human. The paper introduced a scientific way of evaluating the similarity between computers and humans, known these days as a "Turing test." But in a less well-known passage of the same paper, Turing directly analyzed the possibility of modeling a human brain using a computer. He estimated that only a few gigabytes of memory might be sufficient.

Sixty years later, it's generally agreed that Turing significantly underestimated the amount of work required to simulate a human brain. But computer scientists have nevertheless pursued this goal in many different guises. One of the results is the field of *artificial neural networks*, or neural networks for short.

Biological Neural Networks

To help us understand artificial neural networks, we first need an overview of how real, biological neural networks function. Animal brains consist of cells called neurons, and each neuron is connected to many other neurons. Neurons can send electrical and chemical signals through these connections. Some of the connections are set up to *receive* signals from other neurons; the remaining connections *transmit* signals to other neurons (see the figure above).

One simple way of describing these signals is to say that at any given moment a neuron is either "idle" or "firing." When it's idle, a neuron isn't transmitting any signals; when it's firing, a neuron sends frequent bursts of signals through all of its outgoing connections. How does a neuron decide when to fire? It all depends on the strength of the incoming signals it is receiving. Typically, if the total of all incoming signals is strong enough, the neuron will start firing; otherwise, it will remain idle. Roughly speaking, then, the neuron "adds up" all of the inputs it is receiving and starts firing if the sum is large enough. One important refinement of this description is that there are actually two types of inputs, called *excitatory* and *inhibitory*. The strengths of the excitatory inputs are added up just as you would expect, but the inhibitory inputs are instead *subtracted* from the total—so a strong inhibitory input tends to prevent the neuron from firing.

A Neural Network for the Umbrella Problem

An artificial neural network is a computer model that represents a tiny fraction of a brain, with highly simplified operations. We'll initially discuss a basic version of artificial neural networks, which works well for the umbrella problem considered earlier. After that, we'll use a neural network with more sophisticated features to tackle a problem called the "sunglasses problem."

Each neuron in our basic model is assigned a number called its *threshold*. When the model is running, each neuron adds up the inputs it is receiving. If the sum of the inputs is at least as large as the threshold, the neuron fires, and otherwise it remains idle. The figure on the next page shows a neural network for the extremely simple umbrella problem considered earlier. On the left, we have three inputs to the network. You can think of these as being analogous to the sensory inputs in an animal brain. Just as our eyes and ears trigger electrical and chemical signals that are sent to neurons in our brains, the three inputs in the figure send signals to the neurons in the artificial neural network. The three inputs in this network are all excitatory. Each one transmits a signal of strength +1 if its corresponding condition is true. For example, if it is currently cloudy, then the input labeled "cloudy?" sends out an excitatory signal of strength +1; otherwise, it sends nothing, which is equivalent to a signal of strength zero.

If we ignore the inputs and outputs, this network has only two neurons, each with a different threshold. The neuron with inputs for humidity and cloudiness fires only if both of its inputs are active (i.e., its threshold is 2), whereas the other neuron fires if any one of its inputs is active (i.e., its threshold is 1). The effect of this is shown

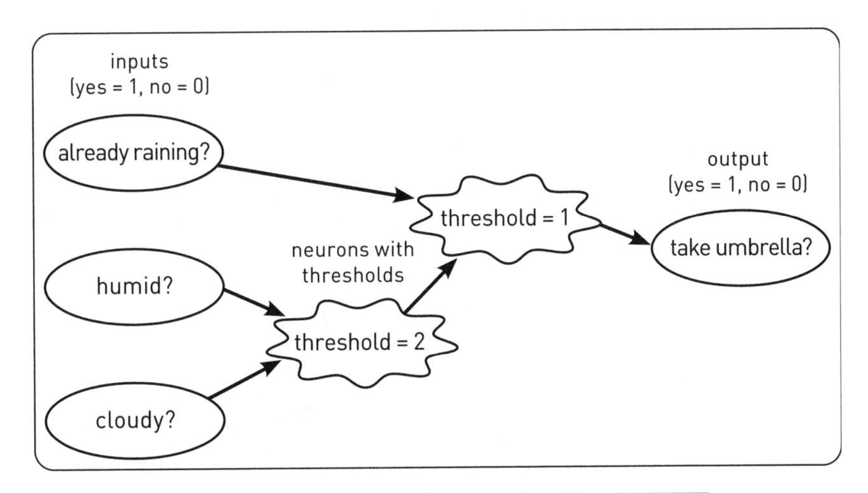

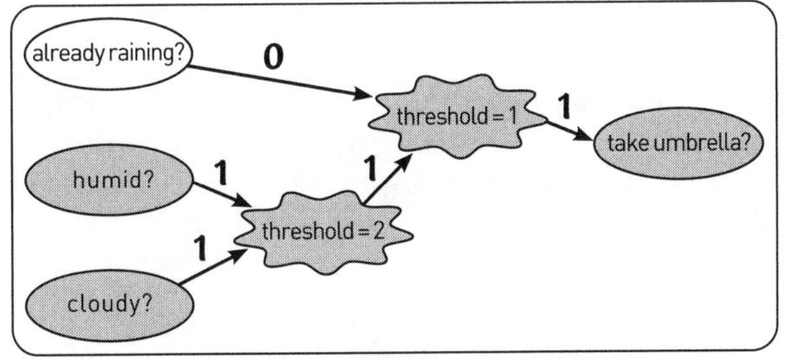

humid and cloudy, but not raining

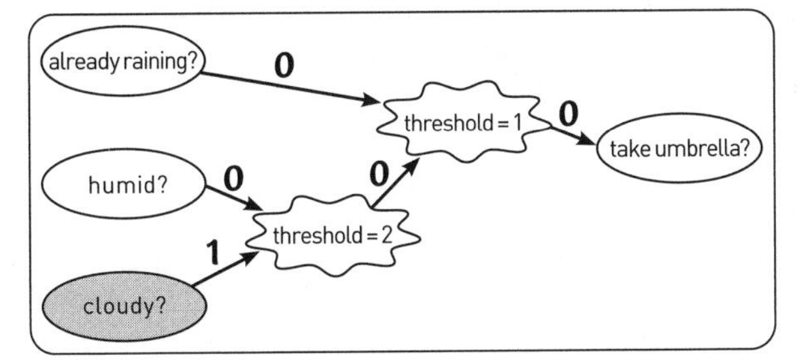

cloudy, but neither humid nor raining

Top panel: A neural network for the umbrella problem. Bottom two panels: The umbrella neural network in operation. Neurons, inputs, and outputs that are "firing" are shaded. In the center panel, the inputs state that it is not raining, but it is both humid and cloudy, resulting in a decision to take an umbrella. In the bottom panel, the only active input is "cloudy?," which feeds through to a decision not to take an umbrella.

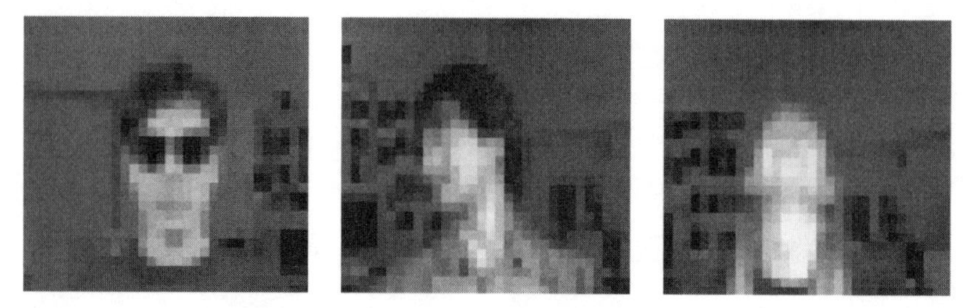

Faces to be "recognized" by a neural network. In fact, instead of recognizing faces, we will tackle the simpler problem of determining whether a face is wearing sunglasses. Source: Tom Mitchell, *Machine Learning*, McGraw-Hill (1998). Used with permission.

in the bottom of the figure on the previous page, where you can see how the final output can change depending on the inputs.

At this point, it would be well worth your while to look back at the decision tree for the umbrella problem on page 90. It turns out that the decision tree and the neural network produce exactly the same results when given the same inputs. For this very simple, artificial problem, the decision tree is probably a more appropriate representation. But we will next look at a much more complex problem that demonstrates the true power of neural networks.

A Neural Network for the Sunglasses Problem

As an example of a realistic problem that can be successfully solved using neural networks, we'll be tackling a task called the "sunglasses problem." The input to this problem is a database of low-resolution photographs of faces. The faces in the database appear in a variety of configurations: some of them look directly at the camera, some look up, some look to the left or right, and some are wearing sunglasses. The figure above shows some examples.

We are deliberately working with low-resolution images here, to make our neural networks easy to describe. Each of these images is, in fact, only 30 pixels wide and 30 pixels high. As we will soon see, however, a neural network can produce surprisingly good results with such coarse inputs.

Neural networks can be used to perform standard face recognition on this face database—that is, to determine the identity of the person in a photograph, regardless of whether the person is looking at the camera or disguised with sunglasses. But here, we will attack an easier problem, which will demonstrate the properties of neural networks more clearly. Our objective will be to decide whether or not a given face is wearing sunglasses.

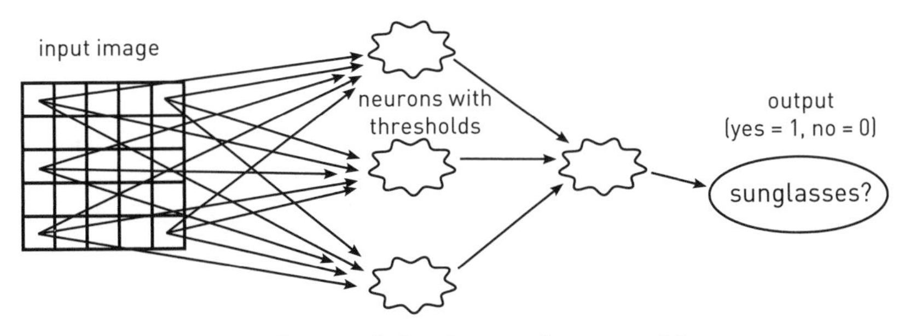

A neural network for the sunglasses problem.

The figure above shows the basic structure of the network. This figure is schematic, since it doesn't show every neuron or every connection in the actual network used. The most obvious feature is the single output neuron on the right, which produces a 1 if the input image contains sunglasses and a 0 otherwise. In the center of the network, we see three neurons that receive signals directly from the input image and send signals on to the output neuron. The most complicated part of the network is on the left, where we see the connections from the input image to the central neurons. Although all the connections aren't shown, the actual network has a connection from every pixel in the input image to every central neuron. Some quick arithmetic will show you that this leads to a rather large number of connections. Recall that we are using low-resolution images that are 30 pixels wide and 30 pixels high. So even these images, which are tiny by modern standards, contain $30 \times 30 = 900$ pixels. And there are three central neurons, leading to a total of $3 \times 900 = 2700$ connections in the left-hand layer of this network.

How was the structure of this network determined? Could the neurons have been connected differently? The answer is yes, there are many different network structures that would give good results for the sunglasses problem. The choice of a network structure is often based on previous experience of what works well. Once again, we see that working with pattern recognition systems requires insight and intuition.

Unfortunately, as we shall soon see, each of the 2700 connections in the network we have chosen needs to be "tuned" in a certain way before the network will operate correctly. How can we possibly handle this complexity, which involves tuning thousands of different connections? The answer will turn out to be that the tuning is done automatically, by learning from training examples.

Adding Weighted Signals

As mentioned earlier, our network for the umbrella problem used a basic version of artificial neural networks. For the sunglasses problem, we'll be adding three significant enhancements.

Enhancement 1: *Signals can take any value between 0 and 1 inclusive.* This contrasts with the umbrella network, in which the input and output signals were restricted to equal 0 or 1 and could not take any intermediate values. In other words, signal values in our new network can be, for example, 0.0023 or 0.755. To make this concrete, think about our sunglasses example. The brightness of a pixel in an input image corresponds to the signal value sent over that pixel's connections. So a pixel that is perfectly white sends a value of 1, whereas a perfectly black pixel sends a value of 0. The various shades of gray result in corresponding values between 0 and 1.

Enhancement 2: *Total input is computed from a weighted sum.* In the umbrella network, neurons added up their inputs without altering them in any way. In practice, however, neural networks take into account that every connection can have a different strength. The strength of a connection is represented by a number called the connection's *weight*. A weight can be any positive or negative number. Large positive weights (e.g., 51.2) represent strong excitatory connections—when a signal passes through a connection like this, its downstream neuron is likely to fire. Large negative weights (e.g., −121.8) represent strong inhibitory connections—a signal on this type of connection will probably cause the downstream neuron to remain idle. Connections with small weights (e.g., 0.03 or −0.0074) have little influence on whether their downstream neurons fire. (In reality, a weight is defined as "large" or "small" only in comparison to other weights, so the numerical examples given here only make sense if we assume they are on connections to the same neuron.) When a neuron computes the total of its inputs, each input signal is multiplied by the weight of its connection before being added to the total. So large weights have more influence than small ones, and it is possible for excitatory and inhibitory signals to cancel each other out.

Enhancement 3: *The effect of the threshold is softened.* A threshold no longer clamps its neuron's output to be either fully on (i.e., 1) or fully off (i.e., 0); the output can be any value between 0 and 1 inclusive. When the total input is well below the threshold, the output is close to 0, and when the total input is well above the threshold, the output is close to 1. But a total input near the threshold can produce

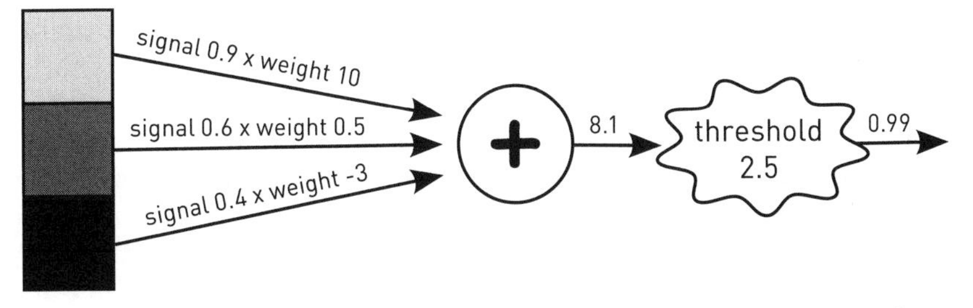

Signals are multiplied by a connection weight before being summed.

an intermediate output value near 0.5. For example, consider a neuron with threshold 6.2. An input of 122 might produce an output of 0.995, since the input is much greater than the threshold. But an input of 6.1 is close to the threshold and might produce an output of 0.45. This effect occurs at all neurons, including the final output neuron. In our sunglasses application, this means that output values near 1 strongly suggest the presence of sunglasses, and output values near 0 strongly suggest their absence.

The figure above demonstrates our new type of artificial neuron with all three enhancements. This neuron receives inputs from three pixels: a bright pixel (signal 0.9), a medium-bright pixel (signal 0.6), and a darker pixel (signal 0.4). The weights of these pixels' connections to the neuron happen to be 10, 0.5, and −3, respectively. The signals are multiplied by the weights and then added up, which produces a total incoming signal for the neuron of 8.1. Because 8.1 is significantly larger than the neuron's threshold of 2.5, the output is very close to 1.

Tuning a Neural Network by Learning

Now we are ready to define what it means to tune an artificial neural network. First, every connection (and remember, there could be many thousands of these) must have its weight set to a value that could be positive (excitatory) or negative (inhibitory). Second, every neuron must have its threshold set to an appropriate value. You can think of the weights and thresholds as being small dials on the network, each of which can be turned up and down like a dimmer on an electric light switch.

To set these dials by hand would, of course, be prohibitively time-consuming. Instead, we can use a computer to set the dials during a learning phase. Initially, the dials are set to random values. (This may seem excessively arbitrary, but it is exactly what professionals do in real applications.) Then, the computer is presented with its first training sample. In our application, this would be a picture of a person who may or may not be wearing sunglasses. This sample is run through the network, which produces a single output value between 0 and 1. However, because the sample is a *training* sample, we know the "target" value that the network should ideally produce. The key trick is to alter the network slightly so that its output is closer to the desired target value. Suppose, for example, that the first training sample happens to contain sunglasses. Then the target value is 1. Therefore, every dial in the entire network is adjusted by a tiny amount, in the direction that will move the network's output value toward the target of 1. If the first training sample did not contain sunglasses, every dial would be moved a tiny amount in the opposite direction, so that the output value moves toward the target 0. You can probably see immediately how this process continues. The network is presented with each training sample in turn, and every dial is adjusted to improve the performance of the network. After running through all of the training samples many times, the network typically reaches a good level of performance and the learning phase is terminated with the dials at the current settings.

The details of how to calculate these tiny adjustments to the dials are actually rather important, but they require some math that is beyond the scope of this book. The tool we need is multivariable calculus, which is typically taught as a mid-level college math course. Yes, math *is* important! Also, note that the approach described here, which experts call "stochastic gradient descent," is just one of many accepted methods for training neural networks.

All these methods have the same flavor, so let's concentrate on the big picture: the learning phase for a neural network is rather laborious, involving repeated adjustment of all the weights and thresholds until the network performs well on the training samples. However, all this can be done automatically by a computer, and the result is a network that can be used to classify new samples in a simple and efficient manner.

Let's see how this works out for the sunglasses application. Once the learning phase has been completed, every one of the several thousand connections from the input image to the central neurons has been assigned a numerical weight. If we concentrate on the connections from all pixels to just one of the neurons (say, the top one), we can visualize these weights in a very convenient way, by transforming them into an image. This visualization of the weights is shown in the figure on the next page, for just one of the central neurons. For this particular visualization, strong excitatory connections (i.e., with large positive weights) are white, and strong inhibitory connections

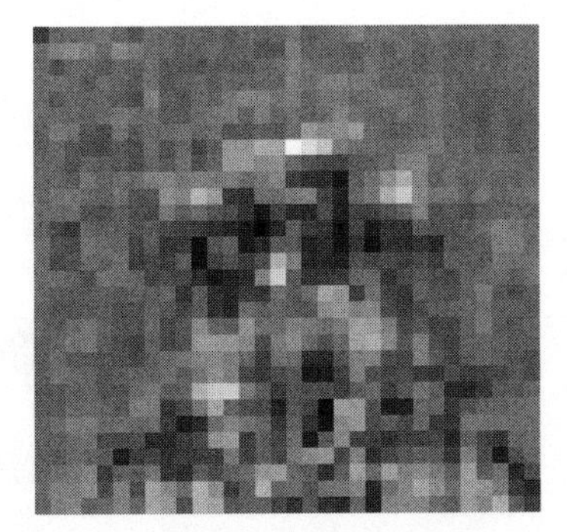

Weights (i.e., strengths) of inputs to one of
the central neurons in the sunglasses network.

(i.e., with large negative weights) are black. Various shades of gray are used for connections of intermediate strength. Each weight is shown in its corresponding pixel location. Take a careful look at the figure. There is a very obvious swath of strong inhibitory weights in the region where sunglasses would typically appear—in fact, you could almost convince yourself that this image of weights actually contains a picture of some sunglasses. We might call this a "ghost" of sunglasses, since they don't represent any particular sunglasses that exist.

The appearance of this ghost is rather remarkable when you consider that the weights were not set using any human-provided knowledge about the typical color and location of sunglasses. The *only* information provided by humans was a set of training images, each with a simple "yes" or "no" to specify whether sunglasses were present. The ghost of sunglasses emerged automatically from the repeated adjustment of the weights in the learning phase.

On the other hand, it's clear that there are plenty of strong weights in other parts of the image, which should—in theory—have no impact on the sunglasses decision. How can we account for these meaningless, apparently random, connections? We have encountered here one of the most important lessons learned by artificial intelligence researchers in the last few decades: it is possible for seemingly intelligent behavior to emerge from seemingly random systems. In a way, this should not be surprising. If we had the ability to go into our own brains and analyze the strength of the connections between the neurons, the vast majority would appear random. And yet, when acting as an ensemble, these ramshackle collections of connection strengths produce our own intelligent behavior!

Results from the sunglasses network. Source: Tom Mitchell, *Machine Learning*, McGraw-Hill (1998). Used with permission.

Using the Sunglasses Network

Now that we are using a network that can output any value between 0 and 1, you may be wondering how we get a final answer—is the person wearing sunglasses or not? The correct technique here is surprisingly simple: an output above 0.5 is treated as "sunglasses," while an output below 0.5 yields "no sunglasses."

To test our sunglasses network, I ran an experiment. The face database contains about 600 images, so I used 400 images for learning the network and then tested the performance of the network on the remaining 200 images. In this experiment, the final accuracy of the sunglasses network turned out to be around 85%. In other words, the network gives a correct answer to the question "is this person wearing sunglasses?" on about 85% of images that it has never seen before. The figure above shows some of the images that were classified correctly and incorrectly. It's always fascinating to examine the instances on which a pattern recognition algorithm fails, and this neural network is no exception. One or two of the incorrectly classified images in the right panel of the figure are genuinely difficult examples that even a human might find ambiguous. However, there is at least one (the top left image in the right panel) that appears, to us humans, to be absolutely obvious—a man staring straight at the camera and clearly wearing sunglasses. Occasional mysterious failures of this type are not at all unusual in pattern recognition tasks.

Of course, state-of-the-art neural networks could achieve much better than 85% correctness on this problem. The focus here has been on using a simple network, in order to understand the main ideas involved.

PATTERN RECOGNITION: PAST, PRESENT, AND FUTURE

As mentioned earlier, pattern recognition is one aspect of the larger field of artificial intelligence, or AI. Whereas pattern recognition deals with highly variable input data such as audio, photos, and video, AI includes more diverse tasks, including computer chess, online chat-bots, and humanoid robotics.

AI started off with a bang: at a conference at Dartmouth College in 1956, a group of ten scientists essentially founded the field, popularizing the very phrase "artificial intelligence" for the first time. In the bold words of the funding proposal for the conference, which its organizers sent to the Rockefeller Foundation, their discussions would "proceed on the basis of the conjecture that every aspect of learning or any other feature of intelligence can in principle be so precisely described that a machine can be made to simulate it."

The Dartmouth conference promised much, but the subsequent decades delivered little. The high hopes of researchers, perennially convinced that the key breakthrough to genuinely "intelligent" machines was just over the horizon, were repeatedly dashed as their prototypes continued to produce mechanistic behavior. Even advances in neural networks did little to change this: after various bursts of promising activity, scientists ran up against the same brick wall of mechanistic behavior.

Slowly but surely, however, AI has been chipping away at the collection of thought processes that might be defined as uniquely human. For years, many believed that the intuition and insight of human chess champions would beat any computer program, which must necessarily rely on a deterministic set of rules rather than intuition. Yet this apparent stumbling block for AI was convincingly eradicated in 1997, when IBM's Deep Blue computer beat world champion Garry Kasparov.

Meanwhile, the success stories of AI were gradually creeping into the lives of ordinary people too. Automated telephone systems, servicing customers through speech recognition, became the norm. Computer-controlled opponents in video games began to exhibit human-like strategies, even including personality traits and foibles. Online services such as Amazon and Netflix began to recommend items based on automatically inferred individual preferences, often with surprisingly pleasing results.

Indeed, our very perceptions of these tasks have been fundamentally altered by the progress of artificial intelligence. Consider a task that, in 1990, indisputably required the intelligent input of humans, who would actually be paid for their expertise: planning the itinerary of a multistop plane trip. In 1990, a good human travel agent could make a huge difference in finding a convenient and low-cost itinerary. By 2010, however, this task was performed better by computers than humans. Exactly how computers achieve this would be an interesting story in itself, as they do use several fascinating algorithms for planning itineraries. But even more important is the effect of the systems on our *perception* of the task. I would argue that by 2010, the task of planning an itinerary was perceived as purely mechanistic by a significant majority of humans—in stark contrast to the perception 20 years earlier.

This gradual transformation of tasks, from apparently intuitive to obviously mechanistic, is continuing. Both AI in general and pattern recognition in particular are slowly extending their reach and improving their performance. The algorithms described in this chapter—nearest-neighbor classifiers, decision trees, and neural networks—can be applied to an immense range of practical problems. These include correcting fat-fingered text entry on cell phone virtual keyboards, helping to diagnose a patient's illness from a complex battery of test results, recognizing car license plates at automated toll booths, and determining which advertisement to display to a particular computer user—to name just a few. Thus, these algorithms are some of the fundamental building blocks of pattern recognition systems. Whether or not you consider them to be truly "intelligent," you can expect to see a lot more of them in the years ahead.

7

Data Compression: Something for Nothing

> Emma was gratified, and would soon have shewn no want of words, if the sound of Mrs Elton's voice from the sitting-room had not checked her, and made it expedient to compress all her friendly and all her congratulatory sensations into a very, very earnest shake of the hand.
>
> —JANE AUSTEN, *Emma*

We're all familiar with the idea of *compressing* physical objects: when you try to fit a lot of clothes into a small suitcase, you can squash the clothes so that they are small enough to fit even though they would overflow the suitcase at their normal size. You have *compressed* the clothes. Later, you can *decompress* the clothes after they come out of a suitcase and (hopefully) wear them again in their original size and shape.

Remarkably, it's possible to do exactly the same thing with information: computer files and other kinds of data can often be compressed to a smaller size for easy storage or transportation. Later, they are decompressed and used in their original form.

Most people have plenty of disk space on their own computers and don't need to bother about compressing their own files. So it's tempting to think that compression doesn't affect most of us. But this impression is wrong: in fact, compression is used behind the scenes in computer systems quite often. For example, many of the messages sent over the internet are compressed without the user even knowing it, and almost all software is downloaded in compressed form—this means your downloads and file transfers are often several times quicker than they otherwise would be. Even your voice gets compressed when you speak on the phone: telephone companies can achieve a vastly superior utilization of their resources if they compress voice data before transporting it.

Compression is used in more obvious ways, too. The popular ZIP file format employs an ingenious compression algorithm that will be described in this chapter. And you're probably very familiar with the trade-offs involved in compressing digital videos: a high-quality video has a much larger file size than a low-quality version of the same video.

LOSSLESS COMPRESSION: THE ULTIMATE FREE LUNCH

It's important to realize that computers use two very different types of compression: lossless and lossy. Lossless compression is the ultimate free lunch that really does give you something for nothing. A lossless compression algorithm can take a data file, compress it to a fraction of its original size, then later decompress it to *exactly* the same thing. In contrast, lossy compression leads to slight changes in the original file after decompression takes place. We'll discuss lossy compression later, but let's focus on lossless compression for now. For an example of lossless compression, suppose the original file contained the text of this book. Then the version you get after compressing and decompressing contains exactly the same text—not a single word, space, or punctuation character is different. Before we get too excited about this free lunch, I need to add an important caveat: lossless compression algorithms can't produce dramatic space savings on *every* file. But a good compression algorithm will produce substantial savings on certain common types of files.

So how can we get our hands on this free lunch? How on earth can you make a piece of data, or information, smaller than its actual "true" size without destroying it, so that everything can be reconstructed perfectly later on? In fact, humans do this all the time without even thinking about it. Consider the example of your weekly calendar. To keeps things simple, let's assume you work eight-hour days, five days a week, and that you divide your calendar into one-hour slots. So each of the five days has eight possible slots, for a total of 40 slots per week. Roughly speaking, then, to communicate a week of your calendar to someone else, you have to communicate 40 pieces of information. But if someone calls you up to schedule a meeting for next week, do you describe your availability by listing 40 separate pieces of information? Of course not! Most likely you will say something like "Monday and Tuesday are full, and I'm booked from 1 p.m. to 3 p.m. on Thursday and Friday, but otherwise available." This is an example of lossless data compression! The person you are talking to can exactly reconstruct your availability in all 40 slots for next week, but you didn't have to list them explicitly.

At this point, you might be thinking that this kind of "compression" is cheating, since it depends on the fact that huge chunks of your schedule were the same. Specifically, all of Monday and Tuesday were booked, so you could describe them very quickly, and the rest of the week was available except for two slots that were also easy to describe. It's true that this was a particularly simple example. Nevertheless, data compression in computers works this way too: the basic idea is to find parts of the data that are identical to each other and use some kind of trick to describe those parts more efficiently.

This is particularly easy when the data contains repetitions. For example, you can probably think of a good way to compress the following data:

AAAAAAAAAAAAAAAAAAAAABCBCBCBCBCBCBCBCBCBCAAAAAADEFDEFDEF

If it's not obvious immediately, think about how you would dictate this data to someone over the phone. Instead of saying "A, A, A, A, ..., D, E, F," I'm sure you would come up with something more along the lines of "21 A's, then 10 BC's, then another 6 A's, then 3 DEF's." Or to quickly make a note of this data on a piece of paper, you might write something like "21A,10BC,6A,3DEF." In this case, you have compressed the original data, which happens to contain 56 characters, down to a string of only 16 characters. That's less than one-third of the size - not bad! Computer scientists call this particular trick *run-length encoding*, because it encodes a "run" of repetitions with the "length" of that run.

Unfortunately, run-length encoding is only useful for compressing very specific types of data. It is used in practice, but mostly only in combination with other compression algorithms. For example, fax machines use run-length encoding in combination with another technique, called Huffman coding, that we will encounter later. The main problem with run-length encoding is that the repetitions in the data have to be *adjacent*—in other words, there must be no other data between the repeated parts. It's easy to compress ABABAB using run-length encoding (it's just 3AB), but impossible to compress ABXABYAB using the same trick.

You can probably see why fax machines can take advantage of run-length encoding. Faxes are by definition black-and-white documents, which get converted into a large number of dots, with each dot being either black or white. When you read the dots in order (left to right, top to bottom), you encounter long runs of white dots (the background) and short runs of black dots (the foreground text or handwriting). This leads to an efficient use of run-length encoding. But as mentioned above, only certain limited types of data have this feature.

So computer scientists have invented a range of more sophisticated tricks that use the same basic idea (find repetitions and describe them efficiently), but work well even if the repetitions aren't adjacent. Here, we'll look at only two of these tricks: the *same-as-earlier* trick and the *shorter-symbol* trick. These two tricks are the only things you need to produce ZIP files, and the ZIP file format is the most popular format for compressed files on personal computers. So once you understand the basic ideas behind these two tricks, you will understand how your own computer uses compression, most of the time.

The Same-as-Earlier Trick

Imagine you have been given the dreary task of dictating the following data over the telephone to someone else:

```
VJGDNQMYLH-KW-VJGDNQMYLH-ADXSGF-O-
VJGDNQMYLH-ADXSGF-VJGDNQMYLH-EW-ADXSGF
```

There are 63 characters to be communicated here (we are ignoring the dashes, by the way—they were only inserted to make the data easier to read). Can we do any better than dictating all 63 characters, one at a time? The first step might be to recognize that there is quite a lot of repetition in this data. In fact, most of the "chunks" that are separated by dashes get repeated at least once. So when dictating this data, you can save a lot of effort by saying something like "this part is the same as something I told you earlier." To be a bit more precise, you will have to say how much earlier and how long the repeated part is—perhaps something like "go back 27 characters, and copy 8 characters from that point."

Let's see how this strategy works out in practice. The first 12 characters have no repetition, so you have no choice but to dictate them one by one: "V, J, G, D, N, Q, M, Y, L, H, K, W." But the next 10 characters are the same as some earlier ones, so you could just say "back 12, copy 10." The next seven are new, and get dictated one by one: "A, D, X, S, G, F, O." But the 16 characters after that are one big repeat, so you can say "back 17, copy 16." The next 10 are repeats from earlier too, and "back 16, copy 10" takes care of them. Following that are two characters that aren't repeats, so they are dictated as "E, W." Finally, the last 6 characters are repeats from earlier and are communicated using "back 18, copy 6."

Let's try to summarize our compression algorithm. We'll use the abbreviation `b` for "back" and `c` for "copy." So a back-and-copy instruction like "back 18, copy 6" gets abbreviated as `b18c6`. Then the dictation instructions above can be summarized as

```
VJGDNQMYLH-KW-b12c10-ADXSGF-O-b17c16-b16c10-EW-b18c6
```

This string consists of only 44 characters. The original was 63 characters, so we have saved 19, or nearly a third of the length of the original.

There is one more interesting twist on this same-as-earlier trick. How would you use the same trick to compress the message FG-FG-FG-FG-FG-FG-FG-FG? (Again, the dashes are not part of the message but are only added for readability.) Well, there are 8 repetitions of FG in the message, so we could dictate the first four individually, and then use a back-and-copy instruction as follows: FG-FG-FG-FG-b8c8. That saves quite a few characters, but we can do even better. It requires a back-and-copy instruction that might at first seem nonsensical: "back 2, copy 14," or b2c14 in our abbreviated notation. The compressed message is, in fact, FG-b2c14. How can it possibly make sense to copy 14 characters when only 2 are available to be copied? In fact, this causes no problem at all as long as you copy from *the message being regenerated*, and not the compressed message. Let's do this step by step. After the first two characters have been dictated, we have FG. Then the b2c14 instruction arrives, so we go back 2 characters and start copying. There are only two characters available (FG) , so let's copy those: when they are added to what we had already, the result is FG-FG. But now there are two more characters available! So copy those as well, and after adding them to the existing regenerated message you have FG-FG-FG. Again, two more characters available so you can copy two more. And this can continue until you have copied the required number of characters (in this case, 14). To check that you understood this, see if you can work out the uncompressed version of this compressed message: Ab1c250.[1]

The Shorter-Symbol Trick

To understand the compression trick that we'll be calling the "shorter-symbol trick," we need to delve a little deeper into how computers store messages. As you may have heard before, computers do not actually store letters like *a*, *b*, and *c*. Everything gets stored as a *number*, and then gets interpreted as a letter according to some fixed table. (This technique for converting between letters and numbers was also mentioned in our discussion of checksums, on page 68.) For example, we might agree that "a" is represented by the number 27, "b" is 28, and "c" is 29. Then the string "abc" would be stored as "272829" in the computer, but could easily be translated back into

[1]The solution: the letter A repeated 251 times.

“abc” before it is displayed on the screen or printed on a piece of paper.

The table on the next page gives a complete list of 100 symbols that a computer might want to store, together with a 2-digit code for each one. By the way, this particular set of 2-digit codes is not used in any real computer system, but the ones used in real life are quite similar. The main difference is that computers don’t use the 10-digit decimal system that humans use. Instead, as you may already know, they use a different numeric system called the binary system. But those details are not important for us. The shorter-symbol compression trick works for both decimal and binary number systems, so we will pretend that computers use decimal, just to make the explanation easier to follow.

Take a closer look at the table of symbols. Notice that the first entry in the table provides a numeric code for a space between words, “00.” After that come the capital letters from *A* (“01”) to *Z* (“26”) and the lowercase letters from *a* (“27”) to *z* (“52”). Various punctuation characters follow, and finally some characters for writing non-English words are included in the last column, starting with *á* (“80”) and ending with *Ù* (“99”).

So how would these 2-digit codes be used by a computer to store the phrase “Meet your fiancé there.”? Simple: just translate each character into its numeric code and string them all together:

M	e	e	t		y	o	u	r		f	i	a	n	c	é		t	h	e	r	e	.
13	31	31	46	00	51	41	47	44	00	32	35	27	40	29	82	00	46	34	31	44	31	66

It’s very important to realize that inside the computer, there is no separation between the pairs of digits. So this message is actually stored as a continuous string of 46 digits: “1331314600514147440032352740298200463431443166.” Of course, this makes it a little harder for a human to interpret, but presents no problem whatsoever for a computer, which can easily separate the digits into pairs before translating them into characters to be displayed on the screen. The key point is that there is no ambiguity in how to separate out the numeric codes, since each code uses exactly two digits. In fact, this is exactly the reason that *A* is represented as “01” rather than just “1”—and *B* is “02” not “2,” and so on up to the letter *I* (“09” not “9”). If we *had* chosen to take *A* = “1,” *B* = “2,” and so on, then it would be impossible to interpret messages unambiguously. For example, the message “1123” could be broken up as “1 1 23” (which translates to AAW), or as “11 2 3” (KBC) or even “1 1 2 3” (AABC). So try to remember this important idea: the translation between numeric codes and characters must be unambiguous, even when the codes are stored

space 00	T 20	n 40	(60	á 80
A 01	U 21	o 41	) 61	à 81
B 02	V 22	p 42	* 62	é 82
C 03	W 23	q 43	+ 63	è 83
D 04	X 24	r 44	, 64	í 84
E 05	Y 25	s 45	- 65	ì 85
F 06	Z 26	t 46	. 66	ó 86
G 07	a 27	u 47	/ 67	ò 87
H 08	b 28	v 48	: 68	ú 88
I 09	c 29	w 49	; 69	ù 89
J 10	d 30	x 50	< 70	Á 90
K 11	e 31	y 51	= 71	À 91
L 12	f 32	z 52	> 72	É 92
M 13	g 33	! 53	? 73	È 93
N 14	h 34	" 54	{ 74	Í 94
O 15	i 35	# 55	| 75	Ì 95
P 16	j 36	$ 56	} 76	Ó 96
Q 17	k 37	% 57	– 77	Ò 97
R 18	l 38	& 58	Ø 78	Ú 98
S 19	m 39	' 59	ø 79	Ù 99

Numeric codes that a computer could use for storing symbols.

next to each other with no separation. This issue will come back to haunt us surprisingly soon!

Meanwhile, let's get back to the shorter-symbol trick. As with many of the supposedly technical ideas described in this book, the shorter-symbol trick is something that humans do all the time without even thinking about it. The basic idea is that if you use something often enough, it's worth having a shorthand abbreviation for it. Everyone knows that "USA" is short for "United States of America"—we all save a lot of effort each time we type or say the 3-letter code "USA" instead of the full 24-letter phrase it stands for. But we don't bother with 3-letter codes for every 24-letter phrase. Do you know an abbreviation for "The sky is blue in color," which also happens to be a 24-letter phrase? Of course not! But why? What is the difference between

"United States of America" and "The sky is blue in color"? The key difference is that one of these phrases is used much more often than the other, and we can save a lot more effort by abbreviating a frequently used phrase instead of one that is rarely used.

Let's try and apply this idea to the coding system shown on the previous page. We already know that we can save the most effort by using abbreviations for things that are used frequently. Well, the letters "e' and "t" are the ones used most often in English, so let's try to use a shorter code for each of those letters. At the moment, "e" is 31 and "t" is 46—so it takes two digits to represent each of these letters. How about cutting them down to only one digit? Let's say "e" is now represented by the single digit 8, and "t" is 9. This is a great idea! Remember how we encoded the phrase "Meet your fiancé there." earlier, using a total of 46 digits. Now we can do it as follows, using only 40 digits:

M e e t y o u r f i a n c é t h e r e .
138 8 9 00514147440032352740298200 9 348 448 66

Unfortunately, there is a fatal flaw in this plan. Remember that the computer does not store the spaces between the individual letters. So the encoding doesn't really look like "13 8 8 9 00 51 ... 44 8 66." Instead it looks like "138890051...44866." Can you see the problem yet? Concentrate on just the first five digits, which are 13889. Notice that the code 13 represents "M," 8 represents "e," and 9 represents "t," so one way of decoding the digits 13889 is to split them up as 13-8-8-9, giving the word "Meet." But 88 represents the accented symbol "ú," so the digits 13889 might also be split up as 13-88-9, which represents "Mút." In fact the situation is even worse, because 89 represents the slightly different accented symbol "ù," so another possible split of 13889 is 13-8-89, representing "Meù." There is absolutely no way to tell which of the three possible interpretations is correct.

Disaster! Our cunning plan to use shorter codes for the letters "e" and "t" has led to a coding system that doesn't work at all. Fortunately, it can be fixed with one more trick. The real problem is that whenever we see a digit 8 or 9, there is no way to tell if it is part of a one-digit code (for either "e" or "t"), or one of the two-digit codes that starts with 8 or 9 (for the various accented symbols like "á" and "è"). To solve this problem, we have to make a sacrifice: some of our codes will actually get *longer*. The ambiguous two-digit codes that start with 8 or 9 will become three-digit codes that *do not* start with 8 or 9. The table on page 114 shows one particular way of achieving this. Some of the punctuation characters got affected too, but we finally have a very nice situation: anything starting with a 7 is a three-digit code, anything starting with an 8 or 9 is a one-digit code, and anything starting with 0, 1, 2, 3, 4, 5 or 6 is the same two-digit code as before. So there is exactly one way to split up the digits 13889 now (13-8-8-9, representing "Meet")—and this is true for any other correctly coded sequence of digits. All ambiguity has been removed, and our original message can be encoded like this:

M e e t y o u r f i a n c é t h e r e .
138 8 9 00 51 41 47 44 00 32 35 27 40 29 782 00 9 348 448 66

The original encoding used 46 digits, and this uses only 41. This might seem like a small saving, but with a longer message the savings can be very significant. For example, the text of this book (that is, just the words, with images excluded) requires nearly 500 kilobytes of storage—that's half a million characters! But when compressed using the two tricks just described, the size is reduced to only 160 kilobytes, or less than one-third of the original.

Summary: Where Did the Free Lunch Come From?

At this point, we understand all the important concepts behind the creation of typical compressed ZIP files on a computer. Here's how it happens:

Step 1. The original uncompressed file is transformed using the same-as-earlier trick, so that most of the repeated data in the file is replaced by much shorter instructions to go back and copy the data from somewhere else.

Step 2. The transformed file is examined to see which symbols occur frequently. For example, if the original file was written in English, then the computer will probably discover that "e" and "t" are the two most common symbols. The computer then constructs a table like the one on the following page, in which frequently used symbols are given short numeric codes and rarely used symbols are given longer numeric codes.

Step 3. The file is transformed again by directly translating into the numeric codes from Step 2.

The table of numeric codes, computed in step 2, is also stored in the ZIP file—otherwise it would be impossible to decode (and hence decompress) the ZIP file later. Note that different uncompressed files will result in different tables of numeric codes. In fact, in a real ZIP file, the original file is broken up into chunks and each chunk can have a different numeric code table. All of this can be done efficiently

space 00	T 20	n 40	(60	**á 780**
A 01	U 21	o 41	) 61	**à 781**
B 02	V 22	p 42	* 62	**é 782**
C 03	W 23	q 43	+ 63	**è 783**
D 04	X 24	r 44	, 64	**í 784**
E 05	Y 25	s 45	- 65	**ì 785**
F 06	Z 26	**t 9**	. 66	**ó 786**
G 07	a 27	u 47	/ 67	**ò 787**
H 08	b 28	v 48	: 68	**ú 788**
I 09	c 29	w 49	; 69	**ù 789**
J 10	d 30	x 50	< **770**	**Á 790**
K 11	**e 8**	y 51	= **771**	**À 791**
L 12	f 32	z 52	> **772**	**É 792**
M 13	g 33	! 53	**? 773**	**È 793**
N 14	h 34	" 54	**{ 774**	**Í 794**
O 15	i 35	# 55	**| 775**	**Ì 795**
P 16	j 36	$ 56	**} 776**	**Ó 796**
Q 17	k 37	% 57	**– 777**	**Ò 797**
R 18	l 38	& 58	**Ø 778**	**Ú 798**
S 19	m 39	’ 59	**ø 779**	**Ù 799**

Numeric codes using the shorter-symbol trick. Changes to the previous table on page 111 are shown in bold. The codes for two common letters have been shortened, at the expense of lengthening the codes for a larger number of uncommon symbols. This results in a shorter total length for most messages.

and automatically, achieving excellent compression on many types of files.

LOSSY COMPRESSION: NOT A FREE LUNCH, BUT A VERY GOOD DEAL

So far, we have been talking about the type of compression known as *lossless*, because you can take a compressed file and reconstruct exactly the same file that you started with, without even one character or one punctuation mark being changed. In contrast, sometimes it is much more useful to use *lossy* compression, which lets you take a compressed file and reconstruct one that is very similar to the original, but not necessarily exactly the same. For example, lossy compression is used very frequently on files that contain images or audio data: as long as a picture *looks* the same to the human eye, it doesn't really matter whether the file that stores that picture on your computer is exactly the same as the file that stores it on your camera. And the same is true for audio data: as long as a song sounds the same to the human ear, it doesn't really matter whether the file storing that song on your digital music player is exactly the same as the file that stores that song on a compact disc.

In fact, sometimes lossy compression is used in a much more extreme way. We have all seen low-quality videos and images on the internet in which the picture is blurry or the sound quality rather bad. This is the result of lossy compression being used in a more aggressive fashion to make the file size of the videos or images very small. The idea here is not that the video looks the same as the original to the human eye, but rather that it is at least recognizable. By tuning just how "lossy" the compression is, website operators can trade off between large, high-quality files that look and sound almost perfect, and low-quality files that have obvious defects but require much less bandwidth to transmit. You may have done the same thing on a digital camera, where you can usually choose different settings for the quality of images and videos. If you choose a high-quality setting, the number of pictures or videos you can store on the camera is smaller than when you choose a lower quality setting. That's because high-quality media files take up more space than low-quality ones. And it's all done by tuning just how "lossy" the compression is. In this section, we will find out a few of the tricks for doing this tuning.

The Leave-It-Out Trick

One simple and useful trick for lossy compression is to simply leave out some of the data. Let's take a look at how this "leave-it-out" trick works in the case of black-and-white pictures. First we need to understand a little about how black-and-white pictures are stored in a computer. A picture consists of a large number of small dots, called "pixels." Each pixel has exactly one color, which could be black, white, or any shade of gray in between. Of course, we are not generally aware of these pixels because they are so small, but you can see the individual pixels if you look closely enough at a monitor or TV screen.

In a black-and-white picture stored in a computer, each possible pixel color is represented by a number. For this example, let's assume that higher numbers represent whiter colors, with 100 being the highest. So 100 represents white, 0 represents black, 50 represents a medium shade of gray, 90 represents a light gray, and so on. The pixels are arranged in a rectangular array of rows and columns, with each pixel representing the color at some very small part of the picture. The total number of rows and columns tells you the "resolution" of the image. For example, many high-definition TV sets have a resolution of 1920 by 1080—that means there are 1920 columns of pixels and 1080 rows of pixels. The total number of pixels is found by multiplying 1920 by 1080, which gives over 2 million pixels! Digital cameras use the same terminology. A "megapixel" is just a fancy name for a million pixels. So a 5-megapixel camera has enough rows and columns of pixels so that when you multiply the number of rows by the number of columns, you get more than 5 million. When a picture is stored in a computer, it is just a list of numbers, one for each pixel.

The picture of a house with a turret shown at the top left of the figure on the next page has a much lower resolution than a high-definition TV: only 320 by 240. Nevertheless, the number of pixels is still rather large ($320 \times 240 = 76{,}800$), and the file that stores this picture in uncompressed form uses over 230 kilobytes of storage space. A kilobyte, by the way, is equivalent to about 1000 characters of text—roughly the size of a one-paragraph e-mail, for instance. Very approximately, then, the top-left picture, when stored as a file, requires the same amount of disk space as around 200 short e-mail messages.

We can compress this file with the following extremely simple technique: ignore, or "leave out," every second row of pixels and every second column of pixels. The leave-it-out trick really is that simple! In this case, it results in a picture with a smaller resolution of 160 by 120, shown below the original picture in the figure. The size of this file is only one-quarter of the original (about 57 kilobytes). This is because there are only one-quarter as many pixels—we reduced both the width *and* the height of the image by one-half. Effectively, the size of the image was reduced by 50% twice—once horizontally and once vertically—resulting in a final size that is only 25% of the original.

And we can do this trick again. Take the new 160 by 120 image, and leave out every second row and column to get another new image, this time only 80 by 60—the result is shown at the bottom left of the figure. The image size is reduced by 75% again, resulting in a final file

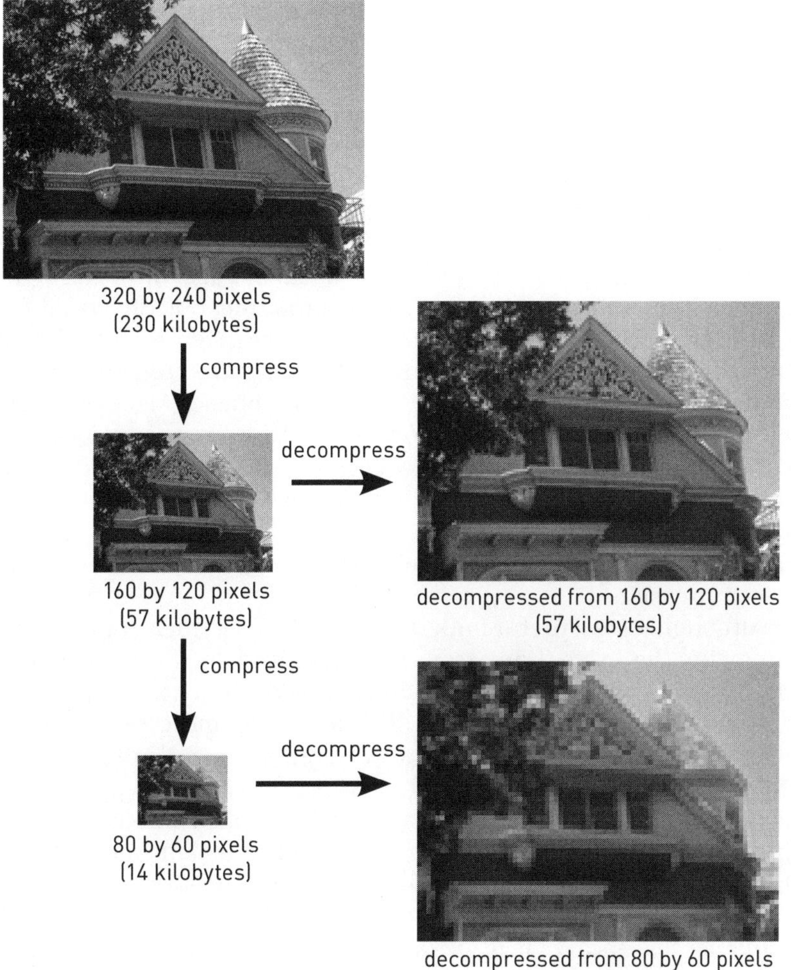

Compression using the leave-it-out trick. The left column shows the original image, and two smaller, reduced versions of this image. Each reduced image is computed by leaving out half of the rows and columns in the previous one. In the right column, we see the effect of decompressing the reduced images to the same size as the original. The reconstruction is not perfect and there are some noticeable differences between the reconstructions and the original.

size of only 14 kilobytes. That's only about 6% of the original—some very impressive compression.

But remember, we are using lossy compression, so we don't get a free lunch this time. The lunch is cheap, but we do have to pay for it. Look at what happens when we take one of the compressed files and decompress it back to the original size. Because some of the rows and columns of pixels were deleted, the computer has to guess what the colors of those missing pixels should be. The simplest possible guess is to give any missing pixel the same color as one of its neighbors. Any choice of neighbor would work fine, but the examples shown here choose the pixel immediately above and to the left of the missing pixel.

The result of this decompression scheme is shown in the right-hand column of the figure. You can see that most of the visual features have been retained, but there is some definite loss of quality and detail, especially in complex areas like the tree, the turret's roof, and the fret-work in the gable of the house. Also, especially in the version decompressed from the 80 by 60 image, you can see some rather unpleasant jagged edges, for example, on the diagonal lines of the house's roof. These are what we call "compression artifacts": not just a loss of detail, but noticeable new features that are introduced by a particular method of lossy compression followed by decompression.

Although it's useful for understanding the basic idea of lossy compression, the leave-it-out trick is rarely used in the simple form described here. Computers do indeed "leave out" information to achieve lossy compression, but they are much more careful about which information they leave out. A common example of this is the JPEG image compression format. JPEG is a carefully designed image compression technique which has far better performance than leaving out every second row and column. Take a look at the figure on the facing page, and compare the quality and size of the images with the previous figure. At the top, we have a JPEG image whose size is 35 kilobytes, and yet it is virtually indistinguishable from the original image. By leaving out more information, but sticking with the JPEG format, we can get down to the 19-kilobyte image in the center, which still has excellent quality although you can see some blurring and loss of detail in the fret-work of the house. But even JPEG suffers from compression artifacts if the compression is too extreme: at the bottom you can see a JPEG image compressed down to only 12 kilobytes, and you'll notice some blocky effects in the sky and some unpleasant blotches in the sky right next to the diagonal line of the house.

Although the details of JPEG's leave-it-out strategy are too technical to be described completely here, the basic flavor of the technique is fairly straightforward. JPEG first divides the whole image into small squares of 8 pixels by 8 pixels. Each of these squares

JPEG (35 kilobytes)

JPEG (19 kilobytes)

JPEG (12 kilobytes)

With lossy compression schemes, higher compression produces lower quality. The same image is shown compressed at three different JPEG quality levels. At the top is the highest quality, which also requires the most storage. At the bottom is the lowest quality, which requires less than half the storage, but now there are noticeable compression artifacts—especially in the sky and along the border of the roof.

is compressed separately. Note that without any compression, each square would be represented by $8 \times 8 = 64$ numbers. (We are assuming that the picture is black-and-white—if it is a color image, then there are three different colors and therefore three times as many numbers, but we won't worry about that detail here.) If the square happens to be all one color, the entire square can be represented by a single number, and the computer can "leave out" 63 numbers. If the square is mostly the same color, with a few very slight differences (perhaps a region of sky that is almost all the same shade of gray), the computer can decide to represent the square by a single number anyway, resulting in good compression for that square with only a small amount of error when it gets decompressed later. In the bottom image of the figure on the previous page, you can actually see some of the 8-by-8 blocks in the sky that have been compressed in exactly this way, resulting in small square blocks of uniform color.

If the 8-by-8 square varies smoothly from one color to another (say, dark gray on the left to light gray on the right), then the 64 numbers might be compressed down to just two: a value for the dark gray and the value for the light gray. The JPEG algorithm does not work exactly like this, but it uses the same ideas: if an 8-by-8 square is close enough to some combination of known patterns like a constant color or a smoothly varying color, then most of the information can be thrown away, and just the level or amount of each pattern is stored.

JPEG works well for pictures, but how about audio and music files? These are also compressed using lossy compression, and they use the same basic philosophy: leave out information that has little effect on the final product. Popular music compression formats, such as MP3 and AAC, generally use the same high-level approach as JPEG. The audio is divided into chunks, and each chunk is compressed separately. As with JPEG, chunks that vary in a predictable way can be described with only a few numbers. However, audio compression formats can also exploit known facts about the human ear. In particular, certain types of sounds have little or no effect on human listeners and can be eliminated by the compression algorithm without reducing the quality of the output.

THE ORIGINS OF COMPRESSION ALGORITHMS

The same-as-earlier trick described in this chapter—one of the main compression methods used in ZIP files—is known to computer scientists as the LZ77 algorithm. It was invented by two Israeli computer scientists, Abraham Lempel and Jacob Ziv, and published in 1977.

To trace the origins of compression algorithms, however, we need to delve three decades further back into scientific history. We have already met Claude Shannon, the Bell Labs scientist who founded the field of information theory with his 1948 paper. Shannon was one of the two main heroes in our story of error-correcting codes (chapter 5), but he and his 1948 paper also figure importantly in the emergence of compression algorithms.

This is no coincidence. In fact, error-correcting codes and compression algorithms are two sides of the same coin. It all comes down to the notion of *redundancy*, which featured quite heavily in chapter 5. If a file has redundancy, it is longer than necessary. To repeat a simple example from chapter 5, the file might use the word "five" instead of the numeral "5." That way, an error such as "fivq" can be easily recognized and corrected. Thus, error-correcting codes can be viewed as a principled way of *adding* redundancy to a message or file.

Compression algorithms do the opposite: they *remove* redundancy from a message or file. It's easy to imagine a compression algorithm that would notice the frequent use of the word "five" in a file and replace this with a shorter symbol (which might even be the symbol "5"), exactly reversing the error-correction encoding process. In practice, compression and error correction do not cancel each other out like this. Instead, good compression algorithms remove inefficient types of redundancy, while error-correction encoding adds a different, more efficient type of redundancy. Thus, it is very common to first compress a message and then add some error correction to it.

Let's get back to Shannon. His seminal 1948 paper, among its many extraordinary contributions, included a description of one of the earliest compression techniques. An MIT professor, Robert Fano, had also discovered the technique at about the same time, and the approach is now known as Shannon-Fano coding. In fact, Shannon-Fano coding is a particular way of implementing the shorter-symbol trick described earlier in this chapter. As we shall soon see, Shannon-Fano coding was rapidly superseded by another algorithm, but the method is very effective and survives to this day as one of the optional compression methods in the ZIP file format.

Both Shannon and Fano were aware that although their approach was both practical and efficient, it was not the best possible: Shannon had proved mathematically that even better compression techniques must exist, but had not yet discovered how to achieve them. Meanwhile, Fano had started teaching a graduate course in information theory at MIT, and he posed the problem of achieving optimal compression as one of the options for a term paper in the course. Remarkably, one of his students solved the problem, producing a method that yields the best possible compression for each individual symbol. The student was David Huffman, and his technique—now known as Huffman coding—is another example of the shorter-symbol trick. Huffman coding remains a fundamental compression algorithm and is widely used in communication and data storage systems.

8

Databases: The Quest for Consistency

> "Data! data! data!" he cried impatiently. "I can't make bricks without clay."
>
> —Sherlock Holmes in Arthur Conan Doyle's *The Adventure of the Copper Beeches*

Consider the following arcane ritual. A person takes from a desk a specially printed pad of paper (known as a *checkbook*), writes some numbers on it, and adds a signature with a flourish. The person then tears the top sheet from the pad, puts it in an envelope, and sticks another piece of paper (known as a *stamp*) on the front of the envelope. Finally, the person carries the envelope outside and down the street, to a large box where the envelope is deposited.

Until the turn of the 21st century, this was the monthly ritual of anyone paying a bill: phone bills, electric bills, credit card bills, and so on. Since then, systems of online bill payment and online banking have evolved. The simplicity and convenience of these systems makes the previous paper-based method seem almost ludicrously laborious and inefficient by comparison.

What technologies have enabled this transformation? The most obvious answer is the arrival of the internet, without which online communication of any form would be impossible. Another crucial technology is public key cryptography, which we already discussed in chapter 4. Without public key crypto, sensitive financial information could not be securely transmitted over the internet. There is, however, at least one other technology that is essential for online transactions: the *database*. As computer users, most of us are blissfully unaware of it, but virtually all of our online transactions are processed using sophisticated database techniques, developed by computer scientists since the 1970s.

Databases address two major issues in transaction processing: efficiency and reliability. Databases provide efficiency through algorithms that permit thousands of customers to simultaneously conduct transactions without leading to any conflicts or inconsistencies. And databases provide reliability through algorithms that allow data to survive intact despite the failure of computer components like disk drives, which would usually lead to severe data loss. Online banking is a canonical example of an application that requires outstanding efficiency (to serve many customers at once without producing any errors or inconsistencies) and essentially perfect reliability. So to focus our discussions, we will often return to the example of online banking.

In this chapter, we will learn about three of the fundamental—and beautiful—ideas behind databases: write-ahead logging, two-phase commit, and relational databases. These ideas have led to the absolute dominance of database technology for storing certain types of important information. As usual, we'll try to focus on the core insight behind each of these ideas, identifying a single trick that makes it work. Write-ahead logging boils down to the "to-do list trick," which is tackled first. Then we move on to the two-phase commit protocol, described here via the simple but powerful "prepare-then-commit trick." Finally, we will take a peek into the world of relational databases by learning about the "virtual table trick."

But before learning any of these tricks, let's try to clear up the mystery of what a database actually is. In fact, even in the technical computer science literature, the word "database" can mean a lot of different things, so it is impossible to give a single, correct definition. But most experts would agree that the key property of databases, the one that distinguishes them from other ways of storing information, is that the information in a database has a predefined structure.

To understand what "structure" means here, let's first look at its opposite—an example of *unstructured* information:

> Rosina is 35, and she's friends with Matt, who is 26. Jingyi is 37 and Sudeep is 31. Matt, Jingyi, and Sudeep are all friends with each other.

This is exactly the type of information that a social networking site, like Facebook or MySpace, would need to store about its members. But, of course, the information would not be stored in this unstructured way. Here's the same information in a structured form:

name	age	friends
Rosina	35	Matt
Jingyi	37	Matt, Sudeep
Matt	26	Rosina, Jingyi, Sudeep
Sudeep	31	Jingyi, Matt

Computer scientists call this type of structure a *table*. Each row of the table contains information about a single thing (in this case, a person). Each column of the table contains a particular type of information, such as a person's age or name. A database often consists of many tables, but our initial examples will keep things simple and use only a single table.

Obviously, it is vastly more efficient for humans and computers alike to manipulate data in the structured form of a table, rather than the unstructured free text in the example above. But databases have much more going for them than mere ease of use.

Our journey into the world of databases begins with a new concept: consistency. As we will soon discover, database practitioners are obsessed with consistency—and with good reason. In simple terms, "consistency" means that the information in the database doesn't contradict itself. If there is a contradiction in the database, we have the worst nightmare of the database administrator: inconsistency. But how could an inconsistency arise in the first place? Well, imagine that the first two rows in the table above were changed slightly, giving:

name	age	friends
Rosina	35	Matt, Jingyi
Jingyi	37	Matt, Sudeep

Can you spot the problem here? According to the first row, Rosina is friends with Jingyi. But according to the second row, Jingyi is not friends with Rosina. This violates the basic notion of friendship, which is that two people are simultaneously friends with each other. Admittedly, this is a rather benign example of inconsistency.

To imagine a more serious case, suppose that the concept of "friendship" is replaced with "marriage." Then we would end up with *A* married to *B*, but *B* married to *C*—a situation that is actually illegal in many countries.

Actually, this type of inconsistency is easy to avoid when new data is added to the database. Computers are great at following rules, so it's easy to set up a database to follow the rule "If *A* is married to *B*, then *B* must be married to *A*." If someone tries to enter a new row that violates this rule, they will receive an error message and the entry will fail. So ensuring consistency based on simple rules doesn't require any clever trick.

But there are other types of inconsistency that require much more ingenious solutions. We'll look at one of these next.

TRANSACTIONS AND THE TO-DO LIST TRICK

Transactions are probably the most important idea in the world of databases. But to understand what they are, and why they are necessary, we need to accept two facts about computers. The first fact is one that you are probably all too familiar with: computer programs crash—and when a program crashes, it forgets everything it was doing. Only information that was explicitly saved to the computer's file system is preserved. The second fact we need to know is rather obscure, but extremely important: computer storage devices, such as hard drives and flash memory sticks, can write only a small amount of data instantaneously—typically about 500 characters. (If you're interested in technical jargon, I'm referring here to the *sector size* of a hard disk, which is typically 512 bytes. With flash memory, the relevant quantity is the *page size*, which may also be hundreds or thousands of bytes.) As computer users, we never notice this small size limit for instantaneously storing data on a device, because modern drives can execute hundreds of thousands of these 500-character writes every second. But the fact remains that the disk's contents get changed only a few hundred characters at a time.

What on earth does this have to do with databases? It has an extremely important consequence: typically, the computer can update only a single row of a database at any one time. Unfortunately, the very small and simple example above doesn't really demonstrate this. The entire table above contains less than 200 characters, so in this particular case, it *would* be possible for the computer to update two rows at once. But in general, for a database of any reasonable size, altering two different rows does require two separate disk operations.

With these background facts established, we can get to the heart of the matter. It turns out that many seemingly simple changes to a database require two or more rows to be altered. And as we now know, altering two different rows cannot be achieved in a single disk operation, so the database update will result in some sequence of two or more disk operations. But the computer can crash at any time. What will happen if the computer crashes *between* two of these disk operations? The computer can be rebooted, but it will have forgotten about any operations it was planning to perform, so it's possible that some of the necessary changes were never made. In other words, the database might be left in an inconsistent state!

At this stage, the whole problem of inconsistency after a crash might seem rather academic, so we'll look at two examples of this extremely important problem. Let's start with an even simpler database than the one above, say:

name	friends
Rosina	none
Jingyi	none
Matt	none

This very dull and depressing database lists three lonely people. Now suppose Rosina and Jingyi become friends, and we would like to update the database to reflect this happy event. As you can see, this update will require changes to both the first and second rows of the table—and as we discussed earlier, this will generally require two separate disk operations. Let's suppose that row 1 happens to get updated first. Immediately after that update, and before the computer has had a chance to execute the second disk operation that will update row 2, the database will look like this:

name	friends
Rosina	Jingyi
Jingyi	none
Matt	none

So far, so good. Now the database program just needs to update row 2, and it will be done. But wait: what if the computer crashes before it gets a chance to do that? Then after the computer has restarted, it will have no idea that row 2 still needs to be updated. The database will be left exactly as printed above: Rosina is friends with Jingyi, but Jingyi is *not* friends with Rosina. This is the dreaded inconsistency.

I already mentioned that database practitioners are obsessed with consistency, but at this point it may not seem like such a big deal. After all, does it really matter if Jingyi is recorded as being a friend in one place and friendless in another place? We could even imagine an automated tool that scans through the database every so often, looking for discrepancies like this and fixing them. In fact, tools like this do exist and can be used in databases where consistency is of secondary importance. You may have even encountered an example of this yourself, because some operating systems, when rebooted after a crash, check the entire file system for inconsistencies.

But there do exist situations in which an inconsistency is genuinely harmful and cannot be corrected by an automated tool. A classic example is the case of transferring money between bank accounts. Here's another simple database:

account name	account type	account balance
Zadie	checking	$800
Zadie	savings	$300
Pedro	checking	$150

Suppose Zadie has requested to transfer $200 from her checking account to her savings account. Just as in the previous example, this is going to require two rows to be updated, using a sequence of two separate disk operations. First, Zadie's checking balance will be reduced to $600, then her savings balance will be increased to $500. And if we are unlucky enough to experience a crash between these two operations, the database will look like this:

account name	account type	account balance
Zadie	checking	$600
Zadie	savings	$300
Pedro	checking	$150

In other words, this is a complete disaster for Zadie: before the crash, Zadie had a total of $1100 in her two accounts, but now she has only $900. She never withdrew any money—but somehow, $200 has completely vanished! And there is no way to detect this, because the database is perfectly self-consistent after the crash. We have encountered a much more subtle type of inconsistency here: the new database is inconsistent with its state *before* the crash.

It's worth investigating this important point in more detail. In our first example of inconsistency, we ended up with a database that was self-evidently inconsistent: A friends with B, but B not friends with A. This type of inconsistency can be detected merely by examining the database (although the detection process could be very time-consuming, if the database contains millions—or even billions—of records). In our second example of inconsistency, the database was left in a state that is perfectly plausible, when considered as a snapshot taken at a particular time. There is no rule that states what the balances of the accounts must be, or any relationships between those balances. Nevertheless, we can observe inconsistent behavior if we examine the state of the database over time. Three facts are pertinent here: (i) before initiating her transfer, Zadie had $1100; (ii) after the crash, she had $900; (iii) in the intervening period, she did not withdraw any money. Taken together, these three facts are inconsistent, but the inconsistency cannot be detected by examining the database at a particular point in time.

To avoid both types of inconsistency, database researchers came up with the concept of a "transaction"—a set of changes to a database that must all take place if the database is to be left consistent. If some, but not all, of the changes in a transaction are performed, then the database might be left inconsistent. This is a simple but extremely powerful idea. A database programmer can issue a command like "begin transaction," then make a bunch of interdependent changes to the database, and finish with "end transaction." The database will guarantee that the programmer's changes will all be accomplished, even if the computer running the database crashes and restarts in the middle of the transaction.

To be absolutely correct, we should be aware that there is another possibility too: it's possible that after a crash and restart, the database will return to the exact state it was in before the transaction began. But if this happens, the programmer will receive a notification that the transaction failed and must be resubmitted—so no harm is done. We'll be discussing this possibility in greater detail later, in the section about "rolling back" transactions. But for now, the crucial point is that the database remains consistent regardless of whether a transaction is completed or rolled back.

From the description so far, it may seem that we are obsessing unnecessarily over the possibility of crashes, which are, after all, very rare on modern operating systems running modern application programs. There are two responses to this. First, the notion of "crash" as it applies here is rather general: it encompasses any incident that might cause the computer to stop functioning and thus lose data. The possibilities include power failure, disk failure, other hardware malfunctions, and bugs in the operating system or application programs. Second, even if these generalized crashes are rather rare, some databases cannot afford to take the risk: banks, insurance companies, and any other organization whose data represents actual money cannot afford inconsistency in their records, under any circumstances.

The simplicity of the solution described above (begin a transaction, perform as many operations as necessary, then end the transaction) might sound too good to be true. In fact, it can be achieved with the relatively simple "to-do list" trick described next.

The To-Do List Trick

Not all of us are lucky enough to be well organized. But whether or not we are well organized ourselves, we've all seen one of the great weapons wielded by highly organized people: the "to-do" list. Perhaps you are not a fan of making lists yourself, but it's hard to argue with their usefulness. If you have 10 errands to get done in one day, then writing them down—preferably in an efficient ordering—makes for a very good start. A to-do list is especially useful if you get distracted (or, shall we say, "crash"?) in the middle of the day. If you forget your remaining errands for any reason, a quick glance at the list will remind you of them.

Database transactions are achieved using a special kind of to-do list. That's why we'll call it the "to-do list" trick, although computer scientists use the term "write-ahead logging" for the same idea. The basic idea is to maintain a log of actions the database is planning to take. The log is stored on a hard drive or some other permanent storage, so information in the log will survive crashes and restarts. Before any of the actions in a given transaction are performed, they are all recorded in the log and thus saved to the disk. If the transaction completes successfully, we can save some space by deleting the transaction's to-do list from the log. So Zadie's money-transfer transaction described above would take place in two main steps. First, the database table is left untouched and we write the transaction's to-do list in the log:

account name	account type	account balance
Zadie	checking	$800
Zadie	savings	$300
Pedro	checking	$150

Write-ahead log

1. Begin transfer transaction
2. Change Zadie checking from $800 to $600
3. Change Zadie savings from $300 to $500
4. End transfer transaction

After ensuring the log entries have been saved to some permanent storage such as a disk, we make the planned changes to the table itself:

account name	account type	account balance
Zadie	checking	$600
Zadie	savings	$500
Pedro	checking	$150

Write-ahead log

1. Begin transfer transaction
2. Change Zadie checking from $800 to $600
3. Change Zadie savings from $300 to $500
4. End transfer transaction

Assuming the changes have been saved to disk, the log entries can now be deleted.

But that was the easy case. What if the computer crashes unexpectedly in the middle of the transaction? As before, let's assume the crash occurs after Zadie's checking account has been debited, but before her savings account is credited. The computer reboots and the database restarts, finding the following information on the hard drive:

account name	**account type**	**account balance**
Zadie	checking	$600
Zadie	savings	$300
Pedro	checking	$150

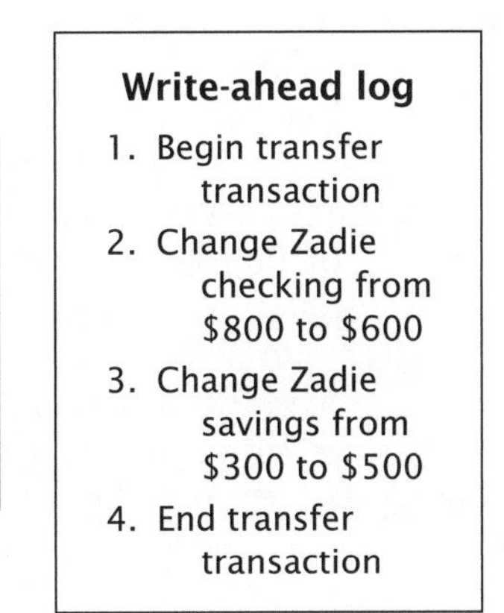

Write-ahead log

1. Begin transfer transaction
2. Change Zadie checking from $800 to $600
3. Change Zadie savings from $300 to $500
4. End transfer transaction

Now, the computer can tell that it may have been in the middle of a transaction when it crashed, because the log contains some information. But there are four planned actions listed in the log. How can we tell which ones have already been performed on the database and which ones remain to be done? The answer to this question is delightfully simple: it doesn't matter! The reason is that every entry in a database log is constructed so that it has the same effect whether it is performed once, twice, or any other number of times.

The technical word for this is *idempotent*, so a computer scientist would say that every action in the log must be idempotent. As an example, take a look at entry number 2, "Change Zadie checking from $800 to $600." No matter how many times Zadie's balance is set to $600, the final effect will be the same. So if the database is recovering after a crash and it sees this entry in the log, it can safely perform the action without worrying about whether it was already performed before the crash too.

Thus, when recovering after a crash, a database can just replay the logged actions of any complete transactions. And it's easy to deal with incomplete transactions too. Any set of logged actions that doesn't finish with an "end transaction" entry simply gets undone in reverse order, leaving the database as if the transaction had never begun. We'll return to this notion of "rolling back" a transaction in the discussion of replicated databases on page 134.

Atomicity, in the Large and in the Small

There is another way of understanding transactions: from the point of view of the database user, every transaction is *atomic*. Although physicists have known how to split atoms for many decades, the original meaning of "atomic" came from Greek, where it means "indivisible." When computer scientists say "atomic," they are referring to this original meaning. Thus, an atomic transaction cannot be divided into smaller operations: either the whole transaction completes successfully, or the database is left in its original condition, as if the transaction had never been started.

So, the to-do list trick gives us atomic transactions, which in turn guarantee consistency. This is a key ingredient in our canonical example: an efficient and completely reliable database for online banking. We are not there yet, however. Consistency does not, by itself, yield adequate efficiency or reliability. When combined with the locking techniques to be described shortly, the to-do list trick maintains consistency even when thousands of customers are simultaneously accessing the database. This *does* yield tremendous efficiency, because many customers can be served at once. And the to-do list trick also provides a good measure of reliability, since it prevents inconsistencies. Specifically, the to-do list trick precludes data *corruption*, but does not eliminate data *loss*. Our next database trick—the prepare-then-commit trick—will produce significant progress toward the goal of preventing any loss of data.

THE PREPARE-THEN-COMMIT TRICK FOR REPLICATED DATABASES

Our journey through ingenious database techniques continues with an algorithm we'll call the "prepare-then-commit trick." To motivate this trick, we need to understand two more facts about databases: first, they are often *replicated*, which means that multiple copies of the database are stored in different places; and second, database transactions must sometimes be canceled, which is also called "rolling back" or "aborting" a transaction. We'll briefly cover these two concepts before moving on to the prepare-then-commit trick.

Replicated Databases

The to-do list trick allows databases to recover from certain types of crashes, by completing or rolling back any transactions that were in progress at the time of the crash. But this assumes all the data that was saved before the crash is still there. What if the computer's hard drive is permanently broken and some or all of the data is lost? This is just one of many ways that a computer can suffer from permanent data loss. Other causes include software bugs (in the database program itself or in the operating system) and hardware failures. Any of these problems can cause a computer to overwrite data that you thought was safely stored on the hard drive, wiping it out and replacing it with garbage. Clearly, the to-do list trick can't help us here.

However, data loss is simply not an option in some circumstances. If your bank loses your account information, you will be extremely upset, and the bank could face serious legal and financial penalties. The same goes for a stockbroking firm that executes an order you've placed, but then loses the details of the sale. Indeed, any company with substantial online sales (eBay and Amazon being prime examples) simply cannot afford to lose or corrupt any customer information. But in a data center with thousands of computers, many components (especially hard drives) fail every day. The data on these components *is* lost every single day. How can your bank keep your data safe in the face of this onslaught?

The obvious, and widely used, solution is to maintain two or more copies of the database. Each copy of the database is called a *replica*, and the set of all copies taken together is called a *replicated database*. Often, the replicas are geographically separated (perhaps in different data centers that are hundreds of miles apart), so that if one of them is wiped out by a natural disaster, another replica is still available.

I once heard a computer company executive describe the experiences of the company's customers after the September 11, 2001 terrorist attacks on the twin towers of New York's World Trade Center. The computer company had five major customers in the twin towers, and all were running geographically replicated databases. Four of the five customers were able to continue their operations essentially uninterrupted on surviving database replicas. The fifth customer, unfortunately, had one replica in each tower and lost both! This customer could only resume operations after restoring its database from off-site archival backups.

Note that a replicated database behaves quite differently to the familiar concept of keeping a "backup" of some data. A backup is a snapshot of some data *at a particular time*—for manual backups, the snapshot is taken at the time you run your backup program, whereas automated backups often take a snapshot of a system at a particular time on a weekly or daily basis, such as every morning at 2 a.m. In other words, a backup is a complete duplicate of some files, or a database, or anything else for which you need a spare copy.

But a backup is, by definition, not necessarily up-to-date: if some changes are made after a backup is performed, those changes are not saved anywhere else. In contrast, a replicated database keeps all copies of the database in sync at all times. Every time the slightest change is made to any entry in the database, all of the replicas must make that change immediately.

Clearly, replication is an excellent way to guard against lost data. But replication has dangers, too: it introduces yet another type of possible inconsistency. What are we going to do if a replica somehow ends up with data that differs from another replica? Such replicas are inconsistent with each other, and it may be difficult or impossible to determine which replica has the correct version of the data. We will return to this issue after investigating how to roll back transactions.

Rolling Back Transactions

At the risk of being a little repetitive, let's try to recall exactly what a transaction is: it's a set of changes to a database that must *all* take place to guarantee the database remains consistent. In the earlier discussion of transactions, we were mostly concerned with making sure that a transaction would complete even if the database crashed in the middle of the transaction.

But it turns out that sometimes it is impossible to complete a transaction for some reason. For example, perhaps the transaction involves adding a large amount of data to the database, and the computer runs out of disk space halfway through the transaction. This is a very rare, but nevertheless important, scenario.

A much more common reason for failing to complete a transaction relates to another database concept called *locking*. In a busy database, there are usually many transactions executing at the same time. (Imagine what would happen if your bank permitted only one customer to transfer money at any one time—the performance of this online banking system would be truly appalling.) But it is often important that some part of the database remains frozen during a transaction. For example, if transaction *A* is updating an entry to record that Rosina is now friends with Jingyi, it would be disastrous if a simultaneously running transaction *B* deleted Jingyi from the database altogether. Therefore, transaction *A* will "lock" the part of the database containing Jingyi's information. This means the data is frozen, and no other transaction can change it. In most databases, transactions can lock individual rows or columns, or entire tables.

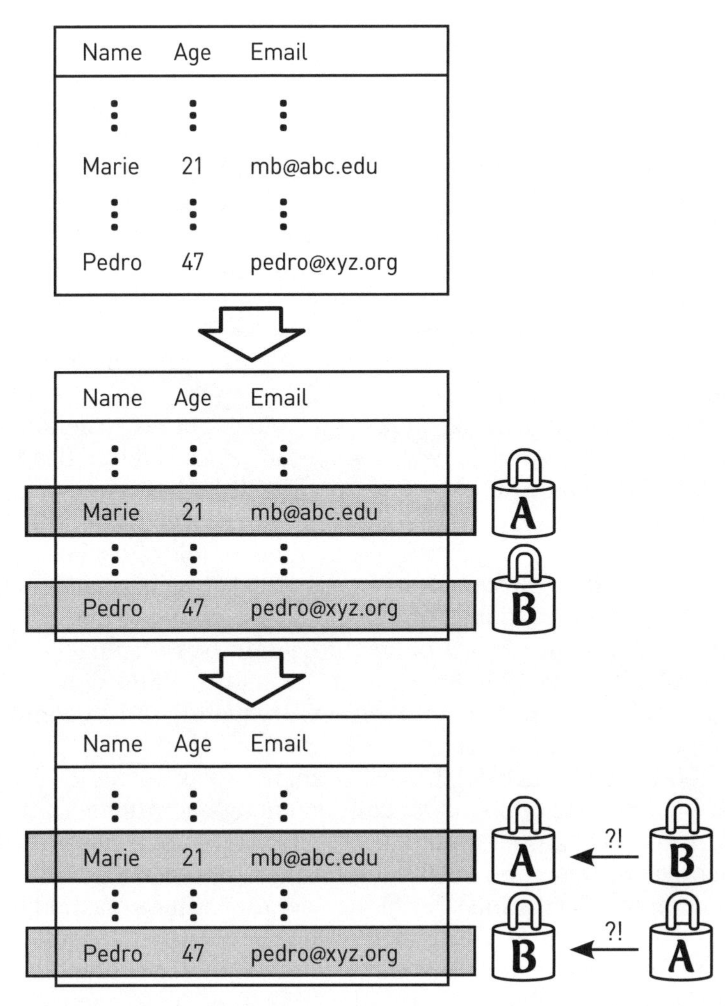

Deadlock: When two transactions, *A* and *B*, both try to lock the same rows—but in the opposite order—they become deadlocked, and neither can proceed.

Obviously, only one transaction can lock a particular part of the database at any one time. Once the transaction completes successfully, it "unlocks" all of the data it has locked, and after this point other transactions are free to alter the previously frozen data.

At first this seems like an excellent solution, but it can lead to a very nasty situation that computer scientists call a *deadlock*, as demonstrated in the figure above. Let's suppose that two long transactions, *A* and *B*, are running simultaneously. Initially, as in the top panel of the figure, none of the rows in the database are locked. Later, as shown in the middle panel, *A* locks the row containing Marie's information, and *B* locks the row containing Pedro's information. Some time after this, *A* discovers that it needs to lock Pedro's row, and *B* discovers that it needs to lock Marie's row—this situation is represented in the bottom panel of the figure. Note that *A* now needs to lock Pedro's row, but only one transaction can lock any row at one time, and *B* has already locked Pedro's row! So *A* will need to wait until *B* finishes. But *B* can't finish until it locks Marie's row, which is currently locked by *A*. So *B* will need to wait until *A* finishes. *A* and *B* are *deadlocked*, because each must wait for the other to proceed. They will be stuck forever, and these transactions will never complete.

Computer scientists have studied deadlocks in great detail, and many databases periodically run a special procedure for deadlock detection. When a deadlock is found, one of the deadlocked transactions is simply canceled, so that the other can proceed. But note that, just as when we run out of disk space in the middle of a transaction, this requires the ability to abort or "roll back" the transaction that has already been partially completed. So we now know of at least two reasons why a transaction might need to be rolled back. There are many others, but there's no need for us to go into details. The fundamental point is that transactions frequently fail to complete for unpredictable reasons.

Rollback can be achieved using a slight tweak to the to-do list trick: the write-ahead log must contain enough additional information to *undo* each operation if necessary. (This contrasts with the earlier description, in which we emphasized that each log entry contains enough information to *redo* the operation after a crash.) This is easy to achieve in practice. In fact, in the simple examples we examined, the undo information and redo information are identical. An entry like "Change Zadie checking from $800 to $600" can easily be "undone"—by simply changing Zadie's checking balance from $600 to $800. To summarize: if a transaction needs to be rolled back, the database program can just work backward through the write-ahead log (i.e., the to-do list), reversing each operation in that transaction.

The Prepare-Then-Commit Trick

Now let's think about the problem of rolling back transactions in a *replicated* database. The big issue here is that one of the replicas might encounter a problem that requires rollback, while the others do not. For example, it's easy to imagine that one replica runs out of disk space while the others still have space available.

A simple analogy will help here. Suppose that you and three friends would all like to see a recently released movie together. To make things interesting, let's set this story in the 1980s, before the days of e-mail, so the movie trip is going to have to be organized by telephone. How do you go about it? One possible approach is as follows. Decide on a day and time for the movie that work for you, and—as far as you know—are likely to be suitable for your friends too. Let's suppose you choose Tuesday at 8 p.m. The next step is to call one of your friends and ask if he or she is free on Tuesday at 8. If the answer is yes, you'll say something like "great, please pencil that in, and I'll call you back later to confirm." Then you'll call the next friend and do the same thing. Finally, you call the third and final friend with the same offer. If everyone is available on Tuesday at 8, you make the final decision to confirm the event and call back your friends to let them know.

That was the easy case. What happens if one of the friends is not available on Tuesday at 8? In this case, you will need to "roll back" all of the work done so far and start again. In reality, you would probably call each friend and immediately propose a new day and time, but to keep things as simple as possible here, let's instead assume that you call each friend and say "Sorry, Tuesday at 8 is no good, please erase that from your calendar, and I'll get back to you soon with a new proposal." Once this is done, you can start the whole procedure all over again.

Notice that there are two distinct phases in your strategy for organizing the movie outing. In the first phase, the date and time have been proposed but are not yet 100% certain. Once you find out that the proposal is feasible for everyone, *you* know that the date and time are now 100% certain, but everyone else does not. Therefore, there is a second phase in which you call back all of your friends to confirm. Alternatively, if one or more friends were unable to make it, the second phase consists of calling back everyone to cancel. Computer scientists call this the *two-phase commit protocol*; we'll call it the "prepare-then-commit trick." The first phase is called the "prepare" phase. The second phase is either a "commit" phase or an "abort" phase, depending on whether the initial proposal has been accepted by everyone or not.

Interestingly, there is a notion of database locking in this analogy. Although we didn't explicitly discuss it, each of your friends makes an implicit promise when they pencil in the movie outing: they are promising not to schedule something else for Tuesday at 8. Until they hear back from you with a confirmation or cancellation, that slot on the calendar is "locked" and cannot be altered by any other "transaction." For example, what should happen if someone else calls your friend, sometime after the first phase but before the second phase, to propose watching a basketball game on Tuesday at 8? Your friend should say something like "Sorry, but I might have another appointment at that time. Until that appointment is finalized, I can't give you a firm answer about the basketball game."

Let's now examine how the prepare-then-commit trick works for a replicated database. The figure on the next page demonstrates the idea. Typically, one of the replicas is the "master" that coordinates the transaction. To be specific, suppose there are three replicas, *A*, *B*, and *C*, with *A* being the master. Suppose the database needs to execute a transaction that inserts a new row of data into a table. The prepare phase begins with *A* locking that table, then writing the new data into its write-ahead log. At the same time, *A* sends the new data to *B* and *C*, which also lock their own copies of the table and write the new data in their logs. *B* and *C* then report back to *A* on whether they succeeded or failed in doing this. Now the second phase begins. If any of *A*, *B*, or *C* encountered a problem (such as running out of disk space or failing to lock the table), the master *A* knows that the transaction must be rolled back and informs all replicas of this—see the figure on page 140. But if all the replicas reported success from their prepare stages, *A* sends a message to each replica confirming the transaction, and the replicas then complete it (as in the figure on the next page).

So far we have two database tricks at our disposal: the to-do list trick and the prepare-then-commit trick. What do they buy us? By combining the two tricks, your bank—and any other online entity—can implement a replicated database with atomic transactions. And this permits simultaneous, efficient service to thousands of customers, with essentially zero chance of any inconsistency or data loss. However, we have not yet looked into the heart of the database: how is the data structured, and how are queries answered? Our final database trick will provide some answers to these questions.

RELATIONAL DATABASES AND THE VIRTUAL TABLE TRICK

In all of our examples so far, the database has consisted of exactly one table. But the true power of modern database technology is unleashed in databases that have multiple tables. The basic idea is that each table stores a different set of information, but that entities in the various tables are often connected in some way. So a company's database might consist of separate tables for customer information, supplier information, and product information. But the

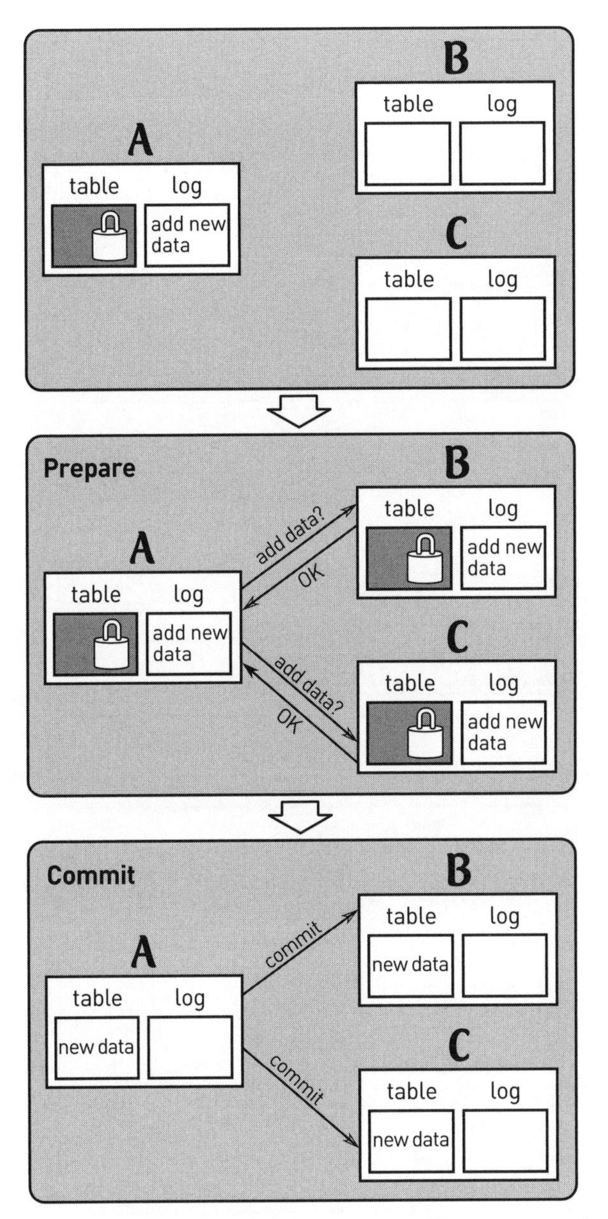

The prepare-then-commit trick: The master replica, *A*, coordinates two other replicas (*B*, *C*) to add some new data to the table. In the prepare phase, the master checks whether all replicas will be able to complete the transaction. Once it gets the all clear, the master tells all replicas to commit the data.

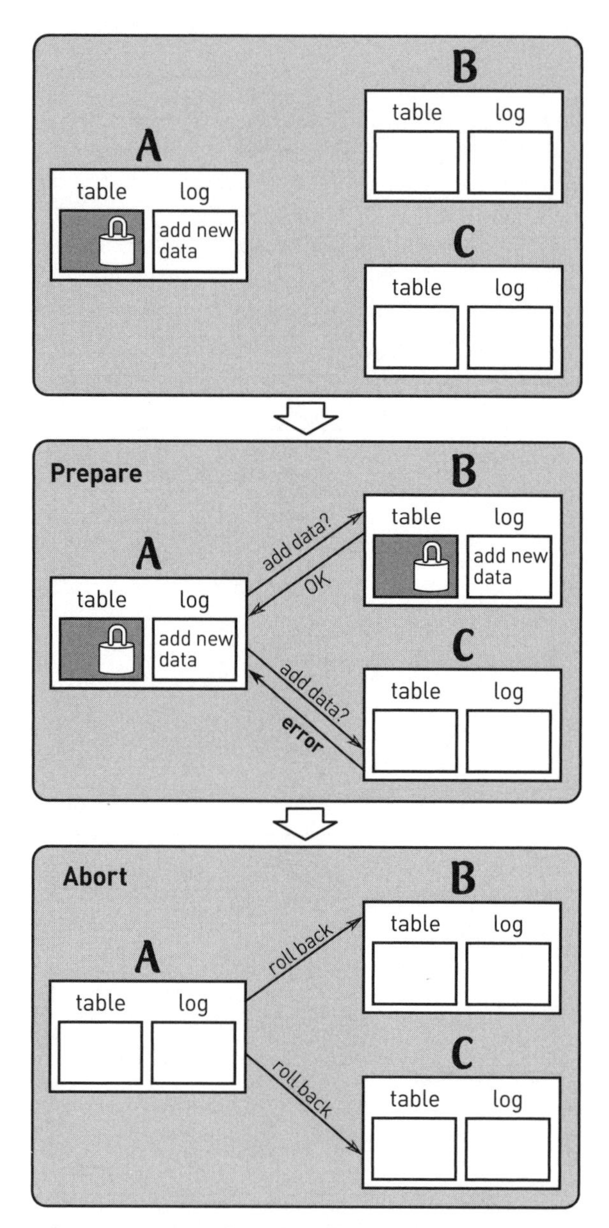

The prepare-then-commit trick with rollback: The top panel of this figure is exactly the same as in the previous figure. But during the prepare phase, one of the replicas encounters an error. As a result, the bottom panel is an "abort" phase in which each replica must roll back the transaction.

customer table might mention items in the product table, because customers order products. And perhaps the product table will mention items in the supplier table, because products are manufactured from the suppliers' goods.

Let's take a look at a small but real example: the information stored by a college, detailing which students are taking which courses. To keep things manageable, the example will have only a handful of students and courses, but hopefully it will be clear that the same principles apply when the amount of data is much larger.

First, let's look at how the data might be stored in the simple, one-table approach we've been using so far in this chapter. This is shown in the top panel of the figure on the following page. As you can see, there are 10 rows in this database and 5 columns; a simple way of measuring the amount of information in the database is to say there are $10 \times 5 = 50$ data items in the database. Spend a few seconds now studying the top panel of the figure on the next page more closely. Is there anything that irks you about the way this data is stored? For instance, can you see any unnecessary repetition of data? Can you think of a more efficient way of storing the same information?

You probably realized that a lot of information about each course is duplicated for each student that takes the course. For example, three students take ARCH101, and the detailed information about this course (including its title, instructor, and room number) is repeated for each of the three students. A much more effective way of storing this information is to use two tables: one to store which courses are taken by which students, and another to store the details about each course. This two-table approach is shown in the bottom panel of the figure on the following page.

We can immediately see one of the advantages of this multitable approach: the total amount of storage required is reduced. This new approach uses one table with 10 rows and 2 columns (i.e., $10 \times 2 = 20$ items), and a second table with 3 rows and 4 columns (i.e., $3 \times 4 = 12$ items), resulting in a total of 32 items. In contrast, the one-table approach needed 50 items to store exactly the same information.

How did this saving come about? It comes from the elimination of repeated information: instead of repeating the course title, instructor, and room number for each course taken by each student, this information is listed exactly once for each course. We have sacrificed something to achieve this, though: now the course numbers appear in two different places, since there is a "course number" column in both tables. So we have traded a *large* amount of repetition (of the course details) for a *small* amount of repetition (of the course numbers). Overall, this works out to be a good deal. The gains in this

student name	course number	course title	instructor	room number
Francesca	ARCH101	Introduction to archeology	Prof Black	610
Francesca	HIST256	European history	Prof Smith	851
Susan	MATH314	Differential equations	Prof Kirby	560
Eric	MATH314	Differential equations	Prof Kirby	560
Luigi	HIST256	European history	Prof Smith	851
Luigi	MATH314	Differential equations	Prof Kirby	560
Bill	ARCH101	Introduction to archeology	Prof Black	610
Bill	HIST256	European history	Prof Smith	851
Rose	MATH314	Differential equations	Prof Kirby	560
Rose	ARCH101	Introduction to archeology	Prof Black	610

student name	course number
Francesca	ARCH101
Francesca	HIST256
Susan	MATH314
Eric	MATH314
Luigi	HIST256
Luigi	MATH314
Bill	ARCH101
Bill	HIST256
Rose	MATH314
Rose	ARCH101

course number	course title	instructor	room number
ARCH101	Introduction to archeology	Prof Black	610
HIST256	European history	Prof Smith	851
MATH314	Differential equations	Prof Kirby	560

Top: Single-table database for students' courses.
Bottom: The same data stored more efficiently, in two tables.

small example are not huge, but you can probably see that if there are hundreds of students taking each course, the storage savings from this approach would be enormous.

There is another big advantage of the multitable approach. If the tables are designed correctly, then changes to the database can be made more easily. For example, suppose the room number for MATH314 has changed from 560 to 440. In the one-table approach (top of the figure on the previous page), four separate rows would need to be updated—and, as we discussed earlier, these four updates would need to be wrapped in a single transaction to ensure that the database remains consistent. But in the multitable approach (bottom of the figure on the facing page), only one change is required, updating a single entry in the table of course details.

Keys

It's worth pointing out here that, while this simple student-courses example is most efficiently represented using only two tables, real databases often incorporate many tables. It is easy to imagine extending our student-courses example with new tables. For example, there could be a table containing details for each student, such as a student ID number, phone number, and home address. There could be a table for each instructor, listing e-mail address, office location, and office hours. Each table is designed so that most of its columns store data that is not repeated anywhere else—the idea is that whenever details about a certain object are required, we can "look up" those details in the relevant table.

In database terminology, any column that is used to "look up" details in a table is called a *key*. For example, let's think about how we would find out the room number for Luigi's history class. Using the single-table approach of the upper panel of the figure on the previous page, we just scan the rows until we find Luigi's history class, look across to the room number column, and observe the answer, which in this case is 851. But in the multitable approach of the same figure's lower panel, we initially scan the first table to find the course number of Luigi's history class—this turns out to be "HIST256." Then we use "HIST256" as a *key* in the other table: we look up the details for this course by finding the row containing "HIST256" as its course number, then move across that row to find the room number (again, 851). This process is shown in the figure on the following page.

The beauty of using keys like this is that databases can look up keys with superb efficiency. This is done in a similar fashion to the way a human looks up a word in a dictionary. Think about how you

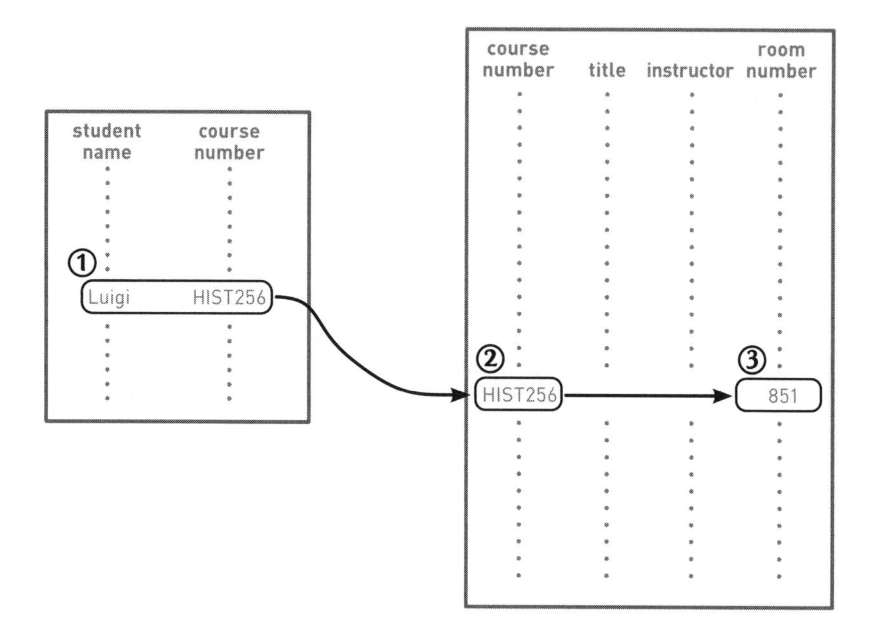

Looking up data using a key: To find out the room number for Luigi's history course, we first find the relevant course number in the left-hand table. This value, "HIST256," is then used as a *key* in the other table. Because the column of course numbers is sorted in alphabetical order, we can find the correct row very quickly, then obtain the corresponding room number (851).

would go about finding the word "epistemology" in a printed dictionary. Naturally, you would *not* start at the first page and scan through every entry looking for "epistemology." Instead, you quickly narrow in on the word by looking at the page headings, initially turning the pages in large clumps and gradually reverting to smaller clumps as you get close to your goal. Databases look up keys using the same technique, but they are even more efficient than humans. This is because the database can precalculate the "clumps" of pages that will be turned and keep a record of the headings at the start and end of each clump. A set of precalculated clumps for fast key lookup is known in computer science as a *B-tree*. The B-tree is yet another crucial and ingenious idea underpinning modern databases, but a detailed discussion of B-trees would, unfortunately, lead us too far afield.

The Virtual Table Trick

We are nearly ready to appreciate the main ingenious trick behind modern multitable databases. The basic idea is simple: although all of a database's information is stored in a fixed set of tables, a database can generate completely new, temporary tables whenever it needs to. We'll call these "virtual tables" to emphasize the fact that they are never really stored anywhere—the database creates them whenever they are needed to answer a query to the database and then immediately deletes them.

A simple example will demonstrate the virtual table trick. Suppose we start with the database of the lower panel of the figure on page 142, and a user enters a query asking for the names of all students taking classes from Professor Kirby. There are actually several different ways a database can proceed with this query; we'll just examine one of the possible approaches. The first step is to create a new virtual table listing students and instructors for all courses. This is done using a special database operation called a *join* of two tables. The basic idea is to combine each row of one table with each corresponding row of the other table, where the correspondence is established by a key column that appears in both tables. For example, when we join the two tables of the bottom panel of the figure on page 142 using the "course number" column as the key, the result is a virtual table exactly like the one in the figure's top panel—each student name is combined with all of the details for the relevant course from the second table, and these details are looked up using the "course number" as a key. Of course, the original query was about student names and instructors, so we don't need any of the other columns. Luckily, databases include a *projection* operation that lets us throw away columns we are not interested in. So after the join operation to combine the two tables, followed by a projection operation to eliminate some unnecessary columns, the database produces the following virtual table:

student name	instructor
Francesca	Prof Black
Francesca	Prof Smith
Susan	Prof Kirby
Eric	Prof Kirby
Luigi	Prof Smith
Luigi	Prof Kirby
Bill	Prof Black
Bill	Prof Smith
Rose	Prof Kirby
Rose	Prof Black

Next, the database uses another important operation called *select*. A select operation chooses some of the rows from a table, based on some criteria, and throws away the other rows, producing a new virtual table. In this case, we are looking for students who take courses from Professor Kirby, so we need to do a "select" operation that chooses only rows in which the instructor is "Prof Kirby." That leaves us with this virtual table:

student name	instructor
Susan	Prof Kirby
Eric	Prof Kirby
Luigi	Prof Kirby
Rose	Prof Kirby

The query is nearly completed. All we need now is another projection operation, to throw away the "instructor" column, leaving us with a virtual table that answers the original query:

student name
Susan
Eric
Luigi
Rose

It's worth adding a slightly more technical note here. If you happen to be familiar with the database query language SQL, you might find the above definition of the "select" operation rather strange, as the "select" command in SQL does much more than merely selecting some rows. The terminology here comes from a mathematical theory of database operations, known as *relational algebra*, in which "select" is used only for selecting rows. Relational algebra also includes the "join" and "project" operations that we used in our query to find Professor Kirby's students.

Relational Databases

A database that stores all of its data in interconnected tables such as the ones we have been using is called a *relational* database. Relational databases were advocated by the IBM researcher E. F. Codd in his extraordinarily influential 1970 paper, "A Relational Model of Data for Large Shared Data Banks." Like many of the greatest ideas in science, relational databases seem simple in retrospect—but at the time, they represented a huge leap forward in the efficient storage and processing of information. It turns out that a mere handful of operations (such as the relational algebra operations "select," "join," and "project" we saw earlier) are sufficient to generate virtual tables that answer essentially any query to a relational database. So a relational database can store its data in tables that are structured for efficiency, and use the virtual table trick to answer queries that seemingly require the data to be in a different form.

That's why relational databases are used to support a large proportion of e-commerce activities. Whenever you buy something online, you are probably interacting with a slew of relational database tables storing information about products, customers, and individual purchases. In cyberspace, we are constantly surrounded by relational databases, often without even realizing it.

THE HUMAN SIDE OF DATABASES

To the casual observer, databases may well be the least exciting topic in this book. It's just hard to get excited about data storage. But under the covers, the ingenious ideas that make databases work tell a different story. Built out of hardware that can fail in the middle of any operation, databases nevertheless give us the efficiency and rock-solid dependability that we have come to expect from online banking and similar activities. The to-do list trick gives us atomic transactions, which enforce consistency even when thousands of customers are simultaneously interacting with a database. This immense level of concurrency, together with rapid query responses via the virtual table trick, make large databases efficient. The to-do list trick also guarantees consistency in the face of failures. When combined with the prepare-then-commit trick for replicated databases, we are left with iron-clad consistency and durability for our data.

The heroic triumph of databases over unreliable components, known by computer scientists as "fault-tolerance," is the work of many researchers over many decades. But among the most important contributors was Jim Gray, a superb computer scientist who literally wrote the book on transaction processing. (The book is *Transaction Processing: Concepts and Techniques*, first published in 1992.) Sadly, Gray's career ended early: one day in 2007, he sailed his yacht out of San Francisco Bay, under the Golden Gate Bridge, and into the open ocean on a planned day trip to some nearby islands. No sign of Gray, or his boat, was ever seen again. In a heart-warming twist to this tragic story, Gray's many friends in the database community used his own tools in an effort to save him: freshly generated satellite imagery of the ocean near San Francisco was uploaded to a database so that friends and colleagues could search for any trace of the missing database pioneer. Unfortunately, the search was not successful, and the world of computer science was left without one of its leading luminaries.

9

Digital Signatures: Who *Really* Wrote This Software?

> To show you how mistaken you are, and what an unfounded assumption yours is, I will lay before you a certificate . . . look at it! You may take it in your hand; it's no forgery.
>
> —CHARLES DICKENS, *A Tale of Two Cities*

Of all the ideas we'll encounter in this book, the concept of a "digital signature" is perhaps the most paradoxical. The word "digital," interpreted literally, means "consisting of a string of digits." So, by definition, anything that is digital can be copied: to do so, just copy the digits one at a time. If you can read it, you can copy it! On the other hand, the whole point of a "signature" is that it can be read, but can't be copied (that is, forged) by anyone other than its author. How could it be possible to create a signature that is digital, yet can't be copied? In this chapter, we will discover the resolution of this intriguing paradox.

WHAT ARE DIGITAL SIGNATURES REALLY USED FOR?

It might seem unnecessary to ask the question: what are digital signatures used for? Surely, you might think, we can use them for the same kinds of things that paper signatures are used for: signing checks and other legal documents, such as the lease on an apartment. But if you think about it for a moment, you will realize that this isn't true. Whenever you make an online payment for something, whether by credit card or through an online banking system, do you provide any kind of signature? The answer is no. Typically, online credit card payments require no signature whatsoever. Online banking systems are a little different, because they require you to log in with a password that helps to verify your identity. But if you later make a payment during your online banking session, no signature of any kind is required.

Internet Explorer - Security Warning

Do you want to run this software?

Name: UltraMon

Publisher: Realtime Soft Ltd

More options Run Don't Run

While files from the Internet can be useful, this file type can potentially harm your computer. Only run software from publishers you trust. What's the risk?

Internet Explorer - Security Warning

The publisher could not be verified. Are you sure you want to run this software?

Name: setup.exe

Publisher: **Unknown Publisher**

Run Don't Run

This file does not have a valid digital signature that verifies its publisher. You should only run software from publishers you trust. How can I decide what software to run?

Your computer checks digital signatures automatically. Top: The message my web browser displays when I attempt to download and run a program that has a valid digital signature. Bottom: The result of an invalid or missing digital signature.

What, then, are digital signatures used for in practice? The answer is the reverse of what you might first think: instead of you signing material that is sent to others, it is typically others who sign material before sending it to you. The reason you are probably not aware of this is that the digital signatures are verified automatically by your computer. For example, whenever you attempt to download and run a program, your web browser probably checks to see if the program has a digital signature and whether or not the signature is valid. Then it can display an appropriate warning, like the ones above.

As you can see, there are two possibilities. If the software has a valid signature (as in the top panel of the figure), the computer can tell you with complete confidence the name of the company that wrote the software. Of course, this doesn't guarantee that the software is safe, but at least you can make an informed decision based on the amount of trust you have in the company. On the other hand, if the signature is invalid or missing (as in the bottom panel of the figure), you have absolutely no reassurance about where the software really came from. Even if you thought you were downloading software from a reputable company, it's possible that a hacker somehow substituted some malicious software for the real thing. Alternatively, maybe the software was produced by an amateur who did not have the time or motivation to create a valid digital signature. It is up to you, the user, to decide whether you trust the software under these circumstances.

Although software-signing is the most obvious application of digital signatures, it is by no means the only one. In fact, your computer receives and verifies digital signatures surprisingly often, because some frequently used internet protocols employ digital signatures to verify the identity of the computers you are interacting with. For example, secure servers whose web addresses begin with "https" typically send your computer a digitally signed certificate before establishing a secure session. Digital signatures are also used to verify the authenticity of many software components, such as browser plugins. You have probably seen warning messages about such things while surfing the web.

There is another type of online signature you may have encountered: some websites ask you to type your name as a signature in an online form. I sometimes have to do this when filling out an online recommendation letter for one of my students, for instance. This is *not* what a computer scientist means by a digital signature! Obviously, this kind of typed signature can be forged effortlessly, by anyone who knows your name. In this chapter, we will learn how to create a digital signature that cannot be forged.

PAPER SIGNATURES

Our explanation of digital signatures is going to be built up gradually, starting with the familiar situation of paper signatures and moving in small steps toward genuine digital signatures. So to start with, let's go back to a world with no computers at all. In this world, the only way to authenticate documents is with handwritten signatures on paper. Notice that in this scenario, a signed document can't be

A paper document with a handwritten signature.

A bank that stores the identities of its customers together with handwritten signatures on file.

authenticated in isolation. For example, suppose you find a piece of paper that says "I promise to pay $100 to Francoise. Signed, Ravi"—just as shown above. How can you verify that Ravi really signed this document? The answer is that you need some trusted repository of signatures, where you can go and check that Ravi's signature is genuine. In the real world, institutions such as banks and government departments perform this role—they really do keep files storing the signatures of their customers, and these files can be physically checked if necessary. In our pretend scenario, let's imagine that a trusted institution called a "paper signature bank" keeps everyone's signature on file. A schematic example of a paper signature bank is shown above.

To verify Ravi's signature on the document promising to pay Francoise, we just need to go to the paper signature bank and ask to see Ravi's signature. Obviously, we are making two important assumptions here. First, we assume the bank can be trusted. In theory, it would be possible for the bank employees to switch Ravi's signature for an imposter's, but we are going to ignore this possibility here. Second, we assume it is impossible for an imposter to forge Ravi's signature. This assumption, as everyone knows, is plain wrong: a skilled forger can easily reproduce a signature, and even amateurs can do a reasonable approximation. Nevertheless, we need the assumption of unforgeability—without it, the paper signature is useless. Later on, we will see how digital signatures are essentially impossible to forge. This is one of the big advantages of digital signatures over paper ones.

SIGNING WITH A PADLOCK

Our first step toward digital signatures is to abandon paper signatures altogether and adopt a new method of authenticating documents that relies on padlocks, keys, and locked boxes. Every participant in the new scheme (in our running example, that means Ravi, Takeshi, and Francoise) acquires a large supply of padlocks. It is crucial that the padlocks belonging to each individual participant are identical—so Ravi's padlocks are all the same. Additionally, each participant's padlocks must be *exclusive*: no one else can make or obtain a padlock like Ravi's. And finally, all padlocks in this chapter have a rather unusual feature: they are equipped with biometric sensors which ensure they can only be locked by their owner. So if Francoise finds an open padlock belonging to Ravi, she can't use it to lock anything. Of course, Ravi also has a supply of keys that will open his padlocks. Because all of his padlocks are identical, all the keys are identical too. The situation so far is shown schematically on the following page. This is the initial setup for what we might call the "physical padlock trick."

Now let's suppose that just as before, Ravi owes Francoise $100, and Francoise would like to record that fact in a verifiable way. In other words, Francoise wants the equivalent of the document on the previous page, but without relying on a handwritten signature. Here is how the trick is going to work. Ravi makes a document saying "Ravi promises to pay $100 to Francoise," and doesn't bother to sign it. He makes a copy of the document and places this document in a lockbox. (A lockbox is just a strongly made box that can be locked with a padlock.) Finally, Ravi locks the box with one of his padlocks and

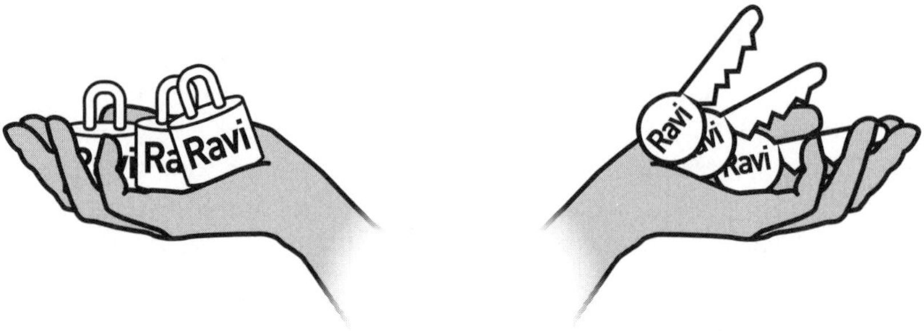

In the physical padlock trick, each participant has
an exclusive supply of identical padlocks and keys.

gives the locked box to Francoise. The complete package is shown in the figure on the facing page. In a sense that will be made precise very soon, the locked box *is* the signature for the document. Note that it would be a good idea for Francoise, or some other trusted witness, to watch while the signature is created. Otherwise, Ravi could cheat by putting a different document into the box. (Arguably, this scheme would work even better if the lockboxes were transparent. After all, digital signatures provide authenticity, not secrecy. However, transparent lockboxes are a little counterintuitive, so we won't pursue this possibility.)

Perhaps you can already see how Francoise can now authenticate Ravi's document. If anyone, perhaps even Ravi himself, tries to deny the authenticity of the document, Francoise can say "Okay Ravi, please lend me one of your keys for a minute. Now I'm going to open this lockbox using your key." In the presence of Ravi and some other witnesses (maybe even a judge in a court of law), Francoise opens the padlock and displays the contents of the lockbox. Then Francoise can continue: "Ravi, as you are the only person with access to padlocks that work with this key, no one else can possibly be responsible for the contents of the lockbox. Therefore, you and only you wrote this note and put it in the lockbox. You *do* owe me $100!"

Although it sounds convoluted when you first encounter it, this method of authentication is both practical and powerful. It does have some drawbacks, however. The main problem is that it requires Ravi's cooperation: before Francoise can prove anything, she has to persuade Ravi to lend her one of his keys. But Ravi could refuse, or even worse, he could pretend to cooperate but in fact give her a different key—a key that will not open his padlock. Then, when Francoise fails to open the lockbox, Ravi can say, "See, that's not one of

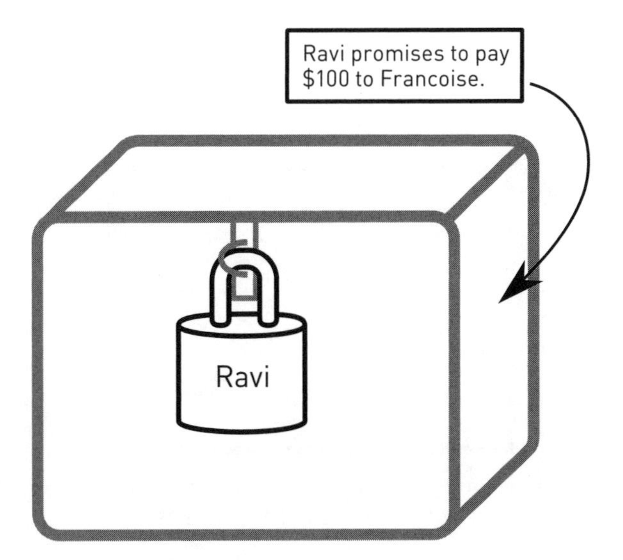

To make a verifiable signature using the physical padlock trick, Ravi places a copy of the document in a lockbox and locks it with one of his padlocks.

my padlocks, so a forger could have created the document and put it in there without my knowledge."

To prevent this cunning approach by Ravi, we still need to resort to a trusted third party such as a bank. In contrast to the paper signature bank on page 152, our new bank will store keys. So instead of giving the bank a copy of their signatures, participants now give the bank a physical key that will open their padlocks. A physical key bank is shown in the figure on the following page.

This bank is the final piece in the puzzle, completing the explanation of the physical padlock trick. If Francoise ever needs to prove that Ravi wrote the IOU, she just takes the lockbox to the bank with some witnesses and opens it there with Ravi's key. The fact that the padlock opens proves that only Ravi could be responsible for the contents of the box, and the box contains an exact copy of the document that Francoise is trying to authenticate.

SIGNING WITH A MULTIPLICATIVE PADLOCK

The key-and-padlock infrastructure that we've built up turns out to be exactly the approach required for digital signatures. Obviously, however, we can't use physical padlocks and physical keys for signatures that must be transmitted electronically. So the next step is to replace the padlocks and keys with analogous mathematical objects

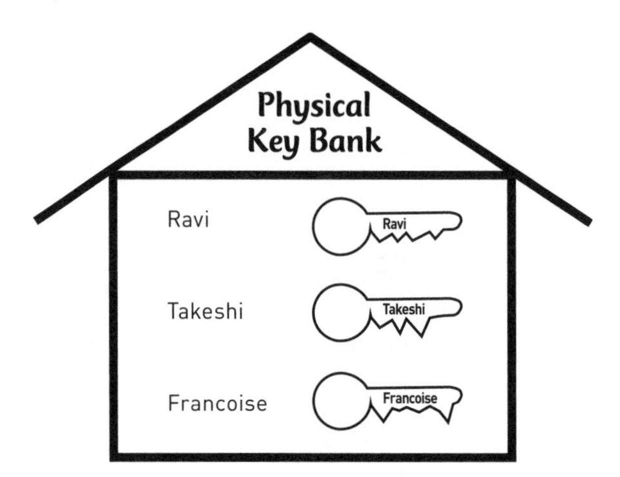

A physical key bank stores keys that will open each participant's padlocks. Note that each of the keys is different.

that can be represented digitally. Specifically, the padlocks and keys will be represented by *numbers*, and the act of locking or unlocking will be represented by *multiplication in clock arithmetic*. If you're not too familiar with clock arithmetic, now would be a great time to reread the explanation given in chapter 4, on page 52.

To create unforgeable digital signatures, computers use absolutely enormous clock sizes—typically tens or hundreds of digits in length. However, in this description, we will be using an unrealistically small clock size to ensure that the calculations are simple.

Specifically, all the examples in this section will use a clock size of 11. Because we will be multiplying numbers together using this clock size quite a bit, I've provided a table on the next page, listing all the values for multiplying together numbers less than 11. As an example, let's compute 7×5. To do it manually, without using the table, we would first compute the answer using regular arithmetic: $7 \times 5 = 35$. Then, we take the remainder after dividing by 11. Now, 11 goes into 35 three times (giving 33) with 2 left over. So the final answer should be 2. Looking at the table, we see the entry in row 7 and column 5 is indeed 2. (You can also use column 7 and row 5—the order doesn't matter, as you can check for yourself.) Try out another couple of multiplication examples for yourself to make sure you understand.

Before going on, we need a slight change to the problem that we're trying to solve. Previously, we've been looking for ways for Ravi to "sign" a message (actually, an IOU) to Francoise. The message was written in plain English. But from now on, it will be much more

	1	2	3	4	5	6	7	8	9	10
1	1	2	3	4	5	6	7	8	9	10
2	2	4	6	8	10	1	3	5	7	9
3	3	6	9	1	4	7	10	2	5	8
4	4	8	1	5	9	2	6	10	3	7
5	5	10	4	9	3	8	2	7	1	6
6	6	1	7	2	8	3	9	4	10	5
7	7	3	10	6	2	9	5	1	8	4
8	8	5	2	10	7	4	1	9	6	3
9	9	7	5	3	1	10	8	6	4	2
10	10	9	8	7	6	5	4	3	2	1

The multiplication table for clock size 11.

convenient to work with numbers only. Therefore, we have to agree that it would be easy for a computer to translate the message into a sequence of numbers for Ravi to sign. Later, if and when someone needs to authenticate Ravi's digital signature of this sequence of numbers, it will be a simple matter to reverse the translation and convert the numbers back into English. We encountered this same problem when talking about checksums (page 68) and the shorter-symbol trick (page 109). If you would like to understand this issue in more detail, look back over the discussion of the shorter-symbol trick—the figure on page 111 gives one simple, explicit possibility for translating between letters and numbers.

So, instead of signing a message written in English, Ravi has to sign a sequence of numbers, perhaps something like "4941381675-43 ... 83271696129149." However, to keep things simple, we will start off by assuming the message to be signed is ridiculously short: in fact, Ravi's message will consist of a single digit, like "8" or "5." Don't worry: we will eventually learn how to sign messages of a more sensible length. For now, however, it's better to stick with single-digit messages.

With these preliminaries out of the way, we are ready to understand the heart of a new trick, called the "multiplicative padlock trick." As with the physical padlock trick, Ravi is going to need a padlock and a key that unlocks the padlock. Obtaining a padlock is surprisingly easy: Ravi first selects a clock size and then chooses essentially any number less than the clock size as his numerical "padlock."

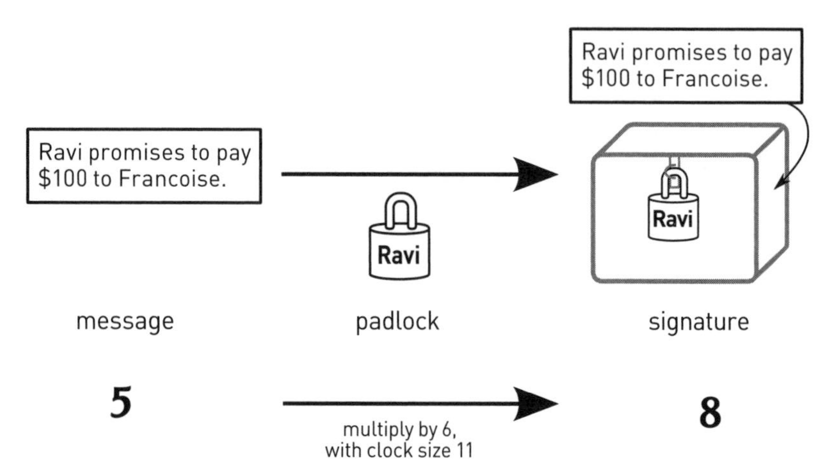

How to "lock" a numeric message using a "padlock," creating a digital signature. The top row shows how to physically lock a message in a box using a physical padlock. The bottom row shows the analogous mathematical operation, in which the message is a number (5), the padlock is another number (6), and the process of locking corresponds to multiplication with a given clock size. The final result (8) is the digital signature for the message.

(Actually, some numbers work better than others, but these details would lead us too far astray.) To make things concrete, let's say Ravi chooses 11 as his clock size and 6 as his padlock.

Now, how can Ravi "lock" his message into a lockbox with this padlock? As strange as it might sound, Ravi is going to use multiplication to do this: the "locked" version of his message will be the padlock multiplied by the message (using clock size 11, of course). Remember, we are dealing with the simple case of a single-digit message right now. So suppose Ravi's message is "5." Then his "locked" message will be 6×5, which is 8—with clock size 11, as usual. (Double-check this using the multiplication table on the previous page.) This process is summarized in the figure above. The final result, "8," is Ravi's digital signature for the original message.

Of course, this type of mathematical "padlocking" would be pointless if we couldn't later unlock the message using a mathematical "key" of some sort. Fortunately, it turns out there is an easy way to unlock messages. The trick is to use multiplication again (applying the clock size, as usual), but this time we'll multiply by a different number—a number selected especially so that it unlocks the previously chosen padlock number.

Let's stick with the same concrete example for the moment, so Ravi is using a clock size of 11, with 6 as his padlock number. It

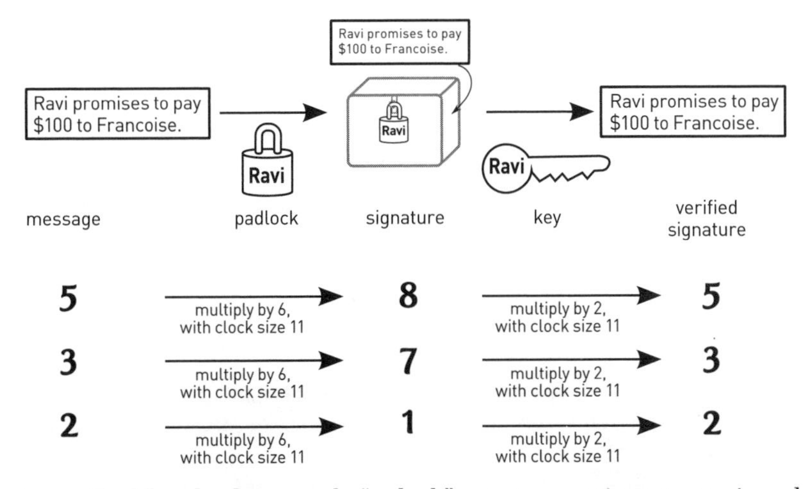

How to "lock" and subsequently "unlock" a message using a numeric padlock and a corresponding numeric key. The top row shows the physical version of locking and unlocking. The next three rows show examples of numerically locking and unlocking messages using multiplication. Note that the locking process produces a digital signature, whereas the unlocking process produces a message. If the unlocked message matches the original message, the digital signature is verified and the original message is authentic.

turns out that the corresponding key is 2. How do we know that? We will come back to this important question later. For the moment, let's stick with the easier task of verifying that the key works once someone else has told us its numeric value. As mentioned earlier, we unlock a padlocked message by multiplying by the key. We have already seen, in the figure on the previous page, that when Ravi locks the message 5 with padlock 6, he gets the locked message (or digital signature) 8. To unlock, we take this 8 and multiply by the key 2, which gives 5 after applying the clock size. Like magic, we have ended up back with the original message, 5! The whole process is shown in the figure above, where you can also see a couple of other examples: the message "3" becomes "7" when padlocked, and reverts to "3" when the key is applied. Similarly, "2" becomes "1" when locked, but the key converts it back to "2."

This figure also explains how to verify digital signatures. You just take the signature and unlock it using the signer's multiplicative key. If the resulting unlocked message matches the original message, the signature is authentic. Otherwise, it must have been forged. This verification process is shown in more detail in the table on the next page. In this table, we stick with a clock size of 11, but to show

Message	**Digital signature** (For genuine signature, multiply message by padlock value 9. To forge, choose a random number.)	**Unlocked signature** (To unlock signature, multiply by key value 5.)	Matches message?	Forged?
4	3	4	Yes	No
8	6	8	Yes	No
8	7	2	No!	Yes!

How to detect a forged digital signature. These examples use a padlock value of 9 and a key value of 5. The first two signatures are genuine, but the third is forged.

that there is nothing special about the numeric padlock and key we have been using up to this point, different values are used for these. Specifically, the padlock value is 9, and the corresponding key value is 5. In the table's first example, the message is "4" with signature "3." The signature unlocks to "4," which matches the original message so the signature is genuine. The next row of the table gives a similar example for the message "8" with signature "6." But the final row shows what happens if the signature is forged. Here, the message is again "8" but the signature is "7." This signature unlocks to "2," which does not match the original message. Hence, the signature is forged.

If you think back to the physical key and padlock scenario, you will remember that the padlocks have biometric sensors preventing use by others—otherwise a forger could use one of Ravi's padlocks to lock any desired message into a box, thus forging a signature of that message. The same reasoning applies to numeric padlocks. Ravi must keep his padlock number *secret*. Each time he signs a message, he can reveal both the message and the signature, but not the padlock number used to produce the signature.

What about Ravi's clock size and his numeric key? Must these also be kept secret? The answer is no. Ravi can announce his clock size and key value to the general public, perhaps by publishing them on a website, without compromising the scheme for verifying signatures. If Ravi does publish his clock size and key value, anyone can obtain these numbers and thus verify his signatures. This approach appears, at first glance, to be very convenient indeed—but there are some important subtleties to be addressed.

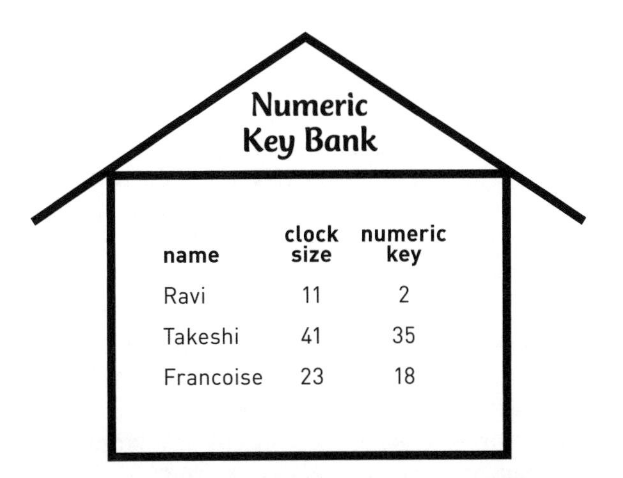

A numeric key bank. The role of the bank is not to keep the numeric keys and clock sizes secret. Instead, the bank is a trusted authority for obtaining the true key and clock size associated with any individual. The bank freely reveals this information to anyone who asks for it.

For example, does the approach eliminate the need for a trusted bank, which was required both for the paper signature technique and for the physical padlock-and-key technique? The answer is no: a trusted third party such as a bank is still required. Without it, Ravi could distribute a false key value that would make his signatures appear invalid. And, even worse, Ravi's enemies could create a new numeric padlock and corresponding numeric key, make a website announcing that this key is Ravi's, and then digitally sign any message they want using their newly minted numeric padlock. Anyone who believes that the new key belongs to Ravi will believe that the enemies' messages were signed by Ravi. Thus, the role of the bank is not to keep Ravi's key and clock size secret. Instead, the bank is a trusted authority for the value of Ravi's numeric key and clock size. The figure above demonstrates this.

A useful way to summarize this discussion would be: numeric padlocks are *private*, whereas numeric keys and clock sizes are *public*. It is, admittedly, a little counterintuitive for a key to be "public," because in our everyday lives we are used to guarding our physical keys very carefully. To clarify this unusual use of keys, think back to the physical padlock trick described earlier. There, the bank kept a copy of Ravi's key and would happily lend it to anyone wishing to verify Ravi's signature. So the physical key was, in some sense, "public." The same reasoning applies to multiplicative keys.

This is a good time to address an important practical issue: what if we want to sign a message longer than one digit? There are several different answers to this question. An initial solution is to use a much larger clock size: if we use a 100-digit clock size, for example, then exactly the same methods allow us to sign 100-digit messages with 100-digit signatures. For a message longer than this, we could just divide it into 100-digit chunks and sign each chunk separately. But computer scientists have a better way of doing this. It turns out that long messages can—for the purposes of signing—be reduced down into a single chunk (of, say, 100 digits), by applying a transformation called a *cryptographic hash function.* We've encountered cryptographic hash functions before, in chapter 5, where they were used as a checksum to ensure the content of a large message (such as a software package) was correct (see page 73). The idea here is very similar: a long message gets reduced to a much smaller chunk before signing takes place. This means that extremely large "messages," such as software packages, can be signed efficiently. To keep things simple, we'll ignore the issue of long messages for the rest of the chapter.

Another important question is: where do these numeric padlocks and keys come from originally? It was mentioned earlier that participants can choose essentially any value for their padlock. The details hiding behind the word "essentially" here require an undergraduate course in number theory, unfortunately. But assuming you haven't had the chance to study number theory, allow me to provide the following teaser: if the clock size is a prime number, then any positive value less than the clock size will work as a padlock. Otherwise, the situation is more complicated. A prime number is a number that has no factors, other than 1 and itself. So you can see that the clock size 11 used so far in this chapter is indeed prime.

Thus, choosing the padlock is the easy part—especially if the clock size is prime. But once the padlock is chosen, we still need to come up with the corresponding numeric key that unlocks the chosen padlock. This turns out to be an interesting—and very old—mathematical problem. Actually, the solution has been known for centuries, and the central idea is even older: it is a technique known as Euclid's algorithm, documented over 2000 years ago by the Greek mathematician Euclid. However, we don't need to pursue the details of key generation here. It is enough to know that, given a padlock value, your computer can come up with the corresponding key value using a well-known mathematical technique called Euclid's algorithm.

If you're still dissatisfied with this explanation, maybe you will be happier once I reveal a dramatic turn that we will be taking soon: the whole "multiplicative" approach to padlocks and keys has a fundamental flaw and must be abandoned. In the next section, we'll be using a different numerical approach to padlocks and keys—an approach that is actually used in practice. So why did I bother to explain the flawed multiplicative system? The main reason is that everyone is familiar with multiplication, which means that the system could be explained without requiring too many new ideas all at once. Another reason is that there are some fascinating connections between the flawed multiplicative approach and the correct approach we will consider next.

But before moving on, let's try to understand the flaw in the multiplicative approach. Recall that padlock values are *private* (i.e., secret), whereas key values are *public*. As just discussed, a participant in a signature scheme freely chooses a clock size (which is made public) and a padlock value (which remains private), and then generates the corresponding key value using a computer (via Euclid's algorithm, in the particular case of the multiplicative keys we have been using so far). The key is stored in a trustworthy bank, and the bank reveals the key's value to anyone who asks. The problem with a multiplicative key is that the same trick—essentially Euclid's algorithm—that is used to generate a key from a padlock works perfectly well in reverse: exactly the same technique allows a computer to generate the padlock value corresponding to a given key value! We can immediately see why this trashes the whole digital signature scheme. Because the key values are public, the supposedly secret padlock values can be computed by anyone. And once you know someone's padlock value, you can forge that person's digital signature.

SIGNING WITH AN EXPONENT PADLOCK

In this section, we will upgrade our flawed multiplicative system to a digital signature scheme, known as RSA, that is actually used in practice. But the new system will use a less-familiar operation called *exponentiation* in place of the multiplication operation. In fact, we went through the same sequence of explanatory steps when building up our understanding of public key cryptography in chapter 4: we first worked through a simple but flawed system that used multiplication, and then looked at the real version using exponentiation.

So, if you're not too familiar with power notation, like 5^9 and 3^4, this would be a great time to go back to page 52 for a refresher. But as a one-line reminder, 3^4 ("3 to the power of 4") means $3 \times 3 \times 3 \times 3$. In

n	n^3	n^7		n	n^3	n^7
1	1	1		11	11	11
2	8	18		12	12	12
3	5	9		13	19	7
4	20	16		14	16	20
5	15	3		15	9	5
6	18	8		16	4	14
7	13	17		17	7	19
8	6	2		18	2	6
9	3	15		19	17	13
10	10	10		20	14	4

Values for exponentiating by 3 and 7 when the clock size is 22.

addition, we need a few more technical terms. In an expression like 3^4, the 4 is called the *exponent* or *power* and the 3 is called the *base*. The process of applying an exponent to a base is called "raising to a power," or, more formally, *exponentiation*. As in chapter 4, we will be combining exponentiation with clock arithmetic. All the examples in this section of the chapter will use clock size 22. The only exponents we will need are 3 and 7, so I've provided a table above showing the value of n^3 and n^7, for every value of n up to 20 (when the clock size is 22).

Let's check a couple of the entries in this table now, to ensure they make sense. Take a look at the row corresponding to $n = 4$. If we weren't using clock arithmetic, then we could work out that $4^3 = 4 \times 4 \times 4 = 64$. But applying the clock size of 22, we see that 22 goes into 64 twice (giving 44), with 20 left over. That explains the entry of 20 in the column for n^3. Similarly, without clock arithmetic you can work out that $4^7 = 16,384$ (okay, you can trust me on that one), which happens to be 16 more than the nearest multiple of 22 (that's $22 \times 744 = 16,368$, just in case you are interested). So that explains the 16 in the column for n^7.

Now we are finally ready to see a genuine digital signature in action. The system works exactly the same as the multiplicative method from the previous section, with one exception: instead of locking and unlocking messages using multiplication, we use exponentiation. As before, Ravi first chooses a clock size that will be made public. Here, Ravi uses clock size 22. Then he selects a secret padlock value, which can be anything less than the clock size (subject to some fine print that we'll discuss briefly later). In our example, Ravi chooses 3 as his padlock value. Then, he uses a computer to work

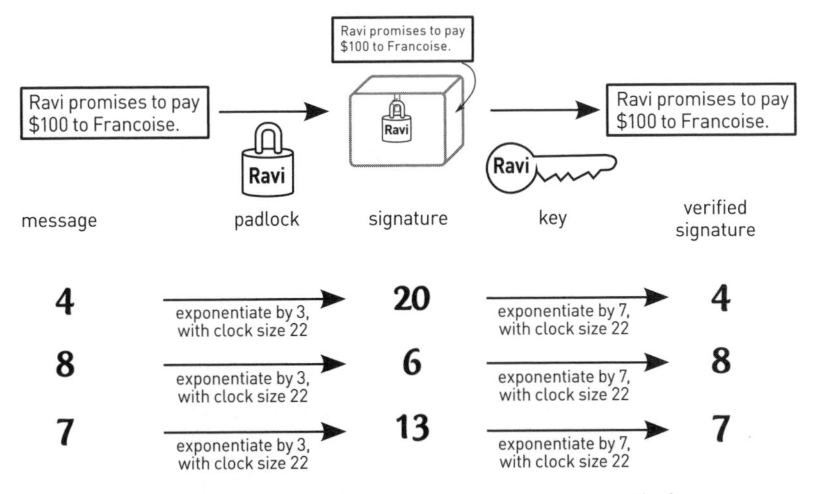

Locking and unlocking messages using exponentiation.

out the corresponding key value for the given padlock and clock size. We'll learn a few more details about this later on. But the only important fact is that a computer can easily compute the key from the padlock and clock size, using a well-known mathematical technique. In this case, it turns out that the key value 7 corresponds to the previously selected padlock value 3.

The figure above shows some concrete examples of how Ravi can sign messages, and how others can unlock the signatures to check them. If the message is "4," the signature is "20": we get this by exponentiating the message with the padlock as exponent. So we need to compute 4^3, which gives 20 once the clock size is taken into account. (Don't forget, you can easily check any of these computations using the table on the previous page.) Now, when Francoise wants to verify Ravi's digital signature "20," she first goes to the bank to get authoritative values for Ravi's clock size and key. (The bank looks the same as before, except with different numbers—see the figure on page 161.) Then Francoise takes the signature, exponentiates by the key value, and applies the clock size: this gives $20^7 = 4$, again using the table on the previous page. If the result matches the original message (and in this case it does), the signature is authentic. The figure shows similar calculations for the messages "8" and "7."

The table on the following page shows the process again, this time emphasizing the verification of the signature. The first two examples in this figure are identical to the previous figure (messages "4" and "8," respectively), and they have genuine signatures. The third example has message "8" and signature "9." Unlocking, by applying the

Message	**Digital signature** (For genuine signature, exponentiate message by padlock value 3. To forge, choose a random number.)	**Unlocked signature** (To unlock signature, exponentiate by key value 7.)	**Matches message?**	**Forged?**
4	20	4	Yes	No
8	6	8	Yes	No
8	9	15	No!	Yes!

How to detect a forged digital signature with exponentiation. These examples use a padlock value of 3, a key value of 7, and a clock size of 22. The first two signatures are genuine, but the third is forged.

key and clock size, gives $9^7 = 15$, which doesn't match the original message. Therefore, this signature is forged.

As mentioned earlier, this scheme of exponent padlocks and exponent keys is known as the *RSA* digital signature scheme, named for its inventors (Ronald **R**ivest, Adi **S**hamir, and Leonard **A**dleman), who first published the system in the 1970s. This may sound eerily familiar, because we already encountered the acronym RSA in chapter 4, on public key cryptography. In fact, RSA is both a public key cryptography scheme and a digital signature scheme—which is no coincidence, as there is a deep theoretical relationship between these two types of algorithms. In this chapter, we have explored only the digital signature aspect of RSA, but you may have noticed some striking similarities to the ideas in chapter 4.

The details of how to choose clock sizes, padlocks, and keys in the RSA system are truly fascinating, but they aren't needed to understand the overall approach. The most important point is that in this system, a participant can easily compute an appropriate key value once the padlock value has been chosen. But it is impossible for anyone else to reverse the process: if you know the key and clock size being used by someone else, you can't work out the corresponding padlock value. This fixes the flaw in the multiplicative system explained earlier.

At least, computer scientists think it does, but nobody knows for sure. The issue of whether RSA is truly secure is among the most fascinating—and vexing—questions in the whole of computer science. For one thing, this question depends on both an ancient unsolved mathematical problem and a much more recent hot topic at the intersection of physics and computer science research. The mathematical problem is known as *integer factorization*; the hot research topic is *quantum computing*. We are going to explore both of these aspects of RSA security in turn, but before we do that, we need a slightly better understanding of what it really means for a digital signature scheme like RSA to be "secure."

The Security of RSA

The security of any digital signature scheme comes down to the question, "Can my enemy forge my signature?" For RSA, this in turn boils down to "Can my enemy compute my private padlock value, given my public clock size and key value?" You might be distressed to learn that the simple answer to this question is "Yes!" In fact, you already knew that: it's *always* possible to work out someone's padlock value by trial and error. After all, we are given a message, a clock size, and a digital signature. We know the padlock value is smaller than the clock size, so we can simply try every possible padlock value in turn, until we find one that produces the correct signature. It's just a matter of exponentiating the message by each trial padlock value. The catch is that, in practice, RSA schemes use absolutely enormous clock sizes—say, thousands of digits long. So even on the fastest existing supercomputer, it would take trillions of years to try all the possible padlock values. Therefore, we are not interested in whether an enemy could compute the padlock value by any means whatsoever. Instead, we want to know if the enemy can do so *efficiently enough* to be a practical threat. If the enemy's best method of attack is trial and error—also known as *brute force* by computer scientists—we can always choose our clock size large enough to make the attack impractical. If, on the other hand, the enemy has a technique that works significantly faster than brute force, we might be in trouble.

For example, going back to the multiplicative padlock and key scheme, we learned that a signer can choose a padlock value and then compute the key value from this using Euclid's algorithm. But the flaw was that adversaries did not need to resort to brute force to reverse this process: it turned out that Euclid's algorithm could also be used to compute the padlock given the key, and this algorithm is vastly more efficient than brute force. That's why the multiplicative approach is considered insecure.

The Connection between RSA and Factoring

I promised earlier to reveal a connection between the security of RSA and an age-old mathematical problem called integer factorization. To understand this connection, we need a few more details about how an RSA clock size is chosen.

First, recall the definition of a *prime number*: it is a number that has no factors other than 1 and itself. For example, 31 is prime because 1×31 is the only way to produce 31 as the product of two numbers. But 33 is not prime, since $33 = 3 \times 11$.

Now we are ready to walk through how a signer such as our old friend Ravi can generate a clock size for RSA. The first thing Ravi does is choose two very large prime numbers. Typically these numbers will be hundreds of digits long, but as usual we will work with a tiny example instead. So let's say Ravi chooses 2 and 11 as his prime numbers. Then he multiplies them together; this produces the clock size. So in our example, the clock size is $2 \times 11 = 22$. As we know, the clock size will be made public along with Ravi's chosen key value. But—and this is the crucial point—the two prime factors of the clock size remain secret, known only to Ravi. The math behind RSA gives Ravi a method of using these two prime factors to compute a padlock value from a key value and vice versa.

The details of this method are described in the panel on the next page, but they are irrelevant for our main purpose. All we need to realize is that Ravi's enemies cannot compute his secret padlock value using the publicly available information (the clock size and key value). But *if* his enemies also knew the two prime factors of the clock size, they could easily compute the secret padlock value. In other words, Ravi's enemies can forge his signature if they can *factorize* the clock size. (Of course, there may be other ways of cracking RSA. Efficient factorization of the clock size is just one possible method of attack.)

In our small example, factoring the clock size (and thus cracking the digital signature scheme) is absurdly easy: everyone knows that $22 = 2 \times 11$. But when the clock size is hundreds or thousands of digits long, finding the factors turns out to be an extremely difficult problem. In fact, although this so-called "integer factorization" problem has been studied for centuries, no one has found a general method of solving it that works efficiently enough to compromise a typical RSA clock size.

The history of mathematics is peppered with unsolved problems that fascinated mathematicians by their aesthetic qualities alone, inspiring deep investigation despite the lack of any practical application. Rather astonishingly, many of these intriguing-yet-apparently-useless problems later turned out to have great practical significance—and in some cases, the significance was discovered only after the problem had been studied for centuries.

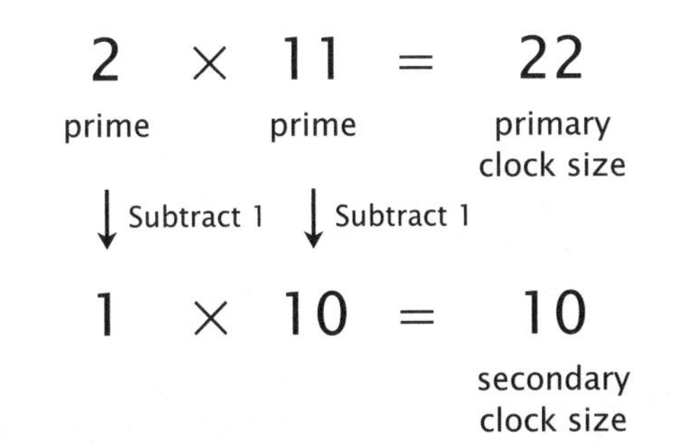

Ravi chooses two prime numbers (2 and 11, in our simple example) and multiplies them together to produce his clock size (22). Let's refer to this as the "primary" clock size for reasons that will soon become apparent. Next, Ravi subtracts one from each of the original two prime numbers, and multiplies *those* numbers together. This produces Ravi's "secondary" clock size. In our example, Ravi is left with 1 and 10 after subtracting one from each of the original primes, so the secondary clock size is $1 \times 10 = 10$.

At this point, we encounter an extremely gratifying connection to the flawed multiplicative padlock-and-key system described earlier: Ravi chooses a padlock and key according to the multiplicative system, but using the secondary clock size instead of the primary. Suppose Ravi chooses 3 as his padlock number. It turns out, when using the secondary clock size of 10, that the corresponding multiplicative key is 7. We can quickly verify that this works: the message "8" padlocks to $8 \times 3 = 24$, or "4" in clock size 10. Unlocking "4" with the key gives $4 \times 7 = 28$, which is "8" after applying the clock size—the same as the original message.

Ravi's work is now done: he takes the multiplicative padlock and key just chosen, and uses them directly as his *exponent* padlock and key in the RSA system. Of course, they will be used as exponents with the *primary* clock size, 22.

The gory details of generating RSA clock, padlock, and key values.

Integer factorization is just such a problem. The earliest serious investigations seem to have been in the 17th century, by the mathematicians Fermat and Mersenne. Euler and Gauss—two of the biggest names in the mathematical canon—made contributions in the centuries immediately following, and many others have built on their work. But it was not until the discovery of public key cryptography in the 1970s that the difficulty of factoring large numbers became the linchpin of a practical application. As you now know, anyone who discovers an efficient algorithm for factoring large numbers will be able to forge digital signatures at will!

Before this begins to sound too alarming, I should clarify that numerous other digital signature schemes have been invented since the 1970s. Although each scheme depends on the difficulty of some fundamental mathematical challenge, the different schemes rely on different mathematical challenges. Therefore, the discovery of an efficient factorization algorithm will break only the RSA-like schemes.

On the other hand, computer scientists continue to be baffled by an intriguing gotcha that applies to all of these systems: none of the schemes has been *proved* secure. Each of them depends on some apparently difficult, much-studied mathematical challenge. But in each case, theoreticians have been unable to prove that no efficient solution exists. Thus, although experts consider it extremely unlikely, it is possible in principle that any one of these cryptography or digital signature schemes could be cracked wide open at any time.

The Connection between RSA and Quantum Computers

I've made good on my promise to reveal a connection between RSA and an old mathematical problem, but I have yet to explain the connection to the hot research topic of quantum computing. To pursue this, we must first accept the following fundamental fact: in quantum mechanics, the motion of objects is governed by *probabilities*—in contrast to the deterministic laws of classical physics. So if you build a computer out of parts that are susceptible to quantum-mechanical effects, the values it computes are determined by probabilities, instead of the absolutely certain sequence of 0s and 1s that a classical computer produces. Another way of viewing this is that a quantum computer stores many different values at the same time: the different values have different probabilities, but until you force the computer to output a final answer, the values all exist simultaneously. This leads to the possibility that a quantum computer can compute many different possible answers at the same time. So for certain special types of problems, you can use a "brute force" approach that tries all of the possible solutions simultaneously!

This does only work for certain types of problems, but it just so happens that integer factorization is one of the tasks that can be performed with vastly greater efficiency on quantum computers than on classical ones. Therefore, if you could build a quantum computer that could handle numbers with thousands of digits, you could forge RSA signatures as explained earlier: factorize the public clock size, use the factors to determine the secondary clock size, and use this to determine the private padlock value from the public key value.

As I write these words in 2011, the theory of quantum computing is far ahead of its practice. Researchers have managed to build real quantum computers, but the biggest factorization performed by a quantum computer so far is $15 = 3 \times 5$—a far cry indeed from factoring a thousand-digit RSA clock size! And there are formidable practical problems to be solved before larger quantum computers can be created. So no one knows when, or if, quantum computers will become large enough to break the RSA system once and for all.

DIGITAL SIGNATURES IN PRACTICE

Early on in this chapter, we learned that end-users like you and me don't have much need to sign things digitally. Some computer-savvy users do sign things like e-mail messages, but for most of us, the primary use of digital signatures is the verification of downloaded content. The most obvious example of this is when you download a new piece of software. If the software is signed, your computer "unlocks" the signature using the signer's public key and compares the results with the signer's "message"—in this case, the software itself. (As mentioned earlier, in practice the software is reduced to a much smaller message called a secure hash before it is signed.) If the unlocked signature matches the software, you get an encouraging message; otherwise, you see a more dire warning: examples of both were shown in the figure on page 150.

As has been emphasized throughout, all of our schemes require some sort of trusted "bank" to store the signers' public keys and clock sizes. Fortunately, as you have probably noticed, you don't need to take a trip to a real bank every time you download some software. In real life, the trusted organizations that store public keys are known as *certification authorities*. All certification authorities maintain servers that can be contacted electronically to download public key information. So when your machine receives a digital signature, it will be accompanied by information stating which certification authority can vouch for the signer's public key.

You have probably already noticed a problem here: sure, your computer can go ahead and verify the signature with the designated certification authority, but how can we trust the authority itself? All we have done is transfer the problem of verifying the identity of one organization (the one that sent you the software, say NanoSoft.com), to the problem of verifying the identity of another organization (the certification authority, say, TrustMe Inc.). Believe

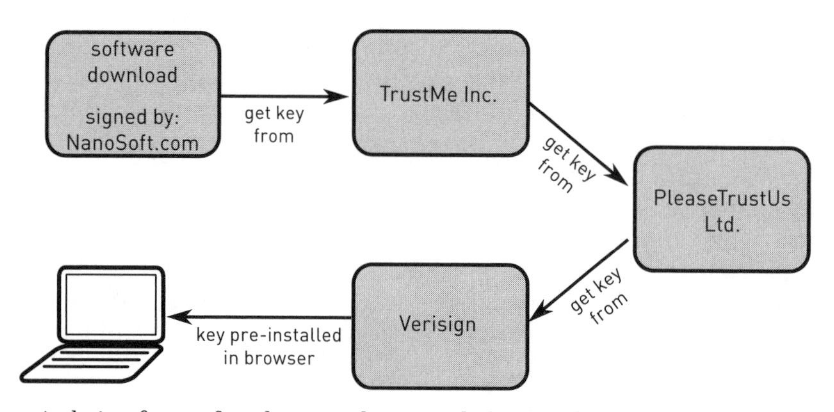

A chain of trust for obtaining keys needed to verify digital signatures.

it or not, this problem is typically solved by the certification authority (TrustMe Inc.) referring you to yet another certification authority (say, PleaseTrustUs Ltd.) for verification, also via a digital signature. This type of chain of trust can be extended indefinitely, but we will always be stuck with the same problem: how can we trust the organization at the end of the chain? The answer, as shown in the figure above, is that certain organizations have been officially designated as so-called *root* certificate authorities, or root CAs for short. Among the better-known root CAs are VeriSign, GlobalSign, and GeoTrust. The contact details (including internet addresses and public keys) of a number of root CAs come pre-installed in your browser software when you acquire it, and that is how the chain of trust for digital signatures becomes anchored in a trustworthy starting point.

A PARADOX RESOLVED

At the start of this chapter, I pointed out that the very phrase "digital signature" could be regarded as an oxymoron: anything digital can be copied, yet a signature should be impossible to copy. How was this paradox resolved? The answer is that a digital signature depends on both a secret known only to the signer and on the message being signed. The secret (which we called a padlock throughout this chapter) stays the same for each message signed by a particular entity, but the signature is different for each message. Thus, the fact that anyone can easily copy the signature is irrelevant: the signature cannot be transferred to a different message, so merely copying it does not create a forgery.

The resolution of this paradox is not just a cunning and beautiful idea. Digital signatures are also of immense practical importance:

without them, the internet as we know it would not exist. Data could still be exchanged securely using cryptography, but it would be far more difficult to verify the *source* of any data received. This combination of a profound idea with such wide practical impact means that digital signatures are, without doubt, one of the most spectacular achievements of computer science.

10

What Is Computable?

> Let me remind you of some of the problems of computing machines.
>
> —RICHARD FEYNMAN (1965 Nobel Prize in physics)

We've now seen quite a number of clever, powerful, and beautiful algorithms—algorithms that turn the bare metal of a computer into a genius at your fingertips. In fact, it would be natural to wonder, based on the rhapsodic rhetoric in the preceding chapters, if there is *anything* that computers cannot do for us. The answer is absolutely clear if we limit ourselves to what computers can do *today*: there are plenty of useful tasks (mostly involving some form of artificial intelligence) that computers can't, at present, perform well. Examples include high-quality translation between languages like English and Chinese; automatically controlling a vehicle to drive safely and quickly in a busy city environment; and (as a teacher, this is a big one for me) grading students' work.

Yet, as we have seen already, it is often surprising what a really clever algorithm can achieve. Perhaps tomorrow, someone will invent an algorithm that will drive a car perfectly or do an excellent job of grading my students' work. These do seem like hard problems—but are they impossibly hard? Indeed, is there any problem at all that is so difficult, no one could ever invent an algorithm to solve it? In this chapter, we will see that the answer is a resounding yes: there *are* problems that can never be solved by computers. This profound fact—that some things are "computable" and others are not—provides an interesting counterpoint to the many algorithmic triumphs we've seen in the preceding chapters. No matter how many clever algorithms are invented in the future, there will always be problems whose answers are "uncomputable."

The existence of uncomputable problems is striking enough on its own, but the story of their discovery is even more remarkable.

The existence of such problems was known before the first electronic computers were ever built! Two mathematicians, one American and one British, independently discovered uncomputable problems in the late 1930s—several years before the first real computers emerged during the Second World War. The American was Alonzo Church, whose groundbreaking work on the theory of computation remains fundamental to many aspects of computer science. The Briton was none other than Alan Turing, who is commonly regarded as the single most important figure in the founding of computer science. Turing's work spanned the entire spectrum of computational ideas, from intricate mathematical theory and profound philosophy to bold and practical engineering. In this chapter, we will follow in the footsteps of Church and Turing on a journey that will eventually demonstrate the impossibility of using a computer for one particular task. That journey begins in the next section, with a discussion of bugs and crashes.

BUGS, CRASHES, AND THE RELIABILITY OF SOFTWARE

The reliability of computer software has improved tremendously in recent years, but we all know that it's still not a good idea to assume software will work correctly. Very occasionally, even high-quality, well-written software can do something it was not intended to do. In the worst cases, the software will "crash," and you lose the data or document you were working on (or the video game you were playing—very frustrating, as I know from my own experience). But as anyone who encountered home computers in the 1980s and 90s can testify, computer programs used to crash an awful lot more frequently than they do in the 21st century. There are many reasons for this improvement, but among the chief causes are the great advances in automated software checking tools. In other words, once a team of computer programmers has written a large, complicated computer program, they can use an automatic tool to check their newly created software for problems that might cause it to crash. And these automated checking tools have been getting better and better at finding potential mistakes.

So a natural question to ask would be: will the automated software-checking tools ever get to the point where they can detect all potential problems in all computer programs? This would certainly be nice, since it would eliminate the possibility of software crashes once and for all. The remarkable thing that we'll learn in this chapter is that this software nirvana will never be attained: it is provably impossible for any software-checking tool to detect all possible crashes in all programs.

It's worth commenting a little more on what it means for something to be "provably impossible." In most sciences, like physics and biology, scientists make hypotheses about the way certain systems behave, and conduct experiments to see if the hypotheses are correct. But because the experiments always have some amount of uncertainty in them, it's not possible to be 100% certain that the hypotheses were correct, even after a very successful experiment. However, in stark contrast to the physical sciences, it *is* possible to claim 100% certainty about some of the results in mathematics and computer science. As long as you accept the basic axioms of mathematics (such as $1 + 1 = 2$), the chain of deductive reasoning used by mathematicians results in absolute certainty that various other statements are true (for example, "any number that ends in a 5 is divisible by 5"). This kind of reasoning does not involve computers: using only a pencil and paper, a mathematician can prove indisputable facts.

So, in computer science, when we say that "X is provably impossible," we don't just mean that X appears to be very difficult, or might be impossible to achieve in practice. We mean that it is 100% certain that X can never be achieved, because someone has proved it using a chain of deductive, mathematical reasoning. A simple example would be "it is provably impossible that a multiple of 10 ends with the digit 3." Another example is the final conclusion of this chapter: it is provably impossible for an automated software-checker to detect all possible crashes in all computer programs.

PROVING THAT SOMETHING ISN'T TRUE

Our proof that crash-detecting programs are impossible is going to use a technique that mathematicians call *proof by contradiction.* Although mathematicians like to lay claim to this technique, it's actually something that people use all the time in everyday life, often without even thinking about it. Let me give you a simple example.

To start with, we need to agree on the following two facts, which would not be disputed by even the most revisionist of historians:

1. The U.S. Civil War took place in the 1860s.
2. Abraham Lincoln was president during the Civil War.

Now, suppose I made the statement: "Abraham Lincoln was born in 1520." Is this statement true or false? Even if you knew nothing whatsoever about Abraham Lincoln, apart from the two facts above, how could you quickly determine that my statement is false?

Most likely, your brain would go through a chain of reasoning similar to the following: (i) No one lives for more than 150 years, so if Lincoln was born in 1520, he must have died by 1670 at the absolute latest; (ii) Lincoln was president during the Civil War, so the Civil War must have occurred before he died—that is, before 1670; (iii) but that's impossible, because everyone agrees the Civil War took place in the 1860s; (iv) *therefore*, Lincoln could not possibly have been born in 1520.

But let's try to examine this reasoning more carefully. Why is it valid to conclude that the initial statement was false? It is because we proved that this claim contradicts some other fact that is known to be true. Specifically, we proved that the initial statement implies the Civil War occurred before 1670—which contradicts the known fact that the Civil War took place in the 1860s.

Proof by contradiction is an extremely important technique, so let's do a slightly more mathematical example. Suppose I made the following claim: "On average, a human heart beats about 6000 times in 10 minutes." Is this claim true or false? You might immediately be suspicious, but how would you go about proving to yourself that it is false? Spend a few seconds now trying to analyze your thought process before reading on.

Again, we can use proof by contradiction. First, assume for argument's sake that the claim is true: human hearts average 6000 beats in 10 minutes. If that were true, how many beats would occur in just one minute? On average, it would be 6000 divided by 10, or 600 beats per minute. Now, you don't have to be a medical expert to know that this is far higher than any normal pulse rate, which is somewhere between 50 and 150 beats per minute. So the original claim contradicts a known fact and must be false: it is *not* true that human hearts average 6000 beats in 10 minutes.

In more abstract terminology, proof by contradiction can be summarized as follows. Suppose you suspect that some statement S is false, but you would like to prove beyond doubt that it is false. First, you assume that S is true. By applying some reasoning, you work out that some other statement, say T, must also be true. If, however, T is known to be false, you have arrived at a contradiction. This proves that your original assumption (S) must have been false.

A mathematician would state this much more briefly, by saying something like "S implies T, but T is false, therefore S is false." That is proof by contradiction in a nutshell. The following table shows how to connect this abstract version of proof by contradiction with the two examples above:

	First example	Second example
S (original statement)	Lincoln was born in 1520	Human heart beats 6000 times in 10 minutes
T (implied by *S*, but known to be false)	Civil War occurred before 1670	Human heart beats 600 times in 1 minute
Conclusion: *S* is false	Lincoln was *not* born in 1520	Human heart does *not* beat 6000 times in 10 minutes

For now, our detour into proof by contradiction is finished. The final goal of this chapter will be to prove, by contradiction, that a program which detects all possible crashes in other programs cannot exist. But before marching on toward this final goal, we need to gain familiarity with some interesting concepts about computer programs.

PROGRAMS THAT ANALYZE OTHER PROGRAMS

Computers slavishly follow the exact instructions in their computer programs. They do this completely deterministically, so the output of a computer program is exactly the same every time you run it. Right? Or wrong? In fact, I haven't given you enough information to answer this question. It's true that certain simple computer programs produce exactly the same output every time they are run, but most of the programs we use every day look very different every time we run them. Consider your favorite word processing program: does the screen look the same every time it starts up? Of course not—it depends on what document you opened. If I use Microsoft Word to open the file "address-list.docx," the screen will display a list of addresses that I keep on my computer. If I use Microsoft Word to open the file "bank-letter.docx," I see the text of a letter I wrote to my bank yesterday. (If the ".docx" here seems mysterious to you, check out the box on the facing page to find out about file name extensions.)

Let's be very clear about one thing: in both cases, I'm running exactly the same computer program, which is Microsoft Word. It's just that the *inputs* are different in each case. Don't be fooled by the fact that all modern operating systems let you run a computer

Throughout this chapter, I'll be using file names like "abcd.txt." The part after the period is called the "extension" of the file name—in this case, the extension of "abcd.txt" is "txt." Most operating systems use the extension of a file name to decide what type of data the file contains. For example, a ".txt" file typically contains plain text, a ".html" file typically contains a web page, and a ".docx" file contains a Microsoft Word document. Some operating systems hide these extensions by default, so you might not see them unless you turn off the "hide extensions" feature in your operating system. A quick web search for "unhide file extensions" will turn up instructions on how to do this.

Some technical details about file name extensions.

program by double-clicking on a document. That is just a convenience that your friendly computer company (most likely Apple or Microsoft) has provided you. When you double-click on a document, a certain computer program gets run, and that program uses the document as its input. The output of the program is what you see on the screen, and naturally it depends on what document you clicked on.

In reality, the input and output of computer programs is quite a bit more complex than this. For instance, when you click on menus or type into a program, you are giving it additional input. And when you save a document or any other file, the program is creating additional output. But to keep things simple, let's imagine that programs accept exactly one input, which is a file stored on your computer. And we'll also imagine that programs produce exactly one output, which is a graphical window on your monitor.

Unfortunately, the modern convenience of double-clicking on files clouds an important issue here. Your operating system uses various clever tricks to guess which program you would like to run whenever you double-click on a file. But it's very important to realize that it's possible to open *any* file using *any* program. Or to put it another way, you can run any program using any file as its input. How can you do this? The box on the next page lists several methods you can try. These methods will not work on all operating systems, or on all choices of input file—different operating systems launch programs in different ways, and they sometimes limit the choice of input file due to security concerns. Nevertheless, I strongly urge you to experiment for a few minutes with your own computer, to convince yourself that you can run your favorite word processing program with various different types of input files.

Here are three ways you could run the program Microsoft Word using `stuff.txt` as the input file:

- Right-click on `stuff.txt`, choose "Open with...," and select Microsoft Word.
- First, use the features of your operating system to place a shortcut to Microsoft Word on your desktop. Then drag `stuff.txt` onto this Microsoft Word shortcut.
- Open the Microsoft Word application directly, go to the "File" menu, choose the "Open" command, make sure the option to display "all files" is selected, then choose `stuff.txt`.

Various ways of running a program with a particular file as its input.

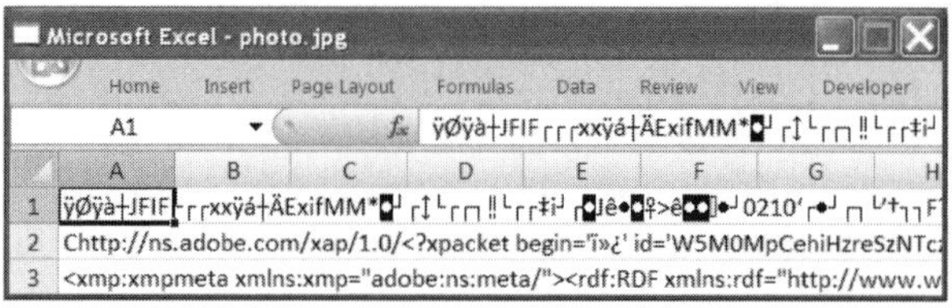

Microsoft Excel run with "photo.jpg" as its input. The output is garbage, but the important point is that you can, in principle, run any program on any input you want.

Obviously, you can get rather unexpected results if you open a file using a program it was not intended for. In the figure above, you can see what happens if I open the picture file "photo.jpg" with my spreadsheet program, Microsoft Excel. In this case, the output is garbage and is no use to anyone. But the spreadsheet program did run, and did produce some output.

This may already seem ridiculous, but we can take the craziness one step further. Remember that computer programs are themselves stored on the computer's disk as files. Often, these programs have a name that ends in ".exe," which is short for "executable"—this just means that you can "execute," or run, the program. So because computer programs are just files on the disk, we can feed one computer program as input to another computer program. As one specific example, the Microsoft Word program is stored on my computer as the file "WINWORD.EXE." So by running my spreadsheet program with the file WINWORD.EXE as input, I can produce the wonderful garbage you see in the figure on the facing page.

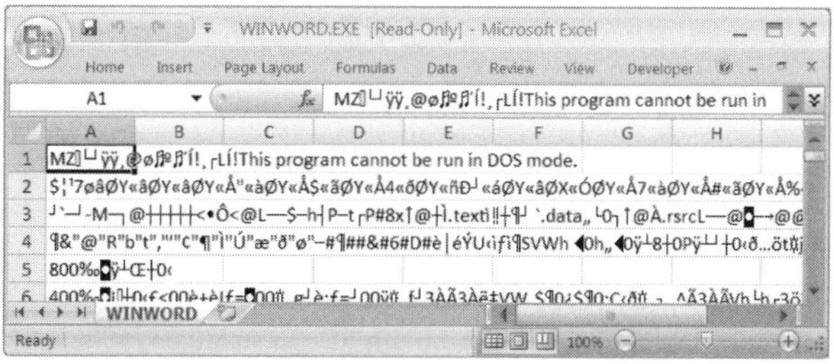

Microsoft Excel examines Microsoft Word. When Excel opens the file WINWORD.EXE, the result is—unsurprisingly—garbage.

Again, it would be well worth trying this experiment for yourself. To do that, you will need to locate the file WINWORD.EXE. On my computer, WINWORD.EXE lives in the folder "C:\Program Files\Microsoft Office\Office12," but the exact location depends on what operating system you are running and what version of Microsoft Office is installed. You may also need to enable the viewing of "hidden files" before you can see this folder. And, by the way, you can do this experiment (and one below) with any spreadsheet and word processing programs, so you don't need Microsoft Office to try it.

One final level of stupidity is possible here. What if we ran a computer program *on itself*? For example, what if I ran Microsoft Word, using the file WINWORD.EXE as input? Well, it's easy enough to try this experiment. The figure on the next page shows the result when I try it on my computer. As with the previous few examples, the program runs just fine, but the output on the screen is mostly garbage. (Once again, try it for yourself.)

So, what is the point of all this? The purpose of this section was to acquaint you with some of the more obscure things you can do when running a program. By now, you should be comfortable with three slightly strange ideas that will be very important later. First, there is the notion that any program can be run with any file as input, but the resulting output will usually be garbage unless the input file was intentionally produced to work with the program you chose to run. Second, we found out that computer programs are stored as files on computer disks, and therefore one program can be run with another program as its input file. Third, we realized that a computer program can be run using its own file as the input. So far, the second and third activities always produced garbage, but in the next section we will see a fascinating instance in which these tricks finally bear some fruit.

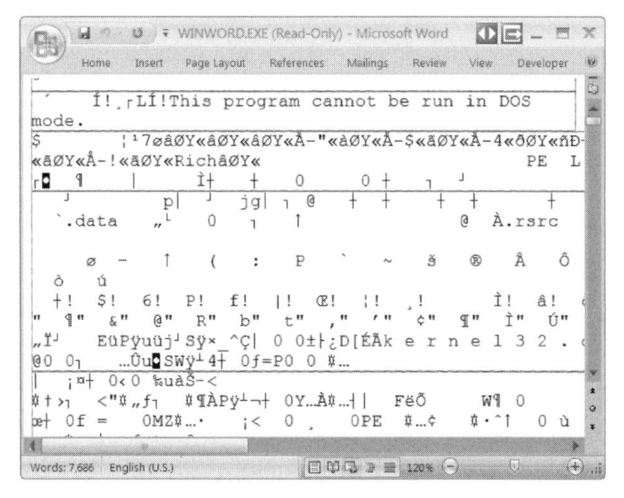

Microsoft Word examines itself. The open document is the file WINWORD.EXE, which is the actual computer program run when you click on Microsoft Word.

SOME PROGRAMS CAN'T EXIST

Computers are great at executing simple instructions—in fact, modern computers execute simple instructions billions of times every second. So you might think that any task that could be described in simple, precise English could be written down as a computer program and executed by a computer. My objective in this section is to convince you that the opposite is true: there are some simple, precise English statements that are literally impossible to write down as a computer program.

Some Simple Yes-No Programs

To keep things as simple as possible in this section, we will consider only a very boring set of computer programs. We'll call these "yes-no" programs, because the only thing these programs can do is pop up a single dialog box, and the dialog box can contain either the word "yes" or the word "no." For example, a few minutes ago I wrote a computer program called ProgramA.exe, which does nothing but produce the following dialog box:

Note that by looking in the title bar of the dialog box, you can see the name of the program that produced this output—in this case, ProgramA.exe.

I also wrote a different computer program called ProgramB.exe, which outputs "no" instead of "yes":

ProgramA and ProgramB are extremely simple—so simple, in fact, that they do not require any input (if they do receive input, they ignore it). In other words, they are examples of programs that really do behave exactly the same every time they are run, regardless of any input they may be given.

As a more interesting example of one of these yes-no programs, I created a program called SizeChecker.exe. This program takes one file as input and outputs "yes" if that file is bigger than 10 kilobytes and otherwise outputs "no." If I right-click on a 50-megabyte video file (say, mymovie.mpg), choose "Open with...," and select SizeChecker.exe, I will see the following output:

On the other hand, if I run the same program on a small 3-kilobyte e-mail message (say, myemail.msg), I will, of course, see a different output:

Therefore, SizeChecker.exe is an example of a yes-no program that sometimes outputs “yes” and sometimes “no.”

Now consider the following slightly different program, which we’ll call NameSize.exe. This program examines the *name* of its input file. If the file name is at least one character long, NameSize.exe outputs “yes”; otherwise, it outputs “no.” What are the possible outputs of this program? Well, by definition, the name of any input file is at least one character long (otherwise, the file would have no name at all, and you couldn’t select it in the first place). Therefore, NameSize.exe will always output “yes,” regardless of its input.

By the way, the last few programs mentioned above are our first examples of programs that do not produce garbage when they are given other programs as input. For example, it turns out that the size of the file NameSize.exe is only about 8 kilobytes. So if I run SizeChecker.exe with NameSize.exe as the input, the output is “no” (because NameSize.exe is not more than 10 kilobytes). We can even run SizeChecker.exe on itself. The output this time is “yes,” because it turns out that SizeChecker.exe is larger than 10 kilobytes—about 12 kilobytes, in fact. Similarly, we could run NameSize.exe with itself as input; the output would be “yes” since the file name “NameSize.exe” contains at least one character. All of the yes-no programs we have discussed this far are admittedly rather dull, but it’s important to understand their behavior, so work through the table on the facing page line by line, making sure you agree with each output.

AlwaysYes.exe: A Yes-No Program That Analyzes Other Programs

We’re now in a position to think about some much more interesting yes-no programs. The first one we’ll investigate is called “AlwaysYes.exe.” This program examines the input file it is given and outputs “yes” if the input file is itself a yes-no program that *always* outputs “yes.” Otherwise, the output of AlwaysYes.exe is “no.” Note that AlwaysYes.exe works perfectly well on any kind of input file. If you give it an input that isn’t an executable program (e.g., addresslist.docx), it will output “no.” If you give it an input that *is* an executable program, but isn’t a yes-no program (e.g., WINWORD.EXE),

program run	input file	output
ProgramA.exe	address-list.docx	yes
ProgramA.exe	ProgramA.exe	yes
ProgramB.exe	address-list.docx	no
ProgramB.exe	ProgramA.exe	no
SizeChecker.exe	mymovie.mpg (50MB)	yes
SizeChecker.exe	myemail.msg (3KB)	no
SizeChecker.exe	NameSize.exe (8KB)	no
SizeChecker.exe	SizeChecker.exe (12KB)	yes
NameSize.exe	mymovie.mpg	yes
NameSize.exe	ProgramA.exe	yes
NameSize.exe	NameSize.exe	yes

The outputs of some simple yes–no programs. Note the distinction between programs that *always* output "yes," regardless of their input (e.g., ProgramA.exe, NameSize.exe), and programs that output "no" either sometimes (e.g., SizeChecker.exe) or always (e.g., ProgramB.exe).

it will output "no." If you give it an input that is a yes–no program, but it's a program that sometimes outputs "no," then AlwaysYes.exe outputs "no." The only way that AlwaysYes.exe can output "yes" is if you input a yes–no program that *always* outputs "yes," regardless of its input. In our discussions so far, we've seen two examples of programs like this: ProgramA.exe, and NameSize.exe. The table on the next page summarizes the output of AlwaysYes.exe on various different input files, including the possibility of running AlwaysYes.exe on itself. As you can see in the last line of the table, AlwaysYes.exe outputs "no" when run on itself, because there are at least some input files on which it outputs "no."

In the next-to-last line of this table, you may have noticed the appearance of a program called Freeze.exe, which has not been described yet. Freeze.exe is a program that does one of the most annoying things a computer program can do: it "freezes" (no matter what its input is). You have probably experienced this yourself, when a video game or an application program seems to just lock up (or "freeze") and refuses to respond to any more input whatsoever. After that, your only option is to kill the program. If that doesn't work, you might even need to turn off the power (sometimes, when using a

AlwaysYes.exe outputs

input file	output
address-list.docx	no
mymovie.mpg	no
WINWORD.EXE	no
ProgramA.exe	yes
ProgramB.exe	no
NameSize.exe	yes
SizeChecker.exe	no
Freeze.exe	no
AlwaysYes.exe	no

The outputs of AlwaysYes.exe for various inputs. The only inputs that produce a "yes" are yes-no programs that *always* output "yes"—in this case, ProgramA.exe and NameSize.exe.

laptop, this requires removing the batteries!) and reboot. Computer programs can freeze for a variety of different reasons. Sometimes, it is due to "deadlock," which was discussed in chapter 8. In other cases, the program might be busy performing a calculation that will never end—for example, repeatedly searching for a piece of data that is not actually present.

In any case, we don't need to understand the details about programs that freeze. We just need to know what AlwaysYes.exe should do when it's given such a program as input. In fact, AlwaysYes.exe was defined carefully so that the answer is clear: AlwaysYes.exe outputs "yes" if its input always outputs "yes"; otherwise, it outputs "no." Therefore, when the input is a program like Freeze.exe, AlwaysYes.exe must output "no," and this is what we see in the next-to-last line of the table above.

YesOnSelf.exe: A Simpler Variant of AlwaysYes.exe

It may have already occurred to you that AlwaysYes.exe is a rather clever and useful program, since it can analyze other programs and predict their outputs. I will admit that I didn't actually write this program—I just described how it would behave, if I had written it. And now I am going to describe another program, called YesOnSelf.exe. This program is similar to AlwaysYes.exe, but simpler.

YesOnSelf.exe outputs

input file	output
address-list.docx	no
mymovie.mpg	no
WINWORD.EXE	no
ProgramA.exe	yes
ProgramB.exe	no
NameSize.exe	yes
SizeChecker.exe	yes
Freeze.exe	no
AlwaysYes.exe	no
YesOnSelf.exe	???

The outputs of YesOnSelf.exe for various inputs. The only inputs that produce a "yes" are yes-no programs that output "yes" when given themselves as input—in this case, ProgramA.exe, NameSize.exe, and SizeChecker.exe. The last line in the table is something of a mystery, since it seems as though either possible output might be correct. The text discusses this in more detail.

Instead of outputting "yes" if the input file *always* outputs "yes," YesOnSelf.exe outputs "yes" if the input file outputs "yes" *when run on itself*; otherwise, YesOnSelf.exe outputs "no." In other words, if I provide SizeChecker.exe as the input to YesOnSelf.exe, then YesOnSelf.exe will do some kind of analysis on SizeChecker.exe to determine what the output is when SizeChecker.exe is run with SizeChecker.exe as the input. As we already discovered (see the table on page 185), the output of SizeChecker.exe on itself is "yes." Therefore, the output of YesOnSelf.exe on SizeChecker.exe is "yes" too. You can use the same kind of reasoning to fill in the outputs of YesOnSelf.exe for various other inputs. Note that if the input file isn't a yes-no program, then YesOnSelf.exe automatically outputs "no." The table above shows some of the outputs for YesOnSelf.exe—try to verify that you understand each line of this table, since it's very important to understand the behavior of YesOnSelf.exe before reading on.

We need to note two more things about this rather interesting program, YesOnSelf.exe. First, take a look at the last line in the table above. What should be the output of YesOnSelf.exe, when it is given the file YesOnSelf.exe as an input? Luckily, there are only two possibilities, so we can consider each one in turn. If the output is "yes," we know that (according to the definition of YesOnSelf.exe), YesOnSelf.exe should output "yes" when run on itself. This is a bit of a tongue twister, but if you reason through it carefully, you'll see that everything is perfectly consistent, so you might be tempted to conclude that "yes" is the right answer.

But let's not be too hasty. What if the output of YesOnSelf.exe when run on itself happened to be "no"? Well, it would mean that (again, according to the definition of YesOnSelf.exe) YesOnSelf.exe should output "no" when run on itself. Again, this statement is perfectly consistent! It seems like YesOnSelf.exe can actually choose what its output should be. As long as it sticks to its choice, its answer will be correct. This mysterious freedom in the behavior of YesOnSelf.exe will soon turn out to be the innocuous tip of a rather treacherous iceberg, but for now we will not explore this issue further.

The second thing to note about YesOnSelf.exe is that, as with the slightly more complicated AlwaysYes.exe, I didn't actually write the program. All I did was describe its behavior. However, note that if we assume I *did* write AlwaysYes.exe, then it would be easy to create YesOnSelf.exe. Why? Because YesOnSelf.exe is simpler than AlwaysYes.exe: it only has to examine one possible input, rather than all possible inputs.

AntiYesOnSelf.exe: The Opposite of YesOnSelf.exe

It's time to take a breath and remember where we are trying to get to. The objective of this chapter is to prove that a crash-finding program cannot exist. But our immediate objective is less lofty. In this section, we are merely trying to find an example of some program that cannot exist. This will be a useful steppingstone on the way to our ultimate goal, because once we've seen *how* to prove that a certain program can't exist, it will be reasonably straightforward to use the same technique on a crash-finding program. The good news is, we are very close to this steppingstone goal. We will investigate one more yes–no program, and the job will be done.

The new program is called "AntiYesOnSelf.exe." As its name suggests, it is very similar to YesOnSelf.exe—in fact, it is identical, except that its outputs are reversed. So if YesOnSelf.exe would output "yes" given a certain input, then AntiYesOnSelf.exe would output "no" on that same input. And if YesOnSelf.exe outputs "no" on an input, AntiYesOnSelf.exe outputs "yes" on that input.

> Whenever the input file is a yes-no program, AntiYesOnSelf.exe answers the question:
>
> **Will the input program, when run on itself, output "no"?**

A concise description of the behavior of AntiYesOnSelf.exe.

Although that amounts to a complete and precise definition of AntiYesOnSelf.exe's behavior, it will help to spell out the behavior even more explicitly. Recall that YesOnSelf.exe outputs "yes" if its input would output "yes" when run on itself, and "no" otherwise. Therefore, AntiYesOnSelf.exe outputs "no" if its input would output "yes" when run on itself, and "yes" otherwise. Or to put it another way, AntiYesOnSelf.exe answers the following question about its input: "Is it true that the input file, when run on itself, will not output 'yes'?"

Admittedly, this description of AntiYesOnSelf.exe is another tongue twister. You might think it would be simpler to rephrase it as "Will the input file, when run on itself, output 'no'?" Why would that be incorrect? Why do we need the legalese about not outputting "yes," instead of the simpler statement about outputting "no"? The answer is that programs can sometimes do something other than output "yes" or "no." So if someone tells us that a certain program does not output "yes," we can't automatically conclude that it outputs "no." For example, it might output garbage, or even freeze. However, there is one particular situation in which we can draw a stronger conclusion: if we are told in advance that a program is a yes-no program, then we know that the program never freezes and never produces garbage—it always terminates and produces the output "yes" or "no." Therefore, *for yes-no programs*, the legalese about not outputting "yes" is equivalent to the simpler statement about outputting "no."

Finally, therefore, we can give a very simple description of AntiYesOnSelf.exe's behavior. Whenever the input file is a yes-no program, AntiYesOnSelf.exe answers the question "Will the input program, when run on itself, output 'no'?" This formulation of AntiYesOnSelf.exe's behavior will be so important later that I have put it in a box above.

Given the work we've done already to analyze YesOnSelf.exe, it is particularly easy to draw up a table of outputs for AntiYesOnSelf.exe. In fact, we can just copy the table on page 187, switching all the

AntiYesOnSelf.exe outputs

input file	output
address-list.docx	yes
mymovie.mpg	yes
WINWORD.EXE	yes
ProgramA.exe	no
ProgramB.exe	yes
NameSize.exe	no
SizeChecker.exe	no
Freeze.exe	yes
AlwaysYes.exe	yes
AntiYesOnSelf.exe	**???**

The outputs of AntiYesOnSelf.exe for various inputs. By definition, AntiYesOnSelf.exe produces the opposite answer to YesOnSelf.exe, so this table—except for its last row—is identical to the one on page 187, but with the outputs switched from "yes" to "no" and vice versa. The last row presents a grave difficulty, as discussed in the text.

outputs from "yes" to "no" and vice versa. Doing this produces the table above. As usual, it would be a good idea to run through each line in this table, and verify that you agree with the entries in the output column. Whenever the input file is a yes-no program, you can use the simple formulation in the box on the previous page, instead of working through the more complicated one given earlier.

As you can see from the last row of the table, a problem arises when we try to compute the output of AntiYesOnSelf.exe on itself. To help us analyze this, let's further simplify the description of AntiYesOnSelf.exe given in the box on the previous page: instead of considering all possible yes-no programs as inputs, we'll concentrate on what happens when AntiYesOnSelf.exe is given itself as input. So the question in bold in that box, "Will the input program, ...," can be rephrased as "Will AntiYesOnSelf.exe, ..."—because the input program *is* AntiYesOnSelf.exe. This is the final formulation we will need, so it is also presented in a box on the facing page.

Now we're ready to work out the output of AntiYesOnSelf.exe on itself. There are only two possibilities ("yes" and "no"), so it shouldn't be too hard to work through this. We'll just deal with each of the cases in turn:

AntiYesOnSelf.exe, when given itself as input, answers the question:

Will AntiYesOnSelf.exe, when run on itself, output "no"?

A concise description of the behavior of AntiYesOnSelf.exe when given itself as input. Note that this box is just a simplified version of the box on page 189, specialized to the single case that the input file is AntiYesOnSelf.exe.

Case 1 (output is "yes"): If the output is "yes," then the answer to the question in bold in the box above is "no." But the answer to the bold question is, by definition, the output of AntiYesOnSelf.exe (read the whole box again to convince yourself of this)—and therefore, the output must be "no." To summarize, we just proved that if the output is "yes," then the output is "no." Impossible! In fact, we have arrived at a *contradiction.* (If you're not familiar with the technique of proof by contradiction, this would be a good time to go back and review the discussion of this topic earlier in this chapter. We'll be using the technique repeatedly in the next few pages.) Because we obtained a contradiction, our assumption that the output is "yes" must be invalid. We have proved that the output of AntiYesOnSelf.exe, when run on itself, cannot be "yes." So let's move on to the other possibility.

Case 2 (output is "no"): If the output is "no," then the answer to the question in bold in the box above is "yes." But, just as in case 1, the answer to the bold question is, by definition, the output of AntiYesOnSelf.exe—and, therefore, the output must be "yes." In other words, we just proved that if the output is "no," then the output is "yes." Once again, we have obtained a contradiction, so our assumption that the output is "no" must be invalid. We have proved that the output of AntiYesOnSelf.exe, when run on itself, cannot be "no."

So what now? We have eliminated the only two possibilities for the output of AntiYesOnSelf.exe when run on itself. This too is a contradiction: AntiYesOnSelf.exe was defined to be a yes-no program—a program that always terminates and produces one of the two outputs "yes" or "no." And yet we just demonstrated a particular input for which AntiYesOnSelf.exe does not produce either of these outputs! This contradiction implies that our initial assumption was false:

thus, it is *not* possible to write a yes–no program that behaves like AntiYesOnSelf.exe.

Now you will see why I was very careful to be honest and admit that I did not actually write any of the programs AlwaysYes.exe, YesOnSelf.exe, or AntiYesOnSelf.exe. All I did was describe how these programs would behave if I did write them. In the last paragraph, we used proof by contradiction to show that AntiYesOnSelf.exe cannot exist. But we can prove even more: the existence of AlwaysYes.exe and YesOnSelf.exe is also impossible! Why is this? As you can probably guess, proof by contradiction is again the key tool. Recall how we discussed, on page 188, that if AlwaysYes.exe existed, it would be easy to make a few small changes to it and produce YesOnSelf.exe. And if YesOnSelf.exe existed, it would be extremely easy to produce AntiYesOnSelf.exe, since we just have to reverse the outputs ("yes" instead of "no," and vice versa). In summary, if AlwaysYes.exe exists, then so does AntiYesOnSelf.exe. But we already know that AntiYesOnSelf.exe can't exist, and, therefore, AlwaysYes.exe can't exist either. The same argument shows that YesOnSelf.exe is also an impossibility.

Remember, this whole section was just a steppingstone toward our final goal of proving that crash-finding programs are impossible. The more modest goal in this section was to give some examples of programs that cannot exist. We've achieved this by examining three different programs, each of which is impossible. Of these three, the most interesting is AlwaysYes.exe. The other two are rather obscure, in that they concentrate on the behavior of programs that are given themselves as input. AlwaysYes.exe, on the other hand, is a very powerful program, since if it existed, it could analyze any other program and tell us whether that program always outputs "yes." But as we've now seen, no one will ever be able to write such a clever and useful-sounding program.

THE IMPOSSIBILITY OF FINDING CRASHES

We are finally ready to begin a proof about a program that successfully analyzes other programs and determines whether or not they crash: specifically, we will be proving that such a program cannot exist. After reading the last few pages, you have probably guessed that we will be using proof by contradiction. That is, we will start off by assuming that our holy grail exists: there is some program called CanCrash.exe which can analyze other programs and tell us whether or not they can crash. After doing some strange, mysterious, and delightful things to CanCrash.exe, we will arrive at a contradiction.

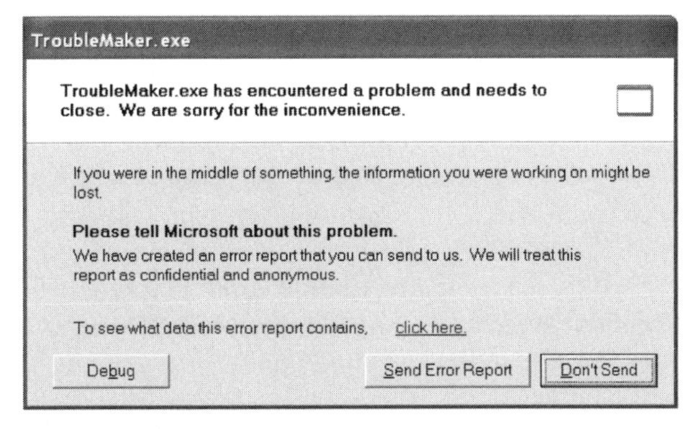

The result of a crash on one particular operating system. Different operating systems handle crashes in different ways, but we all know one when we see one. This TroubleMaker.exe program was deliberately written to cause a crash, demonstrating that intentional crashes are easy to achieve.

One of the steps in the proof requires us to take a perfectly good program and alter it so that it deliberately crashes under certain circumstances. How can we do such a thing? It is, in fact, very easy. Program crashes can arise from many different causes. One of the more common is when the program tries to divide by zero. In mathematics, the result of taking any number and dividing it by zero is called "undefined." In a computer, "undefined" is a serious error and the program cannot continue, so it crashes. Therefore, one simple way to make a program crash deliberately is to insert a couple of extra instructions into the program that will divide a number by zero. In fact, that is exactly how I produced the TroubleMaker.exe example in the figure above.

Now we begin the main proof of the impossibility of a crash-finding program. The figure on the following page summarizes the flow of the argument. We start off assuming the existence of CanCrash.exe, which is a yes-no program that always terminates, outputting "yes" if the program it receives as input can ever crash under any circumstances, and outputting "no" if the input program never crashes.

Now we make a somewhat weird change to CanCrash.exe: instead of outputting "yes," we will make it crash instead! (As discussed above, it's easy to do this by deliberately dividing by zero.) Let's call the resulting program CanCrashWeird.exe. So this program deliberately crashes—causing the appearance of a dialog box similar to the one above—if its input can crash, and outputs "no" if its input never crashes.

The next step shown in the figure is to transform CanCrash-Weird.exe into a more obscure beast called CrashOnSelf.exe. This

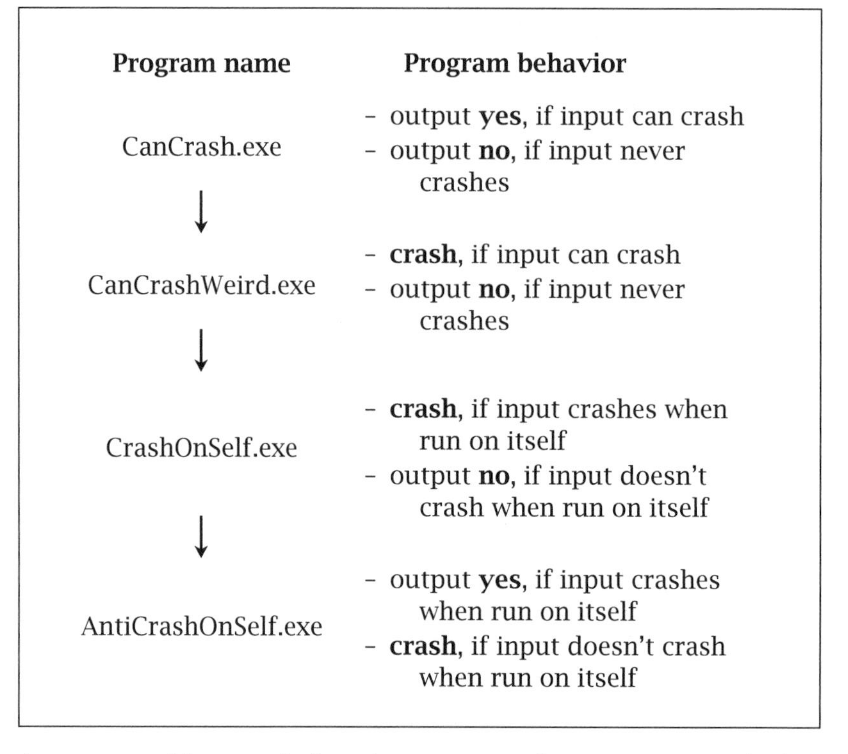

A sequence of four crash-detecting programs that cannot exist. The last program, AntiCrashOnSelf.exe, is obviously impossible, since it produces a contradiction when run on itself. However, each of the programs can be produced easily by a small change to the one above it (shown by the arrows). Therefore, none of the four programs can exist.

program, just like YesOnSelf.exe in the last section, is concerned only with how programs behave when given themselves as input. Specifically, CrashOnSelf.exe examines the input program it is given and deliberately crashes if that program would crash when run on itself. Otherwise, it outputs "no." Note that it's easy to produce CrashOnSelf.exe from CanCrashWeird.exe: the procedure is exactly the same as the one for transforming AlwaysYes.exe into YesOnSelf.exe, which we discussed on page 188.

The final step in the sequence of the four programs in the figure is to transform CrashOnSelf.exe into AntiCrashOnSelf.exe. This simple step just reverses the behavior of the program: so if its input crashes when run on itself, AntiCrashOnSelf.exe outputs "yes." But if the input doesn't crash when run on itself, AntiCrashOnSelf.exe deliberately crashes.

Now we've arrived at a point where we can produce a contradiction. What will AntiCrashOnSelf.exe do when given itself as input? According to its own description, it should output "yes" if it crashes (a contradiction, since it can't terminate successfully with the output "yes" if it has already crashed). And again according to its own description, AntiCrashOnSelf.exe should crash if it doesn't crash—which is also self-contradictory. We've eliminated both possible behaviors of AntiCrashOnSelf.exe, which means the program could not have existed in the first place.

Finally, we can use the chain of transformations shown in the figure on the facing page to prove that CanCrash.exe can't exist either. If it *did* exist, we could transform it, by following the arrows in the figure, into AntiCrashOnSelf.exe—but we already know AntiCrashOnSelf.exe can't exist. That's a contradiction, and, therefore, our assumption that CanCrash.exe exists must be false.

The Halting Problem and Undecidability

That concludes our tour through one of the most sophisticated and profound results in computer science. We have proved the absolute impossibility that anyone will ever write a computer program like CanCrash.exe: a program that analyzes other programs and identifies all possible bugs in those programs that might cause them to crash.

In fact, when Alan Turing, the founder of theoretical computer science, first proved a result like this in the 1930s, he wasn't concerned at all about bugs or crashes. After all, no electronic computer had even been built yet. Instead, Turing was interested in whether or not a given computer program would eventually produce an answer. A closely related question is: will a given computer program ever *terminate*—or, alternatively, will it go on computing forever, without producing an answer? This question of whether a given computer program will eventually terminate, or "halt," is known as the Halting Problem. Turing's great achievement was to prove that his variant of the Halting Problem is what computer scientists call "undecidable." An undecidable problem is one that can't be solved by writing a computer program. So another way of stating Turing's result is: you can't write a computer program called AlwaysHalts.exe, that outputs "yes" if its input always halts, and "no" otherwise.

Viewed in this way, the Halting Problem is very similar to the problem tackled in this chapter, which we might call the Crashing Problem. We proved the undecidability of the Crashing Problem, but you can use essentially the same technique to prove the Halting Problem is also undecidable. And, as you might guess, there are many other problems in computer science that are undecidable.

WHAT ARE THE IMPLICATIONS OF IMPOSSIBLE PROGRAMS?

Except for the conclusion, this is the last chapter in the book. I included it as a deliberate counterpoint to the earlier chapters. Whereas every previous chapter championed a remarkable idea that renders computers even more powerful and useful to us humans, in this chapter we saw one of the fundamental limitations of computers. We saw there are some problems that are literally impossible to solve with a computer, regardless of how powerful the computer is or how clever its human programmer. And these undecidable problems include potentially useful tasks, such as analyzing other computer programs to find out whether they might crash.

What is the significance of this strange, and perhaps even foreboding, fact? Does the existence of undecidable problems affect the way we use computers in practice? And how about the computations that we humans do inside our brains—are those also prevented from tackling undecidable problems?

Undecidability and Computer Use

Let's first address the practical effects of undecidability on computer use. The short answer is: no, undecidability does not have much effect on the daily practice of computing. There are two reasons for this. Firstly, undecidability is concerned only with whether a computer program will ever produce an answer, and does not consider how long we have to wait for that answer. In practice, however, the issue of efficiency (in other words, how long you have to wait for the answer) is extremely important. There are plenty of decidable tasks for which no efficient algorithm is known. The most famous of these is the Traveling Salesman Problem, or TSP for short. Restated in modern terminology, the TSP goes something like this: suppose you have to fly to a large number of cities (say, 20 or 30 or 100). In what order should you visit the cities so as to incur the lowest possible total airfare? As we noted already, this problem *is* decidable—in fact, a novice programmer with only a few days' experience can write a computer program to find the cheapest route through the cities. The catch is that the program could take millions of years to complete its job. In practice, this isn't good enough. Thus, the mere fact that a problem is decidable does not mean that we can solve it in practice.

Now for the second reason that undecidability has limited practical effects: it turns out that we can often do a good job of solving undecidable problems *most of the time.* The main example of the current chapter is an excellent illustration of this. We followed an elaborate proof showing that no computer program can ever be capable of finding all the bugs in all computer programs. But we can still try to write a crash-finding program, hoping to make it find most of the bugs in most types of computer programs. This is, indeed, a very active area of research in computer science. The improvements we've seen in software reliability over the last few decades are partly due to the advances made in crash-finding programs. Thus, it is often possible to produce very useful partial solutions to undecidable problems.

Undecidability and the Brain

Does the existence of undecidable problems have implications for human thought processes? This question leads directly to the murky depths of some classic problems in philosophy, such as the definition of consciousness and the distinction between mind and brain. Nevertheless, we can be clear about one thing: if you believe that the human brain could, in principle, be simulated by a computer, then the brain is subject to the same limitations as computers. In other words, there would be problems that no human brain could solve—however intelligent or well-trained that brain might be. This conclusion follows immediately from the main result in this chapter. If the brain can be imitated by a computer program, and the brain can solve undecidable problems, then we could use a computer simulation of the brain to solve the undecidable problems also—contradicting the fact that computer programs cannot solve undecidable problems.

Of course, the question of whether we will ever be able to perform accurate computer simulations of the brain is far from settled. From a scientific point of view, there do not seem to be any fundamental barriers, since the low-level details of how chemical and electrical signals are transmitted in the brain are reasonably well understood. On the other hand, various philosophical arguments suggest that somehow the physical processes of the brain create a "mind" that is qualitatively different from any physical system that could be simulated by computer. These philosophical arguments take many forms and can be based, for example, on our own capacity for self-reflection and intuition, or an appeal to spirituality.

There is a fascinating connection here to Alan Turing's 1937 paper on undecidability—a paper that is regarded by many as the foundation of computer science as a discipline. The paper's title is, unfortunately, rather obscure: it begins with the innocuous-sounding phrase "On computable numbers..." but ends with the jarring "...with an application to the Entscheidungsproblem." (We won't be concerning ourselves with the second part of the title here!) It is crucial to realize that in the 1930s, the word "computer" had a completely different meaning, compared to the way we use it today. For Turing, a "computer" was a *human*, doing some kind of calculation using a pencil and paper. Thus, the "computable numbers" in the title of Turing's paper are the numbers that could, in principle, be calculated by a human. But to assist his argument, Turing describes a particular type of machine (for Turing, a "machine" is what we would call a "computer" today) that can also do calculations. Part of the paper is devoted to demonstrating that certain calculations cannot be performed by these machines—this is the proof of undecidability, which we have discussed in detail already. But another part of the same paper makes a detailed and compelling argument that Turing's "machine" (read: computer) can perform any calculation done by a "computer" (read: human).

You may be beginning to appreciate why it is difficult to overstate the seminal nature of Turing's "On computable numbers..." paper. It not only defines and solves some of the most fundamental problems in computer science, but also strikes out into the heart of a philosophical minefield, making a persuasive case that human thought processes could be emulated by computers (which, remember, had not been invented yet!). In modern philosophical parlance, this notion—that all computers, and probably humans too, have equivalent computational power—is known as the *Church-Turing thesis*. The name acknowledges both Alan Turing and Alonzo Church, who (as mentioned earlier) independently discovered the existence of undecidable problems. In fact, Church published his work a few months before Turing, but Church's formulation is more abstract and does not explicitly mention computation by machines.

The debate over the validity of the Church-Turing thesis rages on. But if its strongest version holds, then our computers aren't the only ones humbled by the limits of undecidability. The same limits would apply not only to the genius at our fingertips, but the genius behind them: our own minds.

11

Conclusion: More Genius at Your Fingertips?

> We can only see a short distance ahead, but we can see plenty there that needs to be done.
>
> —Alan Turing, *Computing Machinery and Intelligence*, 1950

I was fortunate, in 1991, to attend a public lecture by the great theoretical physicist Stephen Hawking. During the lecture, which was boldly titled "The Future of the Universe," Hawking confidently predicted that the universe would keep expanding for at least the next 10 billion years. He wryly added, "I don't expect to be around to be proved wrong." Unfortunately for me, predictions about computer science do not come with the same 10-billion-year insurance policy that is available to cosmologists. Any predictions I make may well be disproved during my own lifetime.

But that shouldn't stop us thinking about the future of the great ideas of computer science. Will the great algorithms we've explored remain "great" forever? Will some become obsolete? Will new great algorithms emerge? To address these questions, we need to think less like a cosmologist and more like a historian. This brings to mind another experience I had many years ago, watching some televised lectures by the acclaimed, if controversial, Oxford historian A. J. P. Taylor. At the end of the lecture series, Taylor directly addressed the question of whether there would ever be a third world war. He thought the answer was yes, because humans would probably "behave in the future as they have done in the past."

So let's follow A. J. P. Taylor's lead and bow to the broad sweep of history. The great algorithms described in this book arose from incidents and inventions sprinkled throughout the 20th century. It seems reasonable to assume a similar pace for the 21st century, with a major new set of algorithms coming to the fore every two or three decades. In some cases, these algorithms could be stunningly original, completely new techniques dreamed up by scientists. Public key cryptography and the related digital signature algorithms are examples of this. In other cases, the algorithms may have existed in the research community for some time, waiting in the wings for the right wave of new technology to give them wide applicability. The search algorithms for indexing and ranking fall into this category: similar algorithms had existed for years in the field known as information retrieval, but it took the phenomenon of web search to make these algorithms "great," in the sense of daily use by ordinary computer users. Of course, the algorithms also evolved for their new application; PageRank is a good example of this.

Note that the emergence of new technology does not necessarily lead to new algorithms. Consider the phenomenal growth of laptop computers over the 1980s and 1990s. Laptops revolutionized the way people use computers, by vastly increasing accessibility and portability. And laptops also motivated hugely important advances in such diverse areas as screen technology and power management techniques. But I would argue that no great algorithms emerged from the laptop revolution. In contrast, the emergence of the internet is a technology that did lead to great algorithms: by providing an infrastructure in which search engines could exist, the internet allowed indexing and ranking algorithms to evolve toward greatness.

Therefore, the undoubted acceleration of technology growth that continues to unfold around us does not, in and of itself, guarantee the emergence of new great algorithms. In fact, there is a powerful historical force operating in the other direction, suggesting that the pace of algorithmic innovation will, if anything, decrease in the future. I'm referring to the fact that computer science is beginning to mature as a scientific discipline. Compared to fields such as physics, mathematics, and chemistry, computer science is very young: it has its beginnings in the 1930s. Arguably, therefore, the great algorithms discovered in the 20th century may have consisted of low hanging fruit, and it will become more and more difficult to find ingenious, widely applicable algorithms in the future.

So we have two competing effects: new niches provided by new technology occasionally provide scope for new algorithms, while the increasing maturity of the field narrows the opportunities. On balance, I tend to think that these two effects will cancel each other out, leading to a slow but steady emergence of new great algorithms in the years ahead.

SOME POTENTIALLY GREAT ALGORITHMS

Of course, some of these new algorithms will be completely unexpected, and it's impossible to say anything more about them here. But there are existing niches and techniques that have clear potential. One of the obvious trends is the increasing use of artificial intelligence (and, in particular, pattern recognition) in everyday contexts, and it will be fascinating to see if any strikingly novel algorithmic gems emerge in this area.

Another fertile area is a class of algorithms known as "zero-knowledge protocols." These protocols use a special type of cryptography to achieve something even more surprising than a digital signature: they let two or more entities combine information without revealing any of the individual pieces of information. One potential application is for online auctions. Using a zero-knowledge protocol, the bidders can cryptographically submit their bids to each other in such a way that the winning bidder is determined, but no information about the other bids is revealed to anyone! Zero-knowledge protocols are such a clever idea that they would easily make it into my canon of great algorithms, if only they were used in practice. But so far, they haven't achieved widespread use.

Another idea that has received an immense amount of academic research but limited practical use is a technique known as "distributed hash tables." These tables are an ingenious way of storing the information in a peer-to-peer system—a system that has no central server directing the flow of information. At the time of writing, however, many of the systems that claim to be peer-to-peer in fact use central servers for some of their functionality and thus do not need to rely on distributed hash tables.

The technique of "Byzantine fault tolerance" falls in the same category: a surprising and beautiful algorithm that can't yet be classed as great, due to lack of adoption. Byzantine fault tolerance allows certain computer systems to tolerate any type of error whatsoever (as long as there are not too many simultaneous errors). This contrasts with the more usual notion of fault tolerance, in which a system can survive more benign errors, such as the permanent failure of a disk drive or an operating system crash.

CAN GREAT ALGORITHMS FADE AWAY?

In addition to speculating about what algorithms might rise to greatness in the future, we might wonder whether any of our current "great" algorithms—indispensable tools that we use constantly without even thinking about it—might fade in importance. History can guide us here, too. If we restrict attention to particular algorithms, it is certainly true that algorithms can lose relevance. The most obvious example is in cryptography, in which there is a constant arms race between researchers inventing new crypto algorithms, and other researchers inventing ways to crack the security of those algorithms. As a specific instance, consider the so-called cryptographic hash functions. The hash function known as MD5 is an official internet standard and has been widely used since the early 1990s, yet significant security flaws have been found in MD5 since then, and its use is no longer recommended. Similarly, we discussed in chapter 9 the fact that the RSA digital signature scheme will be easy to crack if and when it becomes possible to build quantum computers of a reasonable size.

However, I think examples like this answer our question too narrowly. Sure, MD5 is broken (and, by the way, so is its main successor, SHA-1), but that doesn't mean the central idea of cryptographic hash functions is irrelevant. Indeed, such hash functions are used extremely widely, and there are plenty of uncracked ones out there. So, provided we take a broad enough view of the situation and are prepared to adapt the specifics of an algorithm while retaining its main ideas, it seems unlikely that many of our presently great algorithms will lose their importance in the future.

WHAT HAVE WE LEARNED?

Are there any common themes that can be drawn out from the great algorithms presented here? One theme, which was a great surprise to me as the author of the book, is that all of the big ideas can be explained without requiring previous knowledge of computer programming or any other computer science. When I started work on the book, I assumed that the great algorithms would fall into two categories. The first category would be algorithms with some simple yet clever trick at their core—a trick that could be explained without requiring any technical knowledge. The second category would be algorithms that depended so intimately on advanced computer science ideas that they could not be explained to readers with no background in this area. I planned to include algorithms from this second category by giving some (hopefully) interesting historical anecdotes about the algorithms, explaining their important applications, and vociferously asserting that the algorithm was ingenious even though I couldn't explain how it worked. Imagine my surprise and delight when I discovered that all the chosen algorithms fell into the first category! To be sure, many important technical details were omitted, but in every case, the key mechanism that makes the whole thing work could be explained using nonspecialist notions.

Another important theme common to all our algorithms is that the field of computer science is much more than just programming. Whenever I teach an introductory computer science course, I ask the students to tell me what they think computer science actually is. By far the most common response is "programming," or something equivalent such as "software engineering." When pressed to provide additional aspects of computer science, many are stumped. But a common follow-up is something related to hardware, such as "hardware design." This is strong evidence of a popular misconception about what computer scientists really do. Having read this book, I hope you have a much more concrete idea of the problems that computer scientists spend their time thinking about, and the types of solutions they come up with.

A simple analogy will help here. Suppose you meet a professor whose main research interest is Japanese literature. It is extremely likely that the professor can speak, read, and write Japanese. But if you were asked to guess what the professor spends the most time thinking *about* while conducting research, you would not guess "the Japanese language." Rather, the Japanese language is a necessary piece of knowledge for studying the themes, culture, and history that comprise Japanese literature. On the other hand, someone who speaks perfect Japanese might be perfectly ignorant of Japanese literature (there are probably millions of such people in Japan).

The relationship between computer programming languages and the main ideas of computer science is quite similar. To implement and experiment with algorithms, computer science researchers need to convert the algorithms into computer programs, and each program is written in a programming language, such as Java, C++, or Python. Thus, knowledge of a programming language is essential for computer scientists, but it is merely a prerequisite: the main challenge is to invent, adapt, and understand algorithms. After seeing the great algorithms in this book, it is my hope that readers will have a much firmer grasp of this distinction.

THE END OF OUR TOUR

We've reached the end of our tour through the world of profound, yet everyday, computation. Did we achieve our goals? And will your interactions with computing devices be any different as a result?

Well, it's just possible that next time you visit a secure website, you'll be intrigued to know who vouched for its trustworthiness, and check out the chain of digital certificates that were inspected by your web browser (chapter 9). Or perhaps the next time an online transaction fails for an inexplicable reason, you'll be grateful instead of frustrated, knowing that database consistency should ensure you won't be charged for something you failed to order (chapter 8). Or maybe you'll be musing to yourself one day, "Now wouldn't it be nice if my computer could do *this* for me"—only to realize that it's an impossibility, because your wished-for task can be proved undecidable using the same method as for our crash-finding program (chapter 10).

I'm sure you can think of plenty more examples in which knowledge of the great algorithms might change the way you interact with a computer. However, as I was careful to state in the introduction, this wasn't the primary objective of the book. *My* chief goal was to give readers enough knowledge about the great algorithms that they gain a sense of wonder at some of their ordinary computing tasks—much as an amateur astronomer has a heightened appreciation of the night sky.

Only you, the reader, can know whether I succeeded in this goal. But one thing is certain: your own personal genius is right at your fingertips. Feel free to use it.

ACKNOWLEDGMENTS

> You road I enter upon and look around! I believe you are not all
> that is here;
> I believe that much unseen is also here.
>
> —WALT WHITMAN, *Song of the Open Road*

Many friends, colleagues, and family members read some or all of the manuscript. Among them are Alex Bates, Wilson Bell, Mike Burrows, Walt Chromiak, Michael Isard, Alastair MacCormick, Raewyn MacCormick, Nicoletta Marini-Maio, Frank McSherry, Kristine Mitchell, Ilya Mironov, Wendy Pollack, Judith Potter, Cotten Seiler, Helen Takacs, Kunal Talwar, Tim Wahls, Jonathan Waller, Udi Wieder, and Ollie Williams. Suggestions from these readers resulted in a large number of substantial improvements to the manuscript. The comments of two anonymous reviewers also resulted in significant improvements.

Chris Bishop provided encouragement and advice. Tom Mitchell gave permission to use his pictures and source code in chapter 6.

Vickie Kearn (the book's editor) and her colleagues at Princeton University Press did a wonderful job of incubating the project and bringing it to fruition.

My colleagues in the Department of Mathematics and Computer Science at Dickinson College were a constant source of support and camaraderie.

Michael Isard and Mike Burrows showed me the joy and beauty of computing. Andrew Blake taught me how to be a better scientist.

My wife Kristine was always there and is here still; *much unseen is also here.*

To all these people I express my deepest gratitude. The book is dedicated, with love, to Kristine.

SOURCES AND FURTHER READING

As explained on page 8, this book does not use in-text citations. Instead, all sources are listed below, together with suggestions of further reading for those interested in finding out more about the great algorithms of computer science.

The epigraph is from Vannevar Bush's essay "As We May Think," originally published in the July 1945 issue of *The Atlantic* magazine.

Introduction (chapter 1). For some accessible, enlightening explanations of algorithms and other computer technology, I recommend Chris Bishop's 2008 Royal Institution Christmas lectures, videos of which are freely available online. The lectures assume no prior knowledge of computer science. A. K. Dewdney's *New Turing Omnibus* usefully amplifies several of the topics covered in the present volume and introduces many more interesting computer science concepts—but some knowledge of computer programming is probably required to fully appreciate this book. Juraj Hromkovič's *Algorithmic Adventures* is an excellent option for readers with a little mathematical background, but no knowledge of computer science. Among the many college-level computer science texts on algorithms, three particularly readable options are *Algorithms*, by Dasgupta, Papadimitriou, and Vazirani; *Algorithmics: The Spirit of Computing*, by Harel and Feldman; and *Introduction to Algorithms*, by Cormen, Leiserson, Rivest, and Stein.

Search engine indexing (chapter 2). The original AltaVista patent covering the metaword trick is U.S. patent 6105019, "Constrained Searching of an Index," by Mike Burrows (2000). For readers with a computer science background, *Search Engines: Information Retrieval in Practice*, by Croft, Metzler, and Strohman, is a good option for learning more about indexing and many other aspects of search engines.

PageRank (chapter 3). The opening quotation by Larry Page is taken from an interview by Ben Elgin, published in *Businessweek*, May 3, 2004. Vannevar Bush's "As We May Think" was, as mentioned above, originally published in *The Atlantic* magazine (July 1945). Bishop's lectures (see above) contain an elegant demonstration of PageRank using a system of water pipes to emulate hyperlinks. The original paper describing Google's architecture is "The Anatomy of a Large-Scale Hypertextual Web Search Engine," written by Google's co-founders, Sergey Brin and Larry Page, and presented at the 1998 World Wide Web conference. The paper includes a brief description and analysis of PageRank. A much more technical, wide-ranging analysis appears in Langville and Meyer's *Google's PageRank and Beyond*—but this book requires college-level linear algebra. John Battelle's *The Search* begins with an accessible and interesting history of the web search industry, including the rise of Google. The web spam mentioned on page 36 is discussed in "Spam, Damn Spam, and Statistics: Using Statistical Analysis to Locate Spam Web Pages," by Fetterly, Manasse, and Najork, and published in the 2004 WebDB conference.

Public key cryptography (chapter 4). Simon Singh's *The Code Book* contains superb, accessible descriptions of many aspects of cryptography, including public key. It also recounts in detail the story of the secret discovery of public key cryptography at GCHQ in Britain. Bishop's lectures (see above) contain a clever practical demonstration of the paint-mixing analogy for public key crypto.

Error correcting codes (chapter 5). The anecdotes about Hamming are documented in Thomas M. Thompson's *From Error-Correcting Codes through Sphere Packings to Simple Groups*. The quotation from Hamming on page 60 is also given in this book and derives from a 1977 interview of Hamming by Thompson. Mathematicians will greatly enjoy Thompson's delightful book, but it definitely assumes the reader has a healthy dose of college math. Dewdney's book (see above) has two interesting chapters on coding theory. The two quotations about Shannon on pages 77–78 are taken from a brief biography by N. J. A. Sloane and A. D. Wyner, appearing in *Claude Shannon: Collected Papers* edited by Sloane and Wyner (1993).

Pattern recognition (chapter 6). Bishop's lectures (see above) have some interesting material that nicely complements this chapter. The geographical data about political donations is taken from the Fundrace project of the Huffington Post. All the handwritten digit data is taken from a dataset provided by Yann LeCun, of New York University's Courant Institute, and his collaborators. Details of the dataset, which is known as the MNIST data, are discussed in the 1998 paper by LeCun et al., "Gradient-Based Learning Applied to Document Recognition." The web spam results come from Ntoulas et al., "Detecting Spam Web Pages through Content Analysis," published in the Proceedings of the World Wide Web Conference, 2006. The face database was created in the 1990s by a leading pattern recognition researcher, Tom Mitchell of Carnegie Mellon University. Mitchell has used this database in his classes at Carnegie Mellon and describes it in his influential book, *Machine Learning*. On the website accompanying his book, Mitchell provides a computer program to perform training and classification of neural networks on the face database. All the results for the sunglasses problem were generated using slightly modified versions of this program. Daniel Crevier gives an interesting account of the Dartmouth AI conference in *AI: The Tumultuous History of the Search for Artificial Intelligence*. The excerpt from the conference's funding proposal (on page 103) is quoted in Pamela McCorduck's 1979 book, *Machines Who Think*.

Compression (chapter 7). The story about Fano, Shannon, and the discovery of Huffman coding is taken from a 1989 interview of Fano by Arthur Norberg. The interview is available from the oral history archive of the Charles Babbage Institute. My favorite treatment of data compression is in *Information Theory, Inference, and Learning Algorithms*, by David MacKay, but this book requires college-level math. Dewdney's book (see above) contains a much briefer and more accessible discussion.

Databases (chapter 8). There is an over-abundance of books providing an introduction to databases for beginners, but they typically explain how to *use* databases, rather than explaining how databases *work*—which was the objective of this chapter. Even college-level textbooks tend to focus on the use of databases. One exception is the second half of *Database Systems*, by Garcia-Molina, Ullman, and Widom, which gives plenty of details on the topics covered in this chapter.

Digital signatures (chapter 9). Gail Grant's *Understanding Digital Signatures* provides a great deal of information about digital signatures and is reasonably accessible to those without a computer science background.

Computability (chapter 10). The chapter's opening quotation is from a talk given by Richard Feynman at Caltech on December 29, 1959. The title of the talk is "There's Plenty of Room at the Bottom," and it was later published in Caltech's *Engineering & Science* magazine (February 1960). One unconventional, but very interesting, presentation of the concepts surrounding computability and undecidability is in the form of a (fictional) novel: *Turing (A Novel about Computation)*, by Christos Papadimitriou.

Conclusion (chapter 11). The Stephen Hawking lecture, "The Future of the Universe," was the 1991 Darwin lecture given at the University of Cambridge, also reprinted in Hawking's book *Black Holes and Baby Universes*. The televised A. J. P. Taylor lecture series was entitled *How Wars Begin*, and was also published as a book in 1977.

INDEX